QUEER OPTIMISM

QUEER OPTIMISM

Lyric Personhood and Other Felicitous Persuasions

MICHAEL D. SNEDIKER

MINNESOTA

University of Minnesota Press
Minneapolis • London

An earlier version of the Introduction was excerpted as "Queer Optimism," *Postmodern Culture* 16, no. 3 (May 2006); reprinted with permission by The Johns Hopkins University Press. An earlier version of chapter 1 first appeared as "Hart Crane's Smile," *Modernism/modernity* 12, no. 4 (November 2005): 629–58; reprinted with permission by The Johns Hopkins University Press.

Published by the University of Minnesota Press
111 Third Avenue South, Suite 290
Minneapolis, MN 55401-2520
http://www.upress.umn.edu

Library of Congress Cataloging-in-Publication Data

Snediker, Michael D.
Queer optimism : lyric personhood and other felicitous persuasions / Michael D. Snediker.
p. cm.
Includes bibliographical references and index.
ISBN 978-0-8166-4999-0 (hc : alk. paper) – ISBN 978-0-8166-5000-2 (pb : alk. paper)
1. American poetry – History and criticism. 2. Gay men's writings, American – History and criticism. 3. Homosexuality and literature – United States. 4. Optimism in literature. 5. Crane, Hart, 1899–1932 – Criticism and interpretation. 6. Dickinson, Emily, 1830–1886 – Criticism and interpretation. 7. Spicer, Jack – Criticism and interpretation. 8. Bishop, Elizabeth, 1911–1979 – Criticism and interpretation. I. Title.
PS310.H66S64 2008
811.009′352664 – dc22 2008031434

Printed in the United States of America on acid-free paper

for
J.E.V.

CONTENTS

Acknowledgments

Writing a book about the interests of felicity has felt all the more felicitous in the generous, encouraging support shown the project from its natal stages. *Queer Optimism* is born of a set of impulses and questions first stirred at Johns Hopkins University, and sustained by Mount Holyoke College. To speak thus of schools is to speak metonymically of libraries, offices, stoops, etc., and even more so, to speak of the persons (e.g., Susie Herrmann) who made these spaces vital. There are many to thank for myriad different reasons. Somewhere in *Swann's Way*, Proust writes of concentric waves of gratitude, and my own set of gratitudes, as I type, likewise seems to radiate. There are as many generative forms of closeness as there are generative forms of distance. From first circle to the last, grazie.

While this project surely seeks to cast its own set of ripples across a set of disciplines, its theoretical claims are inseparable from practices of close reading. There are many persons who taught me the *frisson* of readerly fastidiousness (and vice versa). Sharon Cameron, Frances Ferguson, Anita Sokolsky, Eve Kosofsky Sedgwick are among many from whose own practice of rigor I learned my own, and what's more, from whom I learned the inseparability of rigor and adventure, patience and verve. There are many (including the above), directly and indirectly, whose confidence in their own thinking inspired my own, and whose limpid brilliance has set the most alluring of standards of which I might in turn attempt approximation. An incomplete list of the former (whose absence from such a list would make it all the less complete) includes Henry Abelove, Amanda Anderson, Lauren Berlant, Leo Bersani, Judith Butler, Rey Chow, Theo Davis, Wai Chee Dimock, Lee Edelman, Maud Ellmann, Meredith Evans, Elizabeth Freeman, Jason Gladstone, Jonathan Goldberg, Mark Hansen, Stephen Heath, Barbara Hernnstein Smith, Neil Hertz, Virginia Jackson, Barbara Johnson, Peggy

Kamuf, Katie Kent, Stephen Knapp, Wendy Lee, James Longenbach, Fiona Maazel, Walter Benn Michaels, Christian Nagler, Christopher Pye, Daniel Stout, Rei Terada, Sasha Torres, Irene Tucker. I am lucky to count many of these persons as mentors, allies, and friends. May my path in the offing congenially cross and recross those of others who have inspired and spurred this book without perhaps even knowing it.

The thinking and writing of *Queer Optimism* would have been impossible without the great fortune of its being so lovingly and spiritedly directed by Allen Grossman and Michael Moon. Their inimitable providence and perspicacity are nearly dizzying and indelibly luminous. Differently, no less crucially luminous, has been the extraordinary, unflagging support of family and friends. At this point, I think less of who has made *Queer Optimism* possible than who has made these years not just possible but marvelous: Rachel Hadas, nearly singular exception to my anxious relation to telephones; Louise Gluck and Rick Moody, who reminded me time and again that writing is not only an art but its own form of psychoanalysis and sociability; Lauren Voyer, best big sister I never had; my darlingest Shmoo, the very, very, very best little sister one could ever have; Joseph and Emily Vincent, for whom I would cook meal after meal; my parents and twin brother, who make a project such as this plausible at even its most elementary level.

Most of this book was written from an office in the Fitzwilly Building in Northampton, Massachusetts. As wonderful as that office's productivity are my Pioneer Valley friends who unfailingly restored me, after productivity's particular depletions, and whose delights and kindnesses, in all their fulgent immanence, I most heartily miss in this recent move to Ontario. All x's and o's to Nancy Barre, Perry Carter, Peter Gizzi, Binks and Susan Little, Jason Ranker, Ellen Dore Watson *(j'adore)*, Dara Wier, Elizabeth Willis, and the magnificent, motley crue of the *Massachusetts Review*.

Mount Holyoke generously provided financial support for many of the costs of bringing *Queer Optimism* into print. Difficult, on the other hand, to put a price on the kindness of Maryanne Alos, Chris Benfey, Eugene Hill, and Don Weber, and the rest of my South Hadley colleagues. Ditto the ebullient, challenging, and heartening élan of Kate Sulzer and the rest of my Mount Holyoke posse. My affinities and admirations for my new colleagues at Queen's University, while stripling, no less seem to deserve proleptic appreciation.

I can't enough thank the great Richard Morrison for his prodigal editorial gifts. Sincere thanks likewise to Adam Brunner, John Eagleson, the rest of the University of Minnesota Press staff, as well as the editors and managing editors of *Modernism/modernity* and *Postmodern Culture*, who published excerpts, respectively, of *Queer Optimism*'s Introduction and first chapter. There are latecomers to *Queer Optimism* no less crucial for arriving, beneficently, in tenth or eleventh hours. For their confidence and enabling, I thank Christopher Castiglia, Robert Caserio, Bonnie Costello, Elizabeth Freeman, Lanny Hammer, and Robin Schulze. Above all, I thank Tim Dean, whose friendship and guidance most keenly made me believe that a book such as this might matter. I thank the Merrill House Committee for the luxury of living six months in the Merrill House apartment. Final lapidary changes to this book surely bear the trace of the serenity and beauty afforded by my time in Stonington.

And then there are Raymond Izbicki and Grubby, surely the two most welkin-eyed angels in any heaven one could conjure. If ever I could have two watchful souls above me, it would be you two, which of course is no consolation for your no longer being here.

And then the Callahans — Jeff, Babs, Ming, the bunnies, but especially Lynn, whose heart is large as she is small, connoisseur and curator of all things beautiful. For bondo, Lynn, and for Jamesian complexity sans Jamesian heartbreak, thank you, thank you. And dearest Johnny, dream-interlocutor, dream-partner-in-crime, whose influence on this book rises from every page, who makes each day a cause for its own queer optimism, who in the most magnificently Winnicottian way is good-enough, and then some — this one's for you.

QUEER OPTIMISM

An Introduction

I do not believe the main question of our time to be that of horror, suffering, destiny, or dereliction. We are saturated by these notions. . . . Our question instead is that of affirmative courage, of local energy. To seize a point and hold it. . . . The fact that we do not know how to revisit Aristophanes or Plautus is more disquieting than it is heartening to verify that we have once again breathed life into Aeschylus. . . . We want a theater of capacity, not of incapacity.

—Alain Badiou, "Theses on Theater," *Handbook of Inaesthetics*

While optimism, these past decades, has made cameos in the pages of queer theory, "queer" is not itself so readily imaginable as one of optimism's epithets. More epithetically familiar, perhaps, is Lauren Berlant and Michael Warner's invoking of "hegemonic optimism" in their 1998 essay "Sex in Public."[1] Along similar lines, Berlant raises the specter of "dubious optimism" in her 2001 essay "The Subject of True Feeling: Pain, Privacy, and Politics."[2] As epithets, "dubious" and "hegemonic" construe optimism as a tease, a seduction that queer theory might expose—and subsequently if not simultaneously jettison—as that which cozens liberals (queer and nonqueer) into complacency, the extensiveness and lure of which would all the more require optimism's debunking.

In the vernacular, optimism often is imagined epithetically as "premature": as though if the optimist at hand knew all that she might eventually know, she might retract her optimism altogether. Prematurity qualifies optimism as a temporary state of insufficient information. "Woefully optimistic," on the other hand, implies that the knowledge that would warrant optimism's retraction might never arrive. As an epithet, "woefully" (like "hegemonic," "dubious," or "premature") subjects optimism to an outside judgment, the likes of which the optimist in question is presumed unable to make. It is difficult to imagine an optimist, as conventionally understood, denominating her own optimism as woeful or premature. Indeed, the moment at which she is able to characterize her optimism as such might well mark the moment at which being optimistic cedes, as a position, if not to being pessimistic then to something like being realistic. (That being pessimistic potentially could seem equivalent to being realistic is a matter to which my study shall return.) The epithets delineated, that is, do not describe optimism so much as impose a diagnosis external to it that conjectures further characterizations of optimism (and more to the point, attachments to optimism) unnecessary.

For all the lexical and semantic differences between the above epithets ("hegemonic," for instance, hardly seems synonymous with "premature"), the optimism to which these epithets attach fundamentally is the same. To wit, this optimism describes the utopic energy that motivates counterpublics (along the lines drawn by Michael Warner[3]); or more generally, the liberal nation-state; or cynically, the inane recalcitrances of the recent Bush administration;[4] or literarily, the pluck of Pollyanna or Horatio Alger's Ragged Dick. *Queer Optimism* does not seek a new relation (oppositional, proponential) to this optimism. Rather, my book calls for a reconceptualization of optimism itself. The élan that underwrites utopic optimisms can be traced (or mistraced) to Leibniz, and in a subsequent section of this introduction I shall turn to Leibniz, and to the ways Leibnizian optimism differs from that of my own project. Succinctly: utopic optimism — and following, the optimism that crops up both in queer theory and critical theory more generally — attaches to, a future. Not unrelated to its futural (promissory, parousiac) stakes is utopic optimism's allergic relation to knowledge. For Leibniz, optimism's fealty to faith renders knowledge superfluous; in current critical thought, optimism's very sanguinity implies epistemological deficit.[5] This antagonism between optimism and knowledge has had the perhaps unsurprising effect of taking optimism out of critical circulation. Queer optimism, oppositely, is not promissory. It doesn't ask that some future time make good on its own hopes. Rather, *Queer Optimism* asks that optimism, embedded in its own immanent present, might be *interesting*. Queer optimism's interest — its capacity to be interesting, to hold our attention — depends on its emphatic responsiveness to and solicitation of rigorous thinking.

Queer optimism, immanently rather than futurally oriented, does not entail predisposition in the way that conventional optimism entails predisposition. It presents a critical field and asks that this field be taken seriously. Even as my investigation extends, at certain junctures, to the likes of happiness, this is not because if one were more queerly optimistic, one necessarily would feel happier. Queer optimism doesn't aspire toward happiness, but instead finds happiness *interesting*. Queer optimism, in this sense, can be considered a form of meta-optimism: it wants to *think* about feeling good, to make disparate aspects of feeling good thinkable. *Queer Optimism,* then, seeks to take positive affects as serious and interesting sites of critical investigation. Likewise, queer optimism insists on thinking about personhood — as opposed to subjectivity — in terms of a durability neither immediately nor proleptically subject to structuralist or poststructuralist scrutiny. *Queer Optimism* concerns persons, rather than subjects or even selves. The latter categories inhabit (and sometimes unknowingly curate) particular discursive labyrinths (Cartesian, Foucauldian, Althusserian, Hegelian, Lacanian, etc.) of discipline, desire, and knowledge to which my examinations of personhood at best only obliquely speak. My theoretical preference for persons over subjects extends from questions of how personhood — as formulated within the poems on which subsequent chapters' arguments depend — might be characterized, removed from the columbarium of subjectivity. Such an enterprise might signal — to those for whom persons always already are subjects of a certain presumed order — a nostalgia for some sort of prediscursive mode of being. Characterization of my readings along these lines, however, risks the emptying of poetic texts of their own intransigent, idiosyncratic discursive value. Far from invoking persons freed from discursive necessity, *Queer Optimism* scrutinizes the conundra of discursivity at its most local — rather than importing a set of subjectival stipulations extrinsic from the discursive system of a given poem. My collocation of lyric persons with the sorts of subjects marshaled by queer theory will seem, at times, potentially tenuous. To risk this tenuousness nonetheless strikes me as far preferable to (and far less damaging than) the tenuousness of presuming that lyric persons nonproblematically could answer to queer theory's interpellative calls.

My critical project arises from a sense that queer theory, for all its contributions to our understandings of affect, has had far more to say about negative affects than positive ones. Furthermore, that in its attachment to not taking personhood qua personhood for granted, queer theory's suspicious relation to persons has itself become suspiciously routinized, if not taken for granted in its own right. Risking charges of producing but another reductive binary, I shall for present, heuristic purposes be calling this tropaic gravitation toward negative affect and depersonation *queer pessimism*. It's worth noting that queer pessimism has as little truck with conventional pessimism as queer optimism has with optimism, per se. Still, queer theory's habitation of this pessimistic field is cause for real concern. Melancholy, self-shattering, shame, the death drive: these, within queer theory, are categories to conjure with. These terms and the scholarship fueled by them do not in and of themselves comprise queer theory. To argue that they do caricatures both queer theory and the theorists who have put these terms on the map. These terms — this queer-pessimistic constellation — nonetheless have dominated and organized much of queer-theoretical discourse, even as they have often seemed immune to queer theory's own perspicacities.

This introduction conducts a purposive survey of the work of Judith Butler, Leo Bersani, Eve Kosofsky Sedgwick, and Lee Edelman. Without taking as definitive either this survey or my analysis of any given author, I wish these analyses to articulate a certain shape, to describe a current of enchantment that has privileged "suffering" and "dereliction" (to invoke two of Badiou's terms) as sites both of ethics and understanding. Queer theory's analyses of negative affect and ontological instability have been and continue to be both generous and generative. My wish is to clear a space for the possible generosities and generativities of queer optimism's corresponding milieu. As a space-clearing, these pages do not deliver the queer-optimistic "goods," per se: positing a compact or synecdochical account of queer optimism is at cross-purposes with my reluctance to reduce queer optimism's field before the adventure of first expanding it. Such an expansion is the task of the chapters that follow. I offer these introductory pages in the spirit of exordium and invitation.

Of Sadness and Certainty

The year I told my parents I was gay was also the year of my first sustained encounter with depression. At its bleakest, sadness and self-loathing felt like the sole remainders of a self which in all other aspects seemed untrustable and ersatz. Past happiness seemed the feat of terrific mountebanking, moored either to monstrous ulterior motives or to machinically vacant automaticity. Delight was a little boat on a large, sad sea; it was slight and, simultaneously, perversely too heavy to be buoyant, too heavy because so quickly waterlogged.[6]

What Elaine Scarry observed of physical suffering seemed as true of psychological suffering, that "for the person in pain, so incontestably, and unnegotiably present is it that 'having pain' may come to be thought of as the most vibrant example of what it is to 'have certainty.' "[7] Incontestable and unnegotiable, sadness indeed seemed certain—tenaciously and vibrantly so. If sadness seemed certain—if, that is, sadness was the only thing I felt certain about—such an observation dovetailed with the inkling that certainty was itself a kind of sadness. Judith Butler's accounts of melancholy seemed to confirm this latter possibility with an eloquence I had neither will nor skill to contest. "I want to suggest," Butler writes, "that rigid forms of gender and sexual identification, whether homosexual or heterosexual, appear to spawn forms of melancholy."[8] Not just particularly gendered or sexual identities, but "coherent identity position[s]"[9] more generally, were within Butler's account suspect. "Perhaps," Butler continues, "only by risking the *incoherence* of identity is connection possible."[10]

It seemed, in first approaching Butler's texts, that I had two options. I could risk my own incoherence (which is as much to say, accept the originality of that incoherence), or I could attach to coherence; as described by Butler, however, the latter could never really be an option. How could a nascent queer theorist indebted to and inspired by Butler choose the latter, when coherence was constitutively equivalent to reification, naturalization, and congealment? "Further," Butler writes, "this [masculine or feminine] identity is constructed and maintained by the consistent application of this taboo [against homosexuality], not only in the stylization of the body in compliance with discrete categories of sex, but in the production and 'disposition' of sexual desire."[11] To attach to coherence would be to deny this series of "consistent applications," to confuse repetition—amounting to congealment (81)[12] or sedimentation (178)—with a "false foundationalism, the results of affectivity being formed or 'fixed' through the effects of the prohibition [against homosexuality]."[13] The globby abjection of a term like "congealment" did not, for me, go without saying. As though it weren't bad enough that stability could come only on the dragging heels of melancholy, this stability became, within Butler's rhetoric, not just melancholic but potentially disgusting, a sort of ontological aspic.

My particular sadnesses, then, were all the more keenly confusing in so nearly replicating the critical terms for which I, as initiate into queer theory, was falling. My experience of feeling ontologically incoherent, however, had none of the thrill of reading about being incoherent; likewise (to look ahead to another queer paradigm), my experience of feeling shattered lacked all the thrill of reading about being shattered. Stronger than the excitement of radical new possibilities of self-losing, of the vigorous embrace of factitiousness, was the grief of self-loss and consuming repellence of feeling fictive. It felt humiliating to approximate—even literalize—the conditions that in theory seemed so important, even exhilarating, but only to approximate them, to come up short. What I wanted for myself was the opposite of what I found intellectually most interesting and vital.

What I noticed only later, returning to Butler's texts, was the puzzling disjunct between the dubious permanence ascribed to identities and the permanence ascribed to melancholy itself. Whereas identities appeared permanent (or became permanent through a process unsavory as congealment), melancholy simply was permanent:

> This [melancholy] identification is not simply momentary or occasional, but becomes a new structure of identity.[14]

Whereas the identity borne of melancholy required constant, quotidian maintenance, melancholy itself was described as a "permanent internalization."[15] Furthermore, Butler's inclination to describe melancholy's technique as "magical"[16] seemed to render melancholy unimpeachable. Melancholy wasn't like a magic trick, in the manner of debunkable smoke and mirrors. It was simply magic: a process beyond explanation, not entailing a suspension of disbelief, but seducing one *into* belief. Its effects were proof of its reality, and beyond analysis — unlike the identities that both "spawn[ed]"[17] and were spawned by melancholy, whose congealed repetitions and machinic habits were nothing, under Butler's percipient eye, if not susceptible to challenge and revision. Melancholy, that is, produced what would (erroneously) be experienced as coherent or certain identity, even as this false coherence was founded on the certain permanence of a melancholy whose reality remained beyond reproach.

Butler's ingenious resituating of Freudian melancholy intended to monkey-wrench the primacy of the incest taboo's heterosexuality, but there was little assuagement, for me, in thinking that the heterosexuality that had eluded me would itself have been sustained through melancholy magic of which I likely would have remained oblivious. Little assuagement, insofar as this melancholy anterior to incestuous heterosexuality still relied on a heterosexual parental structure: succinctly, a boy desires his father, cannot act on it, and in relinquishing this intergenerational homosexual desire, ends up desiring what his father desires, namely (or at least initially), his mother. This, certainly, would instantiate one form of melancholic constitution. Nonetheless, in the midst of so many other relinquishments (folding and unfolding into each other like an Escher), and so many forms of feeling that seemed to either exceed or shrink from desire, melancholy felt less like what befell other people, than an extravagantly unpredictable landscape into which everyone at some point might fall. Less Sedgwick's mobile proscenium than a mobile trapdoor under which (always already) I was penned.

Ontology under such conditions felt intolerable. No more tolerable, however, seemed Leo Bersani's response to psychical fixity. Whereas Butler advanced an account of melancholy's production of subjects, Bersani advanced an account of subjectival destruction. But if melancholy felt less like being a person than not being a person — if incoherence, that is, seemed to describe my sadness far more coherently than could coherence — how would not being a person feel any different from ruthless, extant self-diminishings? What to choose? What or whom to desire, and how to mobilize an erotic engine that in many ways felt inadequate to all the things desire was expected, within queer theory, to accomplish?

For Leo Bersani, stable identities aren't melancholic, but rather the source of interpsychical aggression. In *Forms of Being: Cinema, Aesthetics, Subjectivity,* Bersani reprises his account of the human subject (earlier developed in his book *The Freudian Body*) as fundamentally destructive, and sexuality as that which underwrites both auto- and allo-destructiveness. Bersani and co-author Ulysse Dutoit write:

> If we dismiss — as it seems to us we should — the more or less optimistic psychoanalytic theories between Freud and Lacan, theories that would make us more or less happy by way of such things as adaptation to the real and genital normalcy, then we may judge the great achievement of psychoanalysis to be its attempt to account for our inability to love others, and ourselves. The promises of adaptive balance and sexual maturity undoubtedly explain the phenomenal appeal of psychoanalysis as therapy, but its greatness may lie in its insistence on an intractable human destructiveness — a destructiveness resistant to any therapeutic endeavours whatsoever. This has little to do with sex, and we can distinguish between the practices normally identified as sex and a permanent, irreducibly destructive disposition which the great figures of psychoanalytic theory — especially Freud, Klein, Laplanche and Lacan — more or less explicitly define as sexuality.[18]

Bersani and Dutoit's qualification of optimism and happiness as "more or less" connotes less optimism's insidiousness — an allegation implicit in Berlant and Warner's affixing of "optimism" and "hegemonic" — than its inconsequentiality. Whether insidious or inconsequential, the result is the same; optimism, for Bersani and Dutoit, calls not for further inquiry, but for "dismiss[al]." The grounds for dismissal, here, lie in the teleological alignment of those "more or less optimistic psychoanalytic theories" with "real and genital normalcy." In its adumbrating of "real and genital normalcy" with the implicit factitiousness of both "real" and "normalcy" (and, in turn, its suggestion of heterosexuality's conscription of this factitiousness as its own perseveratingly veracious prerogative), Bersani's etiolated sketch of psychoanalysis resembles Berlant's own recent analysis of optimism's inextricability from the coercions of love.[19] But even if queer theory positions normativity as heterosexual fantasy (and vice versa), why does it follow that heterosexuality — at its admittedly most reductively sketched — necessarily monopolizes optimism? Why couldn't optimism run in nonnormative circles? Or be conceived as other than universalized and universalizing? The dismissible inconsequentiality of the above passage's optimism contrasts starkly with the passage's subsequent account of "destructive disposition" as "permanent," and "irreducibly so," specifications rhetorically similar to Butler's depictions of melancholy. My frustration with such texts followed—would not have been possible without—an earlier frustration with my own limitations as darkly illuminated by queer theory's midnight sun. In writing *Queer Optimism,* I am turning the tables—considering the possible permanences of optimism, the possible fictions of aggression.

Bersani omits British psychoanalyst D. W. Winnicott from his catalogue of "great figures of psychoanalytic theory," perhaps, in part, because Winnicott's theorizations of aggression challenge the intrinsically negative, malfeasant gist of Bersani's primordial destructiveness. Contrary to Bersani's invocation of "human destructiveness" as commensurate with (if not underwriting) "our inability to love others," Winnicott argues that destructiveness is itself a condition for love. Unlike Bersani's consideration of love's destructive tendencies,[20] Winnicott's insights are not reducible to theorizations of masochism insistent upon desire's inextricability from pain. Rather, Winnicott's insights pertain to a sphere more expansive than that in which desire and masochism so quickly collide. As Winnicott writes in his crucial essay "The Use of an Object and Relating through Identifications,"

> This change (from relating to usage) means that the subject destroys the object. From here it could be argued by an armchair philosopher that there is therefore no such thing in practice as the use of an object: if the object is external, then the object is destroyed by the subject. Should the philosopher come out of his chair and sit on the floor with his patient, however, he will find that there is an intermediate position. In other words, he will find that after 'subject relates to object' comes 'subject destroys object' (as it becomes external); and then may come '*object survives* destruction by the subject.' But there may or may not be survival. A new feature thus arrives in the theory of object-relating. The subject says to the object: 'I destroyed you' and the object is there to receive the communication. From now on the subject says: 'Hullo object!' 'I destroyed you.' 'I love you.' 'You have value for me because of your survival of my destruction of you.' 'While I am loving you I am all the time destroying you in (unconscious) *fantasy.*' Here fantasy begins for the individual. The subject can now *use* the object that has survived. It is important to note that it is not only that the subject

> destroys the object because the object is placed outside the area of omnipotent control. It is equally significant to state this the other way round and to say that it is the destruction of the object that places the object outside the area of the subject's omnipotent control. In these ways the object develops its own autonomy and life, and (if it survives) contributes-in to the subject, according to its own properties.[21] (italics in original)

Winnicott's conception of destructiveness amounts to a theory of love (as opposed to desire), grounded in the possibility of the object's survival of the destructiveness dealt to it. Winnicott's insistence on possibility—"if it survives"—rather than ineluctability differently distinguishes Winnicott's investigative practice from the adamance of Bersani's "irreducibly so." An object's durability as such signals that it *is* an object, and this durability is not recognizable to the Winnicottian subject without the fantasy of destroying it. The destructiveness that an object can withstand, for Winnicott, demonstrates not just the object's own integrity (an integrity from which the subject might subsequently learn), but its own capacity for loving in spite of feeling damaged, or even repelled, by the subject. This form of durability (opposite Butler's "congealment") offers an important psychoanalytic context for my own subsequent readings. Winnicott's work seems indispensable both to future queer negotiations with psychoanalysis and, not unrelatedly, to particularly psychoanalytically conceived modes of optimistic thinking and practice.

Contrary to Winnicottian destructiveness, Bersanian self-shattering amounts to a temporary figurative suicide, a moment's disorganization within a field of intense regulation; or oppositely, an internalization of the destructive, shattering energies otherwise directed outward. Whereas Butler deploys Freud's "Mourning and Melancholia" in the service of producing a genealogy of subjects, Bersani illuminates resistances and impasses internal to *Beyond the Pleasure Principle* that suggest a violence far more capacious than the one Freud's text consciously delineates. "What has been repressed from the speculative second half of Freud's text," Bersani writes in *The Freudian Body,* "is sexuality as productive masochism. *The possibility of exploiting the shattering effects of sexuality in order to maintain the tensions of an eroticized, de-narrativized, and mobile consciousness has been neglected, or refused, in favor of a view of pleasure as nothing more than the reduction of all tension and the evacuation of all excitement*" (italics in original).[22] In "Is the Rectum a Grave?" Bersani more explicitly narrativizes self-shattering and the conditions from which its need arises:

> [T]he self which the sexual shatters provides the basis on which sexuality is associated with power. It is possible to think of the sexual as, precisely, moving beyond a hyperbolic sense of self and a loss of all consciousness of self. But sex as self-hyperbole is perhaps a repression of sex as self-abolition. It inaccurately replicates self-shattering as self-swelling, as psychic tumescence. If, as these words suggest, men are especially apt to "choose" this version of sexual pleasure, because their sexual equipment appears to invite by analogy, or at least to facilitate, the phallicizing of the ego, neither sex has exclusive rights to the practice of sex as self-hyperbole. For it is perhaps primarily *the degeneration of the sexual into a relationship that condemns sexuality to becoming a struggle for power*. As soon as persons are posited, the war begins. It is the self that swells with excitement at the idea of being on top, the self that makes of the inevitable play of thrusts and relinquishments in sex an argument for the natural authority of one sex over the other.[23]

Sex, for Bersani, becomes a spectacular, radical literalization of deconstruction. The "shattering" of sex undoes persons the way queer theory undoes persons.

I might say here that *Queer Optimism* has less to do with my own readings of Freud or Lacan than it does with queer theory's mobilizations of particular psychoanalytic tropes and texts. More to the point, I am concerned with the strains of queer theory that such mobilizations both enable and preempt. Freud's own body of work remains an important site from which to challenge uniforming, simplifying distillations of psychoanalysis. As just one instance of Freud's usefulness in the interrogation of his own reception, one might consider Butler's dependence, in *The Psychic Life of Power*, on a particular passage from *The Ego and the Id*. Freud observes that

> when it happens that a person has to give up a sexual object, there quite often ensues an alteration of his ego which can only be described as a setting up of the object inside the ego, as it occurs in melancholia.[24]

Butler's reading of this passage takes for granted that a process structurally analogous to that of melancholic incorporation ("as it occurs in melancholia") is itself equivalent to melancholia:

> If we accept the notion that heterosexuality naturalized itself by insisting on the radical otherness of homosexuality, then heterosexual identity is purchased through a melancholic incorporation of the love that it disavows: the man who insists upon the coherence of his heterosexuality will claim that he never loved another man, and hence never lost another man. That love, that attachment, becomes subject to a double disavowal, a never having loved, a never having lost. . . . What ensues is a culture of gender melancholy in which masculinity and femininity emerge as the traces of an ungrieved and ungrievable love.[25]

My interest, contra Butler's, lies in the extent to which Freud's account does not literally produce equivalence so much as insist upon similarity. In following a structural pattern that is like melancholia, the process described seems most saliently not to be melancholic; analogy marks a structural similarity but explicitly not an affective one. Such a passage therefore might not merely corroborate Butler's argument that sexual loss effects gender melancholy, but rather pressure Freud's readers to query precisely the differences between the loss of a sexual object and the losses particular to melancholy as such.

There is much in Bersani and Butler with which to differ. Nonetheless, within queer theory (as it has been and currently is being practiced) nobody except Eve Kosofsky Sedgwick (to whom I shall soon turn) has been more influential. The list of essays and books indebted to the insights of Butler and Bersani is a long one, and ever lengthening. To tarry, for instance, within the domain of queer theory as inflected by psychoanalysis, the number of times Butler and Bersani are noted in the index of Tim Dean and Christopher Lane's *Homosexuality and Psychoanalysis* (well over fifty instances) far exceeds references to such seminal psychoanalysts as Sandor Ferenczi (four citations) or Winnicott (zero). While one cannot equate influence with this kind of indexical showing, one nonetheless can get a sense of the extent to which Butler and Bersani have become part of a canon, contested as the category of canonicity (in the context either of queer theory or psychoanalysis) might be.[26]

Even as Butler and Bersani have positioned their work in the context of AIDS, hate-crimes, and other lived domains of crisis,[27] their work, with telling insistence, often depends on abstraction, on metaphor. One doesn't really shatter when one is fucked, despite Bersani's accounts of it as such; millions of persons who imagine their subjectivity as fairly cohesive and nonfictive do not necessarily feel melancholy, even if Butler claims melancholy as the cost of that cohesiveness. If these models of shattering and gender-melancholy seem less than practiceable (or surviveable) in lived experience, they've become ubiquitous in the no less lived (if differently lived) biosphere of the academy.

The alchemy of such figurations demarcates an ever-fluctuating space between (theoretical) scrutiny and (ontological) practice. How to get from one domain to another, without the complex network of figurativity? How might one articulate what happens within the limbo of the figurative? To answer such questions would be tantamount to discerning how theory eventuates its own practical application. This particular problematic of figuration — as syncope between theoretical and practical domains, literary and lived investments — incites many of *Queer Optimism's* own readings. Gilles Deleuze, in the introduction to his book *Essays Critical and Clinical,* writes that "[h]ealth as literature, as writing, consists in inventing a people who are missing. It is the task of the fabulating function to invent a people."[28] What if the people who were missing, the people *Queer Optimism* sought to "invent," were missing optimists? The non-Pollyana, non-Dubya optimists, the queer optimists, with voices differing from both queer theory and optimism, as usually understood?

If Deleuze's turn to literature's "fabulating function" does not exactly illuminate fabulation's particular mechanisms, it nonetheless reminds us that fabulation is a function (of something, on something), whose structures and ends can and ought to prompt explication in ways that figuration, in its slippery whisper of self-evidence, too often theoretically eludes. *Queer Optimism* introduces its own set of explications in order to provide some texture and traction to figuration, as it traverses theoretical and poetic lines. At the same time, it strikes me that the move to figuration within theoretical discourse often is a premature one. The transformation of nonfigurative phenomena into figurative phenomena is often a consequence of saturating cathexes that fetishize (and fetishistically treat) phenomena without acknowledgment of either their cathectic pulsions or the fetishization in which they participate.

Along these lines, I again stress the salutary utility of Winnicott — as, for example, Winnicott's nonironic denomination of adolescent depression as "doldrums." Adumbrated by the gravities of melancholy, doldrums might seem comparably dismissable. Winnicott, however, does not take his nominally nonenthralled category lightly. Doldrums, clinically, are experienced as miserable and, theoretically, are something that psychoanalysis can treat seriously (and compassionately), from which psychoanalysis can learn. For the purposes of *Queer Optimism,* I value the extent to which doldrums resist melancholy's proven capacity to colonize all experiences similar to it. The more there are doldrums, the less of a stronghold melancholy maintains over a field more various and differentiated than one term ever could describe. This Winnicottian defetishization of terms seems all the more salient an intellectual (and therapeutic) model in the context of David Eng and David Kazanjian's edited volume, *Loss* (2003), in which accounts of intense resilience and creativity seem ultimately mischaracterized by their no less intense absorption into the category of melancholia, which, write Eng and Kazanjian, "at the turn of the century has emerged as a crucial touchstone for social and subjective formulations" (23).

There seems in Eng and Kazanjian's collection a conspicuous disparity between innovative scholarship and regression to nominal "touchstones," as though after Freud's dichotomizing of mourning and melancholia, a scholar's choice were de facto only between these two categories. Such a disparity likewise is evident in Ann Cvetkovich's coterminous *An Archive of Feelings.* "What's required," Cvetkovich writes, "is a sex positivity that can embrace negativity, including trauma. Allowing a place for trauma within sexuality is consistent with efforts to keep sexuality queer, to maintain a space for shame and perversion within public discourse rather than purging them of their messiness in order to make them acceptable."[29] Cvetkovich wants a trauma that could describe nearly any lesbian experience,[30] insists on the depathologization of trauma,[31] yet simultaneously wants perversities to sustain their shocking edge. The result is an astute study that seems less energized by its recurrent invoking of trauma than hampered by a misnomer for a range of experiences better left articulated in their specificity, rather than condensed to a single traumatic term. Winnicott speaks of a similar condensation in Freud's original coining of the death drive:

> [W]hen we look anew at the roots of aggression there are two concepts in particular, each of which must be thrown away deliberately, so that we may see whether we are better off without them. One is Freud's

> concept of a death instinct, a by-product of his speculations in which he seemed to be achieving a theoretical simplification that might be compared to the gradual elimination of detail in the technique of a sculptor like Michelangelo. The other is Melanie Klein's setting up of envy in the prominent place that she gave at Geneva in 1955.[32]

Winnicott's polemic helpfully distinguishes the existence of an array of energies and impulses from the eventual attenuation of that array as one "concept." My reservation regarding works such as *Loss* and *An Archive of Feelings* has less to do with any given set of "speculations" than with their resigned gravitation to a single concept that can't possibly do speculations, as such, justice. The more one could resist the transformation of speculations into concepts, the more likely, it seems, one could suspend the flight of observations into figurations. Easy enough, as Eng and Kazanjian demonstrate, to wax lyrical on melancholy.[33] Less easy to wax lyrical about "doldrums." For all its potential banality, "doldrums" hence retreats from a figurative monolith to its own usefully nonfigurative (as well as interestingly, differently figurative) specificity.

Loving Shame

This introduction's previous sections recount, if cursorily, an undertheorization of psychoanalytically derived terms — namely, "melancholy" and "aggression" — whose threading through queer theory nonetheless has galvanized a vital and proliferative body of work. Vital and proliferative, but also foreclosing, in its demarcation of an intellectual field that reinforces the intellectual nonviability of a different terrain, which I am calling queer optimism.

Moving away from considerations of melancholy, aggression, or self-shattering, this next section's engagement with critical revaluations of shame departs from a psychoanalytic rubric, for the sake of making clear that queer pessimism is not, more generally, a psychoanalytic pessimism. I'm likewise moved to write about queer theorizations of shame because much of this work (itself seeking to circumnavigate a psychoanalytic argot) in fact seems optimistically motivated. This is not to say that much of queer theory isn't likewise optimistically motivated: much of Butler's work seems thus energized, even as its optimistic premise nevertheless often trades on the repertoires of melancholy.

I mean, here, to distinguish between the energy that motivates a theoretical enterprise and the subject of that enterprise. Queer optimism attends less to what motivates a project than to a project's content. Optimistic motivations (of Butler, Bersani, and many other theorists[34]) could correspond to Gramsci's "optimism of the will," while queer optimism does not. This is the case because Gramsci's optimism does not seem radically different from optimism as usually conceived, whereas queer optimism, prima facie, seeks to complicate how optimism is conceived. This is not to say that I do not feel solidarity with recent interventions in pessimistic methodology (for instance, challenges to what Paul Ricoeur first termed a hermeneutics of suspicion).[35] *Queer Optimism,* however, calls for a different sort of intervention—on the level of content rather than practice. On the level of practice, then, I am sympathetic toward Butler's recent invoking of hope. "I hope to show," Butler writes in *Giving an Account of Oneself,* "that morality is neither a symptom of its social conditions nor a site of transcendence of them, but rather is essential to the determination of agency and the possibility of hope."[36] The formulation, "possibility of hope," confirms what in a subsequent sentence Butler makes clear: that hope inhabits a horizon, emergent "at the limits of our schemes of intelligibility."[37] This hope differs from queer optimism, in that hope held-as-promissory (as "possibility") or consigned to intelligibility's limits, is only fleetingly intelligible—which is to say, removed from the locus of immanent, fastidious investigation.

Hope is promissory; hope is a horizon. Shame, on the other hand, occurs in a lavish present tense. What if the field of queer optimism were situated as firmly in the present tense as shame? Even as scholarship on shame may arise out of generosity and hopefulness, this work, within queer theory and affect theory, provides shame all the more eloquent and vibrant a vocabulary, while leaving positive affect (itself lexically impoverished) to fend for itself. That positive affect seems innately less available to thinking—or that hope definitionally exists futurally, and shame immanently—is the sort of temporal donnée against which *Queer Optimism* speaks.

I have disarticulated motivation from content because Eve Kosofsky Sedgwick's theorizations of shame are incontestably magnanimous and good-intentioned. Furthermore, the *bon esprit* that suffuses Sedgwick's work—the inseparability, in her writing, of delight and perspicacity—

has inspired my own thinking in ways for which I hardly can account. If ignorance idiomatically attaches to bliss,[38] Sedgwick's trenchant complication of ignorance[39] has made possible my attempt, chiasmatically, to complicate bliss. More specifically, I like to think of my project as a furthering of Sedgwick's account of immanent joy, in Proust:

> In Freud, then, there would be no room — except as an example of self-delusion — for the Proustian epistemology whereby the narrator of *À la recherché,* who feels in the last volume "jostling each other within me a whole host of truths concerning human passions and character and conduct," recognizes them *as* truths insofar as *"the perception of [them] caused me joy...."* In the paranoid Freudian epistemology, it is implausible enough to suppose that truth could be even an accidental occasion of joy; inconceivable to imagine joy as a guarantor of truth. Indeed, from any point of view it is circular, or something, to suppose that one's pleasure at knowing something could be taken as evidence of the truth of the knowledge.[40]

I'm riveted by the idea that joy could be a guarantor of truth — differently put, that joy could be persuasive. While qualifying the above observations with a caveat against tautology ("knowing something... as evidence of the truth of the knowledge"), Sedgwick's later analyses of shame are marvelous in part for their escape of tautology, such that shame is made to yield knowledges not at all equivalent to the sense of shame with which one starts. This new body of knowledge, all the same, defers to a nominal circularity — what no longer resembles shame, in Sedgwick's writing, still is called shame. Why is this the case? Given shame's (or for that matter melancholy's) lability within queer theory, why might queer optimism's subjects not be analogously labile?

In "Shame, Theatricality, and Queer Performativity," Sedgwick charts the exuberant, ambivalent affects of Henry James, as he returns (in writing the prefaces for the New York Edition) to his own earlier novels and characters and to his own earlier authorial selves. In these prefaces (as in everything he writes), James's affective range is punctilious and ravishing, but the affect toward which Sedgwick turns (indeed, the affect, for Sedgwick, that comes to organize, beget, and describe most other affects) is shame:

> The speaking self of the prefaces does not attempt to merge with the potentially shaming or shamed figurations of its younger self, younger

> fictions, younger heroes; its attempt is to love them. That love is shown to occur both in spite of shame and, more remarkably, through it.[41]

The love of shame is the love between a "younger self" and the self that currently is writing; in the distance between selves, the younger self might be experienced not only as having written those "younger fictions," but as a "younger fiction" in his own right. The love of shame, that is, occurs in the disruption of what otherwise might be seen as a continuous self. The love of shame does not "merge," does not synthesize, but flourishes in the very space of personal fissure. This is unsurprising, in that Silvan Tomkins (whose work Sedgwick's extends and to which it pays homage) describes shame as "strik[ing] deepest into the heart of man":

> While terror and distress hurt, they are wounds inflicted from outside which penetrate the smooth surface of the ego; but shame is felt as an inner torment, a sickness of the soul. It does not matter whether the humiliated one has been shamed by derisive laughter or whether he mocks himself. In either event he feels himself naked, defeated, alienated, lacking in dignity and worth.[42]

Tomkins associates shame with guilt and, to a lesser extent, humiliation. I think also of a resonant (if only because so pervasively, campily familiar) articulation of the link between shame and embarrassment: "I could just die!" Kids often say this in movies after they have done something embarrassing, or if their parents have done something terrible in their presence. Less common now than in the fifties (cf. Sandra Dee), the articulation clarifies an implicit relation between shame and the strategies of self-abdication found in Butlerian performative subversion and Bersanian psychosexual askesis. *I could just die!* More often than not a performance of shame rather than a literal threat (shame, after all, is, as Sedgwick suggest, the performative affect par excellence[43]), this articulation of shame nonetheless speaks to the ways shame, as an affect, erupts not just in the space between one version of self and another (as in James), but also in the space where one *wants* another self, and more acutely, wants to give up the self one *has*.[44] Hence, synonymously, our (nonetymological) understanding of feeling mortified, of mortification.

"Shame," Tomkins writes, is "a specific inhibitor of continuing interest and enjoyment."[45] Shame, that is, inhibits not only enjoyment, but continuity. To live without shame, hypothetically, would be to live continuously, without the trauma of wanting to disappear, without the need to reinvent one's "younger self" as a new (if no less fictional) person. Life without shame might approach the stability of Butler's melancholy congealment; even as Tomkins writes that shame, in its renunciation of or abandonment by a loved one, is "not unlike mourning, in which I become exquisitely aware of the self just because I will not surrender the love object which must be surrendered."[46] Here we come to a double bind. The stable self is constitutively melancholic, and yet the unstable self, florid with "its own, powerfully productive and powerfully social metamorphic possibilities"[47] is constituted by an affect that might "not [be] unlike mourning." Why should the opposite paths of ontological stability and instability feel (if not like approaching a rock and a hard place than) like walking in circles?

Shame, for Sedgwick, "generates and legitimates the place of identity . . . but does so without giving that identity space the standing of an essence" (64). While identities are not to be essentialized, however, Sedgwick claims that "at least for certain ('queer') people, shame is simply the first, and remains a permanent, structuring fact of identity" (64). The force of Sedgwick's "simply," "permanent," and "fact" introduces a dissonance between shame's fostering of affective and ontological equivocation (what Sedgwick terms "possibilities") and its own stringent unequivocality. Shame, as conjured by Sedgwick, seldom seems shame-like, per se. This, often, is to Sedgwick's credit, in showing via James how a "potentially paralyzing affect" can be both seen and experienced as "narratively, emotionally, and performatively productive" (44). What Sedgwick identifies in James's writing as "occasions for shame and excitement" (46) do not, however, seem directly to bear on shame. Sedgwick cites this passage from James's preface to *The Wings of the Dove*:

> I haven't the heart now, I confess, to adduce the detail of so many lapsed importances; the explanations of most of which, after all, I take to have been in the crudity of a truth beating full upon me through these reconsiderations, the odd inveteracy with which picture, at almost any turn, is jealous of drama, and drama (though on the whole with greater patience, I think) suspicious of picture. Between them, no doubt, they do much for the theme; yet each baffles insidiously the other's ideals and eats round the edges of its positions. (46)

Why denominate these various affective maneuvers — these odd personifications of aesthetic media — shame, when they are tinged with delight (for instance, the delight of imagining "drama" and "picture" eating around each other's edges)? Such a question, following both the early work of Charles Darwin and more recently, the work of Mark Hansen,[48] attempts to characterize not just what any particular affect is, but how long it lasts, what it cedes to, and why or how it cedes. The degree to which Sedgwick's conception of shame, at this Jamesian juncture, seems more convincing on a nominal rather than affective register recalls, again, the ways Butler's melancholy often doesn't quite seem melancholic (as recounted either in a text such as Julia Kristeva's *Black Sun,* or as experienced by myself or anyone else). Or the way Bersani's self-shattering describes an obliteration that on a somatic level (or even, speculatively, on a psychical one) doesn't occur so much as hover, beguilingly, as an idea.[49]

"Blazons of shame, the 'fallen face' with eyes down and head averted — and, to a lesser extent, the blush — are semaphores of trouble and at the same time of a desire to reconstitute the interpersonal bridge" (Sedgwick 36). I question the inevitable simultaneity ("at the same time") of shame's semaphoric "trouble" and its desire for reconnection. Shame (at its most felicitous) cedes to a desire to reconstitute interpersonality, but this desire seems neither synchronous with nor equivalent to shame's desire to hide.

Sedgwick posits shame as "the first" and "permanent, structuring fact of [certain ('queer')] identity":

> Queers, I'd suggest, might usefully be thought of as referring in the first place to this group or an overlapping group of infants and children, those whose sense of identity is for some reason tuned most durably to the note of shame. . . . The shame-delineated place of identity doesn't determine the consistency or meaning of that identity, and race, gender, class, sexuality, appearance, and abledness are only a few of the defining social constructions that will crystallize there, developing from this originary affect their particular structure of expression, creativity, pleasure, and struggle.[50]

Why, in the midst of all these social constructions, is shame granted originary privilege? Tomkins usefully notes that before shame there exists an even more originary positivity:

> One of the paradoxical consequences of the linkage of positive affect and shame is that the same positive affect which ties the self to the object also ties the self to shame. To the extent to which socialization involves a preponderance of positive affect the individual is made vulnerable to shame and unwilling to renounce either himself or others.[51]

Before one can have shame, before one can be disappointed into blushing (or performative blazoning), one must previously have nursed some "preponderance of positive affect." But why, if positive affect so clearly precedes shame, is shame pronounced foundational? I don't disagree with Sedgwick on the point of shame's interlineation and coloring of queer experiences. I nonetheless challenge the insistence of shame's anteriority at the expense of elaborations of the sorts of positivity that might have preceded it; at the expense of the queer continuities that shame might be able to interrupt, but is unable wholly to address.

Toujours du Jour

I do not take my readings of Butler or Bersani as definitive, nor do I imagine these moments in their respective oeuvres as synecdochically representative of their work. I mean, rather, to articulate some of the ways in which Butler's and Bersani's rigorous thinking itself sometimes seems predicated on curiously nonrigorous attachments to melancholy, or to unqualified aggressions calling for no less qualified a resort to self-shattering. My account of Sedgwick — by my own appraisal, even less definitive — does not critique Sedgwick's analyses of shame for lack of scrutiny (the sort of scrutiny I find lacking in Butler's and Bersani's respective accounts of melancholy or aggression). Rather, I've sought to note how Sedgwick's thinking makes available an affective territory far more interesting and various than the denomination "shame" could (or further, should) describe.

Juxtaposed with Lee Edelman's 2004 book, *No Future,* the orchestratively powerful but more or less latent queer pessimisms of the above theorists seem like kid stuff (to invoke Edelman's own charged co-opting of this formulation). The queer pessimism of Butler and Bersani, circuited from text to text in an eloquence inseparable from its occludedness, brings to mind Jean Laplanche's enigmatic signifier.[52] Edelman's queer pessimism, by contrast, insistent on its own absolute nonenigmatic unequivocality, might suggest the draconian bravura of a superego were Edelman's project not so pitted against the superego, pitted against all forms of stable psychic identity except the "irreducible"[53] identity of the death drive. Though it breeches the basic divisions of psychoanalysis, it is difficult for me not to hear in the sheer absoluteness of Edelman's dicta something like a superego's militancy.

Edelman insists that "the only oppositional status to which our queerness could ever lead would depend on our taking seriously the place of the death drive we're called on to figure" (30). Edelman, as the passage I've cited might suggest, doesn't seem to leave queers a lot of options, even as the option he adjures hardly seems self-evident. The egregious militancy of *No Future* presents an apogee of what I've been calling queer pessimism. Or if not apogee, then pessimism-in-drag. My own thinking differs from Edelman's in many ways, and might surfacially seem self-evident.[54] How, for instance, could a project attached to queer optimism not bristle at a book that insists that "the only oppositional status" available to queers demands fealty to the death drive? Edelman's book certainly trounces optimism, but the optimism he trounces is not the optimism for which my own project lobbies. Against queer optimism's proliferation of local specificities[55] — and no less, against queer optimism's resistance to foreclosing futural entrapment — Edelman writes,

> The structuring optimism of politics to which the order of meaning commits us, installing as it does the perpetual hope of reaching meaning through signification, is always, I would argue, a negation of this primal, constitutive, and negative act. And the various positivities produced in its wake by the logic of political hope depend on the mathematical illusion that negated negations might somehow escape, and not redouble, such negativity. My polemic thus stakes its fortunes on a truly hopeless wager: that taking the Symbolic's negativity to the very letter of the law . . . that turning the force of queerness against all subjects, however queer, can afford an access to the *jouissance* that at once defines us and negates us. Or better: can expose the constancy, the inescapability, of such access to jouissance in the social order itself, even if that order can access its constant access to jouissance only in the process of abjecting that constancy of access onto the queer. (5)

As I've made clear and, as a later section of this introduction will make clearer, *Queer Optimism* is no more attached to "the logic of political hope" than is *No Future*. Even as I think there are some forms of hope worth defending, I'm not interested, for present purposes, in demarcating good and bad hopes, hegemonic and nonhegemonic attachments to futurity. To the extent that my own project seeks to recuperate optimism's potential critical interest by arguing for its separability from the promissory, I'm here insisting that there are ways of resisting a pernicious logic of "reproductive futurism" besides embodying the death drive. If Edelman opines that all forms of optimism eventually lead to Little Orphan Annie singing "Tomorrow," and therefore that all forms of optimism must be met with queer death-driven irony's "always explosive force" (31), I oppositely insist that optimism's limited cultural and theoretical intelligibility calls not for its grandiose excoriation, but for its (no less grandiosely) being rethought along nonfutural lines. Edelman's hypostasization of optimism accepts optimism as at best simplistic and at worst fascistic. This hypostasization leaves unthinkable *Queer Optimism's* own proposition that the reduction of optimism to a diachronic, futurally bound axis is itself the outcome of a machinery that spits out optimism as junk and renders suspicious any form of "enjoyment" that isn't a (mis)translation of *jouissance,* "a violent passage beyond the bounds of identity, meaning, and law" (25), production of "identity as mortification." Enjoyment, anyone?[56]

Edelman's might be one way of refusing the logic of reproductive futurism, but not the only one. That there be many possible queer courses of action might indeed seem to follow from Edelman's invoking of Lacanian truth (*Wunsch*) as characterized by nothing so much as its extravagant, recalcitrant particularity. "The *Wunsch,*" Lacan writes in a passage cited in *No Future's* introduction, "does not have the character of a universal law but, on the contrary, of the most particular of laws—even if it is universal that this particularity is to be found in every human being" (6). Edelman, for all his attentiveness to the Lacanian "letter of the law," glosses Lacan's own argument with symptomatic liberality. "Truth, like queerness," Edelman writes, "finds its value not in a good susceptible to generalization, but only in the stubborn particularity that voids every notion of a general good. The embrace of queer negativity, then, can have no justification if justification requires it to reinforce some positive social value" (6). Lacan, however, does not speak of a "general good." He speaks of a universal, which might be good *or bad.* Furthermore, if the only characteristic universally applicable to this "truth, like queerness" is its particularity, what sort of particularity voids every notion of a general good? Might so intransigent a particularity sometimes not void a universal, good or bad?[57]

My line of inquiry might seem petty, but my question, in fact, illuminates how little Edelman's argument is able to hold on to the particularity on which it partly is premised. "[T]he queer," Edelman insists, "insists that politics is always a politics of the signifier" (6). Edelman likewise contends that "queer theory must always insist on its connection to the vicissitudes of the sign" (7). The ubiquity of "always" and "every," in Edelman's argument, is stunning, and both contrary to Lacan's insistence on particularity, and indicative of *No Future's* coerciveness, as a different passage from *No Future's* introduction handily demonstrates:

> Rather than rejecting, with liberal discourse, this ascription of negativity to the queer, we might, as I argue, do better to consider accepting and even embracing it. Not in the hope of forging thereby some more perfect social order — such a hope, after all, would only reproduce the constraining mandate of futurism, just as any such order would equally occasion the negativity of the queer — but rather to refuse the insistence of hope itself as affirmation, which is always affirmation of an order whose refusal will register as unthinkable, irresponsible, inhumane. And the trump card of affirmation? Always the question: If not this, what? Always the demand to translate the insistence, the pulsive *force,* of negativity into some determinate stance or "position" whose determination would negate it: always the imperative to immure it in some stable and positive form. (4)

Always this, always this, always that. This absoluteness, meant to rally and provoke, recalls Sedgwick's incredulous reading of Frederic Jameson's ukase, "Always historicize." "What could have less to do," Sedgwick rightly asks, "with historicizing than the commanding, atemporal adverb 'always'?"[58] What, for that matter, could have less to do with particularization? The axiomatic thrust of Edelman's "always" makes the world so irrevocably one thing that response to the world amounts to one thing. But still: why does rejection of a primary attachment to futurity (regardless of what this futurity always does or doesn't do) necessarily require the embodiment of negativity?[59]

Edelman's queer pessimism positions itself as "our" only option without having exhausted what other options might glimmeringly look like. This glimmer doesn't conjure the sort of horizon Edelman is so quick to dismantle. It suggests that not all optimisms are a priori equivalent to each other. And as importantly, that not all queer theories need look like Edelman's. "As a particular story . . . of why storytelling fails," Edelman writes, "queer theory, as I construe it, marks the 'other' side of politics . . . the 'side' outside all political sides, committed as they are, on every side, to futurism's unquestioned good" (7). This account of queer theory, even as construed by one theorist, hardly seems like a "particular" story, not at least particular enough. Queer theory, on this account, doesn't seem like an escape from the political's claustrophobically refracted unavailing sides, but a claustrophobia unto itself.[60]

"If Not This, What?"

To return to Edelman's own question, "if not this, what?" The structure of such a question allows possible answers beyond the foreclosing choices that queer theory, these past decades, often has been asked to make. Mourning or melancholia? Gay pride or queer shame? Utopic or nonutopic? Even as the diacritical assertion of queer pessimism versus queer optimism might seem yet another reductive binary, queer optimism, as an answer to "if not this, what?" first and foremost resists the self-evidence of the diverse things this "what" *is*. For instance, Butler reiterates in *Giving an Account of Oneself* what she earlier maintains in *The Psychic Life of Power* as the ethical value of "affirm[ing] what is contingent and incoherent in oneself."[61] It seems crucial, in affirming what is incoherent in oneself, to understand likewise what is coherent and, furthermore, crucial to have a vocabulary as adequate to coherence as to coherence's disruption. Why take coherence for granted? Why presume coherence as characterizable only in the attenuated, noncritical terms against which queer theory and other poststructuralist disciplines inveigh? Dissatisfaction with a given regime of coherence might sponsor a critical commitment to dismantling coherence *tout court*. Such a dissatisfaction, however, might likewise productively sponsor a reconfiguration of coherence — the cultivation of a vocabulary of coherence that more precisely does justice to the ways in which coherence isn't expansively, unilaterally destructive, reductive, or ideological.

To imagine a reevaluation of something like personal coherence as a queer-optimistic project requires, as I have been arguing, a reevaluation of optimism itself. Disdain for optimism (as commonly practiced or invoked) might solicit optimism's wholesale repudiation (à la Edelman) — or it might solicit optimism's own redress. Optimism's queer contents seem inaccessible so long as optimism is sustained as futural, as allergic to scrupulous thinking. To account for what in optimism heretofore has seemed unthinkable, it is useful to return to Leibniz, insofar as Leibniz's writing — and more to the point, his writing's reception — underpins many of the ways in which optimism has been thought (or more to the point, not thought) about. I do not pretend to do Leibniz's theodicy justice so much as to note where Leibnizian optimism most veers from my own investigations. My critique of Leibniz is not necessarily completely commensurate with my critique of queer theory. And as this introduction wishes already to have made clear, one of the ends of reconceiving optimism as an intellectual venture is to open the possibility of a criticism — even skepticism — that is itself optimistically motivated. I turn to this account of Leibniz — and by extension, Leibnizian and non-Leibnizian happiness — to suggest the penuries of our current repertoires for optimism and happiness. Again: what if these penuries compelled us to think harder about optimism or happiness, rather than accept their straw-figure hypostasizations as grounds for their dismissal or too easy excoriation?

Before turning to what in Leibniz sponsors the modes of optimism from which my own project diverges, I wish to note one extraordinary way in which Leibnizian optimism itself differs from the optimisms invoked by Berlant, Bersani, Edelman, or Warner. Leibnizian optimism is not, in fact, futurally oriented. Optimism, etymologically evoking one who hopes, might somehow have come to name one strain of Leibniz's philosophy, but Leibniz's writing — even when most resembling Panglossian caricature of it — has as little staked in hope or future as Edelman's antioptative *No Future*. In his 1686 *Discourse on Metaphysics,* Leibniz delineates the tenets of what would later be described as his optimism. "Therefore," Leibniz writes,

> it is sufficient to have the confidence that God does everything for the best and that nothing can harm those who love him. But to know in detail the reasons that could have moved him to choose this order of the universe — to allow sins, to dispense his saving grace in a certain way — surpasses the power of a finite mind, especially when it has not yet attained the enjoyment of the vision of God.[62]

As Deleuze notes, "Leibniz's optimism is really strange."[63] Really strange, in that "miseries are not what was missing; the best of all possibilities only blossoms amid the ruins of Platonic Good. If this world exists, it is not because it is the best, but because it is rather the inverse; it is the best because it is, because it is the one that is. The philosopher is still not the Inquisitor he will soon become with empiricism. . . . He is a Lawyer, or God's attorney. He defends God's Cause, following the word that Leibniz invents, 'theodicy.' "[64] That is, when Leibniz exhorts that we find all God's works excellent and in complete conformity with what we might have desired, he neither claims that any given work would seem manifestly delightful, nor that our desires only retroactively could be known.

Related but not equivalent to Leibnizian tautology is a more familiarly teleological model of wishful thinking, whereby time could reveal the commensurability of God's work and our desire. Leibniz, however, doesn't need time to prove what faith simply makes known,[65] faith being that which posits optimism not as practice but as given. Following Leibniz, a struggle to remain optimistic in the face of calamity or distress signals not a wavering of optimism, per se, but a wavering of faith, whose digital robustness forecloses faith as analogic sliding-scale. One believes or one does not, without gradation. Similarly, either one is optimistic, or one is not. To struggle to remain optimistic belies that one is not optimistic, that one already has fallen from the logic by which optimism is upheld. To believe in the goodness of God makes optimism not a choice, or even an attitude, but that faith's inevitable extension. Faith's capacity to convert all crises (past, present, future) into manifestations of the good indicates the extent to which Leibniz's theodicy is as imperializing as the pessimisms of queer theory. That is, the *semper* of Leibniz and the *semper* of Edelman are equivalently suspect, even if programatically opposed.

At the same time, however, this Leibnizian *semper* is exactly that which countermands any privileging of futurity. Faith subordinates human experience of time (past, present, future) to a divine temporality in which temporal distinctions all but vanish; God already has orchestrated what will happen no less than what already has happened. As Leibniz writes,

> The whole future is doubtless determined: but since we know not what it is, nor what is foreseen or resolved, we must do our duty, according to the reason that God has given us and according to the rules that he has prescribed for us; and therefore we must have a quiet mind, and leave to God himself the care for the outcome.[66]

Humans perhaps equivocate, but Leibniz's God does not, and in the fundamental nonequivocality of what divinely will happen, the future consequently for all practical purposes lies beyond engagement, revision, or hope — contrary to the ways optimism, after Leibniz, is not beyond hope but generated by it.

My turn from Leibniz, then, does not stem from his valuation of futurity; optimism as valuation of futurity seems a gross mischaracterization of both Leibniz's *Discourse* and his *Theodicy.* Queer optimism is non-Leibnizian in its resistance to faith at the expense of thinking. Leibnizian optimism lies beyond theorization not because it consigns determination or delight to a futural horizon, but because the faith that underwrites it looms beyond interrogation. This brand of optimistic unimpeachability characterized both the exasperating contumaciousness of George W. Bush's two terms in office, as well as Howard Dean's infamously Whitmanian barbaric yawp of January 2004. The former — now as much as then — lies beyond theorization because (among myriad less glib reasons) Bush is incapable of theorizing; the latter, beyond theorization to the extent that Dean's whoop came on the heels of defeat, what J. L. Austin might characterize as an optimistic performative utterance executed under infelicitous conditions. A person (e.g., George W. Bush) might possess the faith that makes credible the divinely infinite logic that to his finite mind is otherwise incomprehensible, or he might not. I raise the examples of Bush and Dean to note the ways in which optimism in past years has saturated the American political field, determining the fate of presidential campaigns, initiating and sustaining otherwise untenable-seeming policies and positions (not to mention wars). Optimism's political power (if not eloquence) makes its critical reexamination — as opposed to its critical eschewal — all the more timely, and crucial.

Leibnizian happiness is chronic and beyond question, even as the means of this interminable happiness remain, secularly speaking, altogether unavailable. Leibnizian optimism purports a structure in which nonhappiness might arise as an erosion of faith, as an erosion, that is, of a happiness that is otherwise structurally inescapable. I find the possible ordeal of inescapable happiness fascinating, in part because such an understanding so extravagantly revises how happiness ordinarily is considered. If optimism eludes or renders gratuitous theorization via a tautology (Deleuze's "it is the one that is") that fashions optimism as conceptually expansive and indelible as the world itself, happiness — plain old happy, not Leibniz's mega-happy — oppositely eludes theorization because it is so transient. Non-Leibnizian happiness isn't inextricable from structure (for instance, Leibnizian faith) but experienced as a disruption of structure.

Disruption, in fact, is how the psychoanalyst Jonathan Lear describes happiness in his account not of Leibniz, but of Aristotle:

> If contemplation were a state that one could achieve and sustain indefinitely and unproblematically, then Aristotle would have been led to feel discontent within it — and he would start to fantasize a *real* happiness which lies just outside.[67]

Continuing his discussion of contemplation as a site of happiness happier than that derived from living ethically, Lear observes that "those few who do manage to find time to contemplate will experience that time as precious and short-lived."[68] The supreme happiness afforded by contemplation, that is, lies outside the realm of ethics, outside the structures in which a person usually operates. More than this, this moment in which contemplation occurs is "precious and short-lived." In Leibniz's model, happiness is the structure from which one falls. In Lear's non-Leibnizian (Aristotelian) model, happiness lies outside of structure. Indeed, in Lear's work, happiness more closely resembles Edelman's death drive (in its disruption of life-as-lived), than it does the pleasure principle (despite happiness's quotidian associations with pleasure), whose status as principle Lear finds antithetical to happiness's propensity to disrupt principles as such:

> Here we need to go back to an older English usage of "happiness" in terms of happenstance: the experience of chance things' working out well rather than badly. Happiness, in this interpretation . . . is a lucky break. . . . If one thinks about it, I think one will see that in such fleeting moments we do find real happiness.[69]

Despite Lear's chiasmatic invoking of thinking, it seems unclear how such fleeting happiness could be thought about. One could recollect it, but could one articulate it beyond the fact that it feels good, quickly? Or that it feels so different from life that it approaches something like death? As Lear writes, "The fantasy of a happy life becomes tinged with the suggestion of a life beyond life—a certain kind of living death."[70] It is not surprising, given this early claim, that Lear concludes that "certain structural similarities exist between Aristotle's treatment of happiness and Freud's treatment of death. Happiness and death are each invoked as the purported aim of all striving."[71] The difficulty of really thinking about happiness (as opposed to the ease of thinking that real happiness arrives fleetingly) is a function of its presumed fleetingness. Were one able to articulate happiness more thoroughly or even imagine it as less fleeting, would it seem as authentically happy?

Queer Optimism involves a thought-experiment. What if happiness could outlast fleeting moments, without that persistence attenuating the quality of happiness? What if instead of attenuating happiness, this extension of happiness opened it up to critical investigations that didn't a priori doubt it, but instead made happiness complicated, and strange? (That is, what if the "quality of happiness" were not itself a given?) If the insights of the past few decades have mobilized shame, shattering, or melancholy as *interesting* (as opposed to instances of fear and trembling) what if we could learn from those insights and critical practices, and imagine happiness as theoretically mobilizable, as conceptually difficult? Which is to ask, what if happiness weren't merely, self-reflexively happy, but interesting? *Queer Optimism* cannot guarantee what such a happiness would look like, how such a happiness would feel. And while it does not promise a road to an Emerald City, *Queer Optimism* avails a new terrain of critical inquiry, which seems a felicity in its own right.

Persons and Poetry

There are many reasons why *Queer Optimism* situates its interventions in queer theory within extended analyses of poetry. Were *Queer Optimism* solely a critique of queer theory, it wouldn't necessarily need an archive beyond queer theory's own. As a critique of certain theoretical limitations and an effort to think beyond those limitations, *Queer Optimism* necessitates a critical vocabulary exceeding those otherwise available. The poems from which I have culled and cultivated this queer-optimistic vocabulary are striking as experiments in the very forms of affect and personhood I seek to rescue from short shrift. As experiments, these poems bear patient curiosity toward their own unfamiliarities; that is, these poems treat as unfamiliar that with which criticism prematurely has dispensed as exhausted. Even in their diverse assertiveness, these poems raise questions (of themselves, of readers) about both the grounds on which such assertions might be made, as well as such assertions' consequences. Assertion, within these poems, suggests neither initial hypothesis nor subsequent conclusion, but rather constitutes the time and form of lyric experimentation, itself.[72]

I understand my own readings of these poems as attempts to retrace their own exacting, often disorienting procedures. I intend less to resolve lyric difficulty than adequately to describe it. My motives, in this regard, follow Bersani's early account of the rigorous sensitivity for which Mallarmé's poetry calls.[73] As a critical endeavor, resolution seems less remunerative, less yielding, than the resolve of articulating and sustaining formal difficulty — against resolution's opposing lures. Such resolve acquires all the more relevance, given *Queer Optimism's* critical ambition to restore complexity to a queer-optimistic field already under the duress of preemptively resolving simplification.

I've turned to poetic phenomena as both instantiations of queer optimism in practice and as the impetus for my own articulations of queer-optimistic theory. In this way, *Queer Optimism* posits — on a register different from queer-theoretical critique or supplement — the utility of poetry as an archive. Following the liquidation of New Criticism and in the ambivalent wake of Paul de Man, lyric poetry has become a genre susceptible to many of the charges likewise leveled against optimism, positive affect, and nonincoherent persons. Lyric poetry, like optimism or joy, solipsistically disengages from or flits above the crises of lived experience. Lyric poetry, like nonincoherent personhood, forges the semblance of coherence only in its severance from the conditions by which it is produced. Both of the above pronouncements—which I find equally fatuous—rehearse indictments of lyric poetry, and even more so, of the New Criticism that continues to organize lyric reception.[74] *Queer Optimism's* argument on behalf of the utility of poetry does not, in fact, ask for lyric poetry's detachment from New Critical methodology. As subsequent chapters make clear, my frustration with queer theory might be characterized as frustration with the distorting lenses by which queer theory often reads (misreads and underreads) itself, distortions that formalist attention renders both discernable and inhabitable. Engagement predicated on formalist attention entails a mode of scholarship beholden to New Critical close reading practices, and that challenges the ineluctability of New Criticism's caricatured attachment to detachment.

My readings of Hart Crane, Emily Dickinson, Jack Spicer and Elizabeth Bishop gravitate toward those moments in their writing where poetry's particular rhetorical repertoire vividly strains. *Queer Optimism*—following Edelman's important argument in *Homographesis* for the deep rhetorical ligatures of desire and panic—extends earlier examinations of queer rhetoric into the margins of metaphor, personification, and repetition, pushed to their own conventional limit: to the points at which metaphoricity and nonmetaphoricity, personification and nonpersonification, most confoundingly buckle. My analysis of rhetorical difficulty intends to complicate and contextualize queer theory's understanding of figuration. What does it mean, for instance, when Edelman's *No Future* exhorts queers to "figure" the death drive? What would it mean to imagine oneself as a figure, granted figuration's various capacities? Such questions reflect the extent to which New Critical and de Manian parsings of rhetoric already are engaged with a lived world; all the more so, as queer theory limns lived experience (however one understands such a formulation) not only as metaphorically figurative, but literally so.

Queer theory is not the only line of inquiry suspicious of the status of persons and personhood. Poetry nonetheless is especially suited to respond to queer theory's suspicions, insofar as the latter replicate conceptions of impersonality on which much contemporary poetry criticism turns. Poetry criticism's conception of impersonality, in turn, stems from T. S. Eliot's 1919 essay, "Tradition and the Individual Talent."[75] Eliot's essay is an inaugurating moment in the history of poetry criticism's reevaluation of individual personality. Even as Eliot can't be made to stand as origin for all of the reading and writing practices the following chapters will claim under the rubric of pessimism, he nonetheless is never too far from their wings. His essay is useful as one of the earliest delineations of what has come to be understood as modernist impersonality.[76]

Published a year before *Beyond the Pleasure Principle,* "Tradition and the Individual Talent" importunes a poetics of impersonality with a rhetorical aggressiveness as uncompromising as Bersani's own. At the same time, the scientific rhetoric to which Eliot turns—a conceit whose enacted neutrality recapitulates on a different register the impersonality that the essay manifestly urges—turns on itself, instantiating a resistance to the impersonal inseparable from the latter's articulation:

> What happens is a continual surrender of himself as he is at the moment to something which is more valuable. The progress of an artist is a continual self-sacrifice, a continual extinction of personality.
>
> There remains to define this process of depersonalization and its relation to the sense of tradition. It is in this depersonalization that art may be said to approach the condition of science. I shall, therefore, invite you to consider, as a suggestive analogy, the action which takes place when a bit of finely filiated platinum is introduced into a chamber containing oxygen and sulphur dioxide.[77]

Eliot charges the processes that "depersonalization" requires—"continual surrender," "continual self-sacrifice," "continual extinction"—with a ruthless theatricality that is absent from Eliot's corresponding descriptions of the "artist" who wills them. Whereas surrender, self-sacrifice, and extinction (intend to) clarify what art demands of an artist, the particular qualities of "an artist" remain unspecified. It is unclear how we are to understand the artist in relation to the absolute vagueness of "himself as he is at the moment," a conception of an artist so nonspecific as to suggest he already has been subjected to the depersonalization that Eliot goes on to describe. Even as "artist" denotes a particularity greater than "himself as he is," "artist" (like "art") dilates the particular sort of artist (poet) and art (poetry) that is Eliot's immediate concern. Even the essay's nearly iconic title is susceptible to (or colludes in) the dilations enacted in the above passage. "Tradition," after all, isn't juxtaposed with an individual poet (or writer, or artist), but with "talent," which only metonymically describes "himself as he is," winnowing the poet to the aptitudes that might make him a poet in the first place.

Eliot's circumnavigations, in these instances, perhaps trouble the idea that there is a poet to speak of — insofar as the essay seems to present at outset what it otherwise purports as its terminus. Where is the poet here? Where is the person that would save "this process of depersonalization" from gratuitousness? That a person (a poet any more particular than artist-as-himself-as-he-is) is missing might as much suggest that Eliot himself can't quite imagine (or bring himself to) subjecting persons any less abstract than those invoked to the processes of extinction that he claims poetry requires. And if Eliot's essay is able to demand allegiance to depersonalization only if persons themselves safely are evacuated from its premises, why (or how) should *we* be able to conceive of impersonality in terms any less fraught, any less qualified?

Personhood, within the above passage, arises most enigmatically in an etymological error. Sapient classicist that he was, Eliot might have known that "filiated" derives from the Latin nouns "filius" or "filia," and not the neuter "filum." Eliot's platinum, etymologically speaking, thus has more to do with affiliation — with having a child, or being a son or daughter — than with the shreds of filaments. Furthermore, the contingencies of filiation proffer a model of tradition that is constituted by the particularities of persons, rather than the erasures of them. "Filiated platinum" both participates in and resists a scientism whose own neutrality art "may be said to approach." In this manner, the progression of Eliot's analogy both advances and withdraws from its own exorbitant claims:[78]

> The analogy was that of the catalyst. When the two gases previously mentioned [oxygen and sulphur dioxide] are mixed in the presence of a filament of platinum, they form sulphurous acid. The combination takes place only if the platinum is present; nevertheless the newly formed acid contains no trace of platinum, and the platinum itself

> is apparently unaffected; has remained inert, neutral, and unchanged. The mind of the poet is the shred of platinum. It may partly or exclusively operate upon the experience of the man himself; but, the more perfect the artist, the more completely separate in him will be the man who suffers and the mind which creates; the more perfectly will the mind digest and transmute the passions which are its material.[79]

"Continual self-sacrifice" and "continual extinction" result in a poem, which, within the analogy, corresponds to "the newly formed" sulphurous acid. "Suggestive[ly]" absent from Eliot's metaphor, however, are the qualities of this sulphurous acid, which can cause pulmonary edema, and if "digest[ed]" corrode the mouth, throat, and esophagus. Upon ingestion, uncontrolled vomiting may occur. To parse the analogy Eliot "invite[s]" us "to consider," the poem produced along such lines would be nothing if not uningestable; and if ingested, capable of corrosions far more extended, far more wrenching, than the invisible interactions of "the two gases." Eliot's analogy is confusing, and becomes more so as one tries to grasp it.[80] To what within the realm of poetry, for example, do these two gases correspond? "[T]he elements which enter the presence of the transforming catalyst," Eliot continues, "are of two kinds: emotions and feelings."[81] Are these two "elements" the two gases? Or are we elsewhere within Eliot's scientism?[82] As the paragraph progresses, it seems these two elements, "emotions and feelings," might not be analogous to "oxygen and sulphur dioxide" (fair enough, since the analogy seems to require that one of the gases correspond to something like tradition?), because sometimes "great poetry may be made without the direct use of any emotion whatever: composed out of feelings solely."[83]

What if "emotions and feelings" still somehow corresponded to the gases of Eliot's filiated experiment? A poetry "composed out of feelings solely" might amount to platinum in a chamber of sulphur dioxide (or more happily, platinum left with nothing but oxygen) — that is to say, a poetry safe from its own textual correlatives to toxic corrosion. Such scientific speculation intimates within Eliot's essay a possible compassion for the poet exempt from the analogy's thick scientific rhetoric, but which that rhetoric risks occluding:

> the more perfect the artist, the more completely separate in him will be the man who suffers and the mind which creates.

A poet, then, works not only toward his own self-sacrifice, but toward a sequestering "in him" of "the man who suffers." Is this suffering—anticipating Edelman or Bersani—that of self-sacrifice itself, or that of simply being "himself as he is?" Along these latter lines, Eliot's essay serves as precedent for *Queer Optimism*'s own enterprise, in reconceiving poetry as the space from which one might escape (or at least temporarily suspend) the nonnecessary interlineations of suffering and being: suffering and writing, suffering and thinking. Personhood as conceived in this Eliotic manner lyrically can experiment with conceptions of itself, released from suffering's own extinguishing, surrendering ultimata. Personhood, in this context, no more opposes "the mind which creates" than it apposes "the man who suffers." Even within Eliot's call for impersonality, we find the possibility for reunderstanding a mind's creativeness not as that which requires depersonalization, but as something synonymous with personality itself. In the spirit of this reprieve at the heart of impersonality's self-corroding energies, the next paragraphs outline what the subsequent chapters conceive as the optimistic poetics of Hart Crane, Emily Dickinson, Jack Spicer, and Elizabeth Bishop.[84]

My investigation begins with Hart Crane, a poet as famous for his alcoholism and eventual suicide as for his difficult poems. This difficulty (often cited as evidence of his poetic failure) coupled with his biography's trail of dissipations, has made Crane uniquely available to the sorts of pessimistic readings already outlined. Against such readings, I explore the proliferation, within Hart Crane's poetry, of the figure of the smile. More vexing than any one of these smiles is their mysterious, collective force as a serial trope. The collective force of these incessantly iterated smiles is matched by the force of even a single smile's given instance, in that many of these smiles (for instance, those of Crane's famously difficult poem, "Possessions," or the late, less well known poem "The Circumstance") are explicitly associated with the petrifactions and resistances of stone. Something like rocky durability is differently signaled in other Cranian smiles (for instance, those of "Lachrymae Christi"), described as "unyielding" and "unmangled." Adjectives, in Crane's poems, suggest personal contexts more than the smiles that they modify: in the textual space between such an adjective and a smilerless smile, Crane conjures a personal will that yields or doesn't yield, a body that has survived some violence unmangled (and simultaneously, the bodies that have not). I argue that these perdurable smiles bear an important relation to the project of poetic optimism (which Crane himself conceived in opposition to what he perceived as T. S. Eliot's poetic pessimism) to which Crane's lyrics aspire; and furthermore, that both Crane's smiles and his articulations of optimism have thus far been overlooked, due to preemptive commitments (on the parts of even his best critics) to tropes of impermanence and negativity.

Emily Dickinson, like Crane, explores within her poetry the phenomenon of a smile that outlasts its ordinary duration. In Dickinson as in Crane, a lyric smile's persistence beyond initial cause (or even stranger, *before* initial cause) does not metonymically gesture toward any correlatively persistent or resilient happiness. Such an inference is less interesting in Dickinson and Crane than the fact of affective durability itself. Crane's smiles seem to exist not only apart from persons (i.e., smilers), but devoid of the personal contexts that make smiles intelligible. Dickinson's smiles, and more generally, her accounts of pleasure and pain, likewise exist without persons; in the Dickinson lyrics I explore, however, the absence of recognizable persons or personal contexts occasions the personification of feelings. For instance, in a poem such as "Delight's despair at setting" Dickinson not only asks what it would mean for "setting" to signal durability, as opposed to evanescence, but imagines a "delight" that could itself experience "despair." The lability characteristic of Dickinson's accounts of feelings (a lability partly derived from the texts' specific personificatory practices) not only is instrumental to Dickinson's analyses of pain (as illuminated by critics such as Sharon Cameron and Jane Eberwein), but amounts to a critique of pain as such. Poems such as "Pain—Expands the Time—" and "I can wade Grief—" describe experiences of pain or grief, but also challenge the inevitability of pain's persuasiveness. In delineating the components of pain's persuasiveness, Dickinson is able to imagine versions of delight or pleasure analogously composed. Such an enterprise is most evident in a poem such as "I got so I could take his name," which invents a secular form of grace capable of intervening in recursive misery, by endowing grace with misery's recursiveness.

My third chapter treats a more explicit (though no less enigmatic) experiment in poetic personhood, that of Jack Spicer's 1958 serial poem

Billy The Kid. My discussions of Crane and Dickinson approach problematics of personhood or personality asymptotically. From those poets' theorizations of personate duress and invention, I turn to Jack Spicer, to challenge what usually is identified as Spicer's own vociferous attachment to a practice of poetic impersonality. In a much-cited lecture given months before his death, Spicer claimed seriality as a crucial means toward achieving poetic impersonality, emptying one's self in a manner similar to that described by T. S. Eliot. In *Billy The Kid,* however, the poem's formal seriality works not to undo the poet, but to preserve the poet's subject, the serially reproduced eponymous cowboy figure. Spicer's relation to this cowboy registers neither the idealizing identifications of Walt Whitman, nor the self-ironizing detachments of Frank O'Hara, nor, for that matter, the ambivalent self-loathing remarked upon by Bersani. Rather, Spicer's love for Billy becomes legible as an effect of the poem's serial practice. As Dickinson renders pain interesting but also subject to critique, Spicer, I argue, experiments with a mode of seriality that might sustain lyrically inscribed persons, even as seriality (from Jean-Paul Sartres to Mark Seltzer) previously has been located only within spheres of depersonalization.[85]

My study of Elizabeth Bishop differently problematizes categories of personality and love in claiming that Bishop's poetry bears a sustained and as yet unremarked attachment both to Hart Crane's poetry and to Hart Crane as a person. Beginning with the early poem "Casabianca," I suggest that that poem's title resonates as a translation of the title of Crane's first book of poems, *White Buildings,* and furthermore, that the subject of "Casabianca," a burning boy caught in the fires of a sinking ship, resonates with Crane's own ship-deck suicide. Tracing poetic intersections between Bishop and Crane raises the question of how best to account for or even describe the relationship between Bishop, who once wrote in a letter that she was "disintegrating just like Hart Crane,"[86] and Crane himself, a gay poet who committed suicide just years before Bishop was coming into her own as a poet in her own right. Bishop's attempt, within her poetry, to save Crane from a fate already suffered resembles Spicer's attempt to save Billy the Kid. Recalling the techniques of Dickinson, Bishop seeks to poetically sustain Crane by allegorizing him. Specifically, Bishop allegorizes Crane as Love, and in so doing, calls for a reexamination of both the terms by which we understand poetic influence, and the domain of queer love itself. I argue, finally, that Bishop's poetic love for Crane offers a way of differently thinking poetic influence in terms of familial structures — not, as Harold Bloom would have it, between Oedipus and Laius, but between Antigone and her dead brother Polyneices. This is to return in a different way to Eliot's inadvertently beautiful invoking of the "finely filiated."

In ending with a reading of Antigone and Polyneices, I end with a burial of the dead. While such a turn might seem a reversion to the critical pessimisms against which I argue, I think of Antigone's attachment to Polyneices as demonstrative of queer optimism at its most radical: born of Antigone's own coherent intensities, impelled by the jeopardized singularity of her dead brother. Whereas Lacan views Sophocles' tragedy as a paradigmatic expression of the death drive, I argue that *Antigone* teaches us something in excess of the death drive. Beyond the pleasure principle, beyond the death drive, lies the terrain of queer optimism I have begun to outline. An optimism that has learned from death, learned its vocabularies to the point of saturation, and in an act of bravery so unfamiliar as to seem impossible, departs from them.

Envoi

To turn, once more, to "Tradition and the Individual Talent," where we last left it: directly following his reference to "great poetry . . . made without the direct use of any emotion," Eliot gives what would seem to be an example of such poetry. The example (whatever, in the end, it might be said for Eliot to exemplify) is relevant to a discussion of queer theory, not only for its allusion to the *Inferno's* seventh circle of sodomites. I begin the citation from Eliot with the line already mentioned:

> Or great poetry may be made without the direct use of any emotion whatever: composed out of feelings solely. Canto XV of the *Inferno* (Brunetto Latini) is a working up of the emotion evident in the situation: but the effect, though single as that of any work of art, is obtained by considerable complexity of detail. The last quatrain gives an image, a feeling attaching to an image, which "came," which did not develop simply out of what precedes, but which was probably in suspension in the poet's mind until the proper combination arrived for it to add itself to.[87]

The stanza in question itself pertains to optimism — if not queer optimism — insofar as the "feeling attaching to an image" is one of victory over loss. "And he went off," the preceding stanza ends,

> Seeming to me like one of those who run
> Competing for the green cloth in the races
> Upon Verona's field — and of them, like one
>
> Who gains the victory, not one who loses.[88]

What interests me more than these lines of Canto XV, however, are earlier ones, in which Dante thanks Latini, the dead sodomite, for teaching a lesson almost entirely contrary to the ostensible lesson of Eliot's essay. Contrary to the surface claims of "Tradition and the Individual Talent," but inseparable from the ambitions of my book, Dante wishes that Latini might not have to endure his infernal exile. Or in Eliot's own words, not have to live out the sentence of "the man who suffers":

> "Could I have everything for which I long,
>
> You would not still endure this banishment
> Away from human nature," I replied.
> "Your image — dear, fatherly, benevolent —
>
> Being fixed inside my memory, has imbued
> My heart; when in the fair world, hour by hour
> You taught me, patiently, it was you who showed
>
> The way man makes himself feel eternal; therefore,
> The gratitude I feel toward you makes fit
> That while I live, I should declare it here."[89]

Dante's words to Latini are in ways my own words to Crane, Dickinson, Spicer, and Bishop. "You taught me, patiently, it was you who showed / The way man makes himself feel eternal."[90] This is as much to say that these poets — these dead sodomites[91] — have taught and continue to teach me, patiently extending disorientingly persuasive departures from the lesson of Eliot — "the continual surrender of [a poet, or artist, or person] . . . to something which is more valuable" — this, in recent decades, has become a lesson (if not *the* lesson) of queer theory. Poetry criticism and queer theory, the following chapters will argue, have intersected in their mutual insistence that poets and persons aestheticize their own self-abdication for something (prematurely or preemptively designated as) "more valuable," a self-immersion in the naturalized entanglements of knowledge and pain, stability and sadness. *Queer Optimism* differently investigates how Crane, Dickinson, Spicer, and Bishop introduce epistemologies not of pain, but of pleasure; aestheticize not the abdication of personhood, but its sustenance. These poets, to paraphrase Dante, show the way one might feel eternal, but also the way one might, more generally, differently, *feel*.

Chapter One

HART CRANE'S SMILE

Affirming Certain Things

The first creatures on Earth to become aware of time, were the first creatures to smile. —Jean-Luc Godard, *Hélas pour Moi*

Have we the patience to endure? I say YES!
—Hart Crane, in a letter to Samuel Grunberg, February 8, 1932

This chapter offers an investigation[1] — rather than exegesis — of the myriad smiles found throughout the poetry of Hart Crane. Exegesis lies beyond my aims, insofar as my ambition is less to explain these smiles (at worst, tantamount to explaining them away) than to argue for their collective value as a subject of inquiry. The sheer multitude of Crane's poetic smiles is only slightly less extraordinary than the fact that these smiles have hitherto been so cursorily broached by an otherwise sophisticated and burgeoning tradition of Crane scholarship. Extant criticism of Crane's smiles seems cursory to the extent that it seldom takes Crane's smiles as such, so much as co-opt them into neutralizing temporal registers (the nostalgically preterite or untenably futural) or contiguous (but nonequivalent) affective categories. Exemplary of this critical dismissiveness is Eric Sundquist's conflation of smiles and smirks, even as a "smirk" appears in only one of Crane's poem: "Lodged throughout Crane's poetry," Sundquist writes, "in enigmatic postures of martyred comedy, the 'smirk' or 'smile'...has always the questionable status which Freud assigns to the joke." Although smiles are indeed "lodged," enigmatically, "throughout Crane's poetry,"[2] Sundquist's analysis is misleading in its production of equivalence between smiling and smirking — an equivalence that Crane's poetry, taken on its own terms, does not support.

Likewise indicative of Crane criticism's *meconnaissance* of Crane's lyric smiles is Sundquist's presumption that a Cranian smile, when not smirking, is the screen for a more interesting or authentic emotional state: "What is concealed by these smiling facades is a prophetic suffering."[3] Why presume the indistinguishability of smiles and smirks? Why presume that a smile not only is a façade, but a façade for suffering? What does it say about Crane scholarship, and criticism more generally, that a smile, critically speaking, so seldom is allowed to be a smile? As such questions suggest, my subject is not only Crane's poetry, but also the specific manner in which this poetry has been understood and misunderstood. In its recalibration of a smile's epistemological value, this chapter entails a suspension of the counterproductive inevitabilities of a smile-as-we-know-it, and to that end takes as point of departure that smiles can and do surface and function in ways less familiar than heretofore allowed.

Crane's smiles require a queer-optimistic repertoire as flexible and potentially perplexing as the smiles themselves. Queer optimism challenges the narrative that smiles signal some nonproblematic happiness — a narrative of which I'm suspicious not because some smiles do not arise out of such happiness, but because this narrative too often takes smiles out of critical circulation. Queer optimism no less challenges opposite narratives that renominate smiles as "smirk" or "façade," that transmute smiles as the lacquer of some more authentic mode of suffering. Along similar lines, I am wary of these latter narratives not because some smiles are not smirks (et cetera) — they as often might be. Rather, because these narratives (no less familiar and routinized than those that map smiles along an axis of happiness) equally (if contrarily) establish smiles as critically unavailable, reinscribing them as screens of or entries to a field of critical pessimism of which smiles are not (at least a priori) necessarily a part.

Crane's profound importance to queer theory registers, in shorthand, in the fact that two of Crane's earliest and most innovative queer readers, Tim Dean and Lee Edelman, have since become important and prolific contributors to the field of queer theory, writ large. That Sundquist's nonqueer scholarship is susceptible to the same limitations as queer Crane criticism (and, I elsewhere argue, queer theory more generally) indicates that a resistance to Crane's smiles — or correlatively, a critical suspicion of optimism — is not a uniquely queer blindspot. I nevertheless have positioned my analysis as an intervention in queer theory because it is to an idea of queer theory to which my book is principally attached. Queer theory, at its most exciting and provocative, has propagated new vocabularies for understanding not just queer persons, but persons; not just queer affect, but affect. I am indebted to a queer theory that has parsed and parses the interlineations of person and affect with the capacities, caprices, constraints, and lures of writing. I wish to contribute to this body of work from which other disciplines have benefited and learned (as much as queer theory has learned from them), and, in turn, hope that other disciplines and enterprises might benefit (by synecdoche, analogy, or kindred spirit) from my own undertaking.

If my discriminations between what is and is not queer theory sometimes seem prematurely hypostasizing, this hypostasis is motivated by and responsive to the particular poetic oeuvres that I take as *Queer Optimism*'s archive. For instance, queer theory's fetishization of self-shattering — inaugurated in Leo Bersani's 1987 essay "Is the Rectum a Grave?" — illuminates (or adumbrates?) most queer readings of Crane. Such readings take Crane's biographical suicide, or notorious poetic failure, or no less notorious textual difficulty, as paradigmatic of queer self-dissolution. This chapter will extricate Crane from such narratives of *jouissance* and self-destruction. As I shall argue in a subsequent section of this chapter, the nonacknowledgment of Crane's smiles within Crane criticism coincides with analogous nonacknowledgments in texts by Bersani and Michel Foucault. Crane's smiles posit not only a problematic that the work of Bersani or Foucault cannot sufficiently address, but also a site from which to elaborate upon and supplement a queer vocabulary already available. This is not to say that I'm using Crane as the occasion for making a purely theoretical argument. I hope to recover in Crane what criticism has previously overlooked. Such a recovery involves a differently conceived optimism, the consequences and possibilities of which extend beyond the purview of queer theory and speak to any person who, like myself, might be inclined to imagine smiles, or optimism, as sites of critical interest — as opposed to sites of suspicion, conversion, or outright eschewal.

As the following section will make clear, "optimism" is Crane's term as much as it is my own. While it perhaps strains credulity to stump for optimism in the poetics of a suicidal alcoholic, Crane specifically invokes optimism in his correspondence, nearly as frequently as his poems invoke smiles. Again, like Crane's smiles, this optimism has yet been given due critical attention. Optimism, like smiles, elicits in Crane scholarship a critical nervousness, as discernible in Christopher Nealon's account of Crane in *Foundlings: Lesbian and Gay Historical Emotion before Stonewall.* My reservations with Nealon's analysis are local, as are my reservations with Sundquist's: my truck with these and other scholars does not question their interests and contributions to their respective fields. Nevertheless, Nealon's treatment of Crane's optimism seems conceptually limited, analogous to Sundquist's foreclosure of smiles as always already smirked, or façade.

Following an analysis of the final section of T. S. Eliot's *The Waste Land,* Nealon writes that

> Eliot's poem handily illuminates some key differences between his poetic grasp of history and Crane's—and not the reductive difference between some poetic "pessimism" of Eliot's and Crane's "optimism," however Crane himself might have imagined the difference that way.[4]

Nealon's use of quotation marks might simply denote that optimism and pessimism are Crane's particular terms — as indeed they are. On this register, however, the work of the quotation marks would be superfluous since Nealon immediately explains that these are the terms in which Crane "imagine[s] the difference" between Eliot's poetics and his own. Signaling the extent to which Crane's terms are not Nealon's own, Nealon's quotation marks function as scare quotes. The quotation marks reenact the a priori reductiveness, for Nealon, of Crane's terms—qualified in the manner other scholars qualify "reality" or "natural" as dubious if not ideologically suspect. Because he is able to locate a difference between Eliot and Crane presumably more interesting than the one Crane himself articulates, Nealon seems willing, if gingerly, to allow Crane his insistence on optimism. But admitting Crane's optimism is a strange critical move, not incommensurate, for instance, with admitting Eliot's anti-Semitism. Nealon's accommodation of Crane's optimism amounts to a polite overlooking of it. Scare quotes gratuitously consolidate and kowtow to a reductiveness already imputed as inarguable and innate. This chapter suspends this presumption of optimism's reductiveness, frees optimism from scare quotes, and investigates how Crane's sense of optimism bears on his poetry's proliferation of intensely unfamiliar smiles.

Affirming Certain Things

In letters coterminous with much of the *White Buildings* poems, Crane describes his poetic project as a departure from the pessimism of T. S. Eliot. In the context of his poetry's difficulties, Crane's epistolary descriptions of poetic optimism are tantalizingly intelligible. In a 1922 letter to Allen Tate, Crane writes that "one *does* have joys" (emphasis in original) and that "the vocabulary of damnations and prostrations has been developed at the expense of these other moods . . . so that it is hard to dance in proper measure."[5] In a letter written to Gorham Munson in January 1923, Crane identifies this vocabulary of "prostrations" as T. S. Eliot's. "I take Eliot as a point of departure," Crane writes, "toward an almost complete reverse of direction. His pessimism is amply justified, in his own case. But I would apply as much of his erudition and technique as I can absorb and assemble toward a more positive, or (if [I] must put it so in a sceptical [*sic*] age) ecstatic goal. . . . All I know through very much suffering and dullness (somehow I seem to twinge more all the time) is that it interests me to still affirm certain things."[6]

Crane's letter to Munson designates at least two important components of this "complete reverse" of Eliot's pessimism. Crane's "positive," here, denotes not only the positive outlook of more familiar conceptions of optimism ("one *does* have joys"), but more peculiarly implies the interlineation of this recognition of happiness with a commitment to recognition more generally. The positive of Crane's antipessimism invokes not only the smiles of positive affect, but a stranger smile of positivity, if positivity is taken to signal a certain receptivity to fact. Crane's positive predisposes him to "still affirm certain things." The litany of smiles in Crane's poetry obliquely indicates an affirmation of joy, but also an affirmation that smiles *are* "certain things." The smiles of Crane's poetry resemble the smile of the Cheshire cat, which outlasts the cat, and seems not only to have its own autonomy, but retroactively to constitute the cat itself. Crane's poetic project, then, involves not only a recuperation of optimism — i.e., that optimism, as much as Eliotic pessimism, could yield, say, truth or beauty — but a recuperation of the unequivocal objectness of the positive.

Positive, for Crane, is not equivalent to ecstatic. Ecstasy might describe the first component of Crane's project ("one *does* have joys"), but not the second. Ecstasy, like *jouissance* or masochism, teeters between joy and pain; ecstasy lets pessimists eat their pain-cake and have it, too. Crane's positive, on the other hand, is nonecstatic and unequivocal. *The certainty of having joys, within this poetics, is inextricable from the joy of having certainty ("to still affirm certain things").* Ecstasy, in Crane's letter, amounts not to an apotheosis of positive feeling, but a mistranslation of positive feeling for an age whose skepticism distrusts that feeling's self-containment.[7] Crane's attempt to save affirmation from the demands of skepticism counts as one of the most singularly important and as yet unacknowledged contributions made by Crane, to both poetry and criticism.

About halfway through Hart Crane's 1926 book of poems, *White Buildings,* and without recognizable reason, Crane's poems begin registering the peculiar affective fact of a smile. "Possessions" ends with the line "All but bright stones wherein our smiling plays."[8] The first stanza of "Lachrymae Christi" ends with the "sluice" of "one unyielding smile" (19), and the poem itself ends with "Thy / Unmangled target smile" (20). The speaker of the next poem asks of another figure, "Why are you back here — smiling an iron coffin?" (21). And the speaker of the next poem, "The Wine Menagerie," directs the reader to "[r]egard the forceps of the smile that takes her (23)" and, later, invokes a time when "my blood dreams a receptive smile" (24). The smiles of *White Buildings* continue, from "this much-exacting fragment smile" ("Recitative," 25) to "stenographic smiles" ("For the Marriage of Faustus and Helen," 26), the "counted smile of hours and days" ("Voyages IV," 37), "[o]ne frozen, trackless smile" ("Voyages V," 38), and "[t]hat smile unsearchable repose" ("Voyages VI," 39). This proliferation of smiles demands to be read, if only because such repetitions suggest a spoor of intent, an entry into meaning, within poems which otherwise seem unabatingly opaque. With each poem read, and each smile added to the collection, it seems all the more evident that Crane is up to something.

The adjectives appended to Crane's smiles, as already listed, include "unyielding," "unmangled," "frozen," and "trackless." In not yielding, in being frozen without tracks (which might tell either from where the smile has come, where it is going, or where it has gone), Crane's smiles assert an unequivocality at seeming odds with metaphoricity. If metaphor describes the transformation of one thing into another, these smiles, on the level of adjective, refuse legibility beyond what they literally (if ponderously) are. The nonmetaphorical quality of these smiles is all the more puzzling, embedded in a Cranian poetics that is (by all accounts, including Crane's) grounded in (or rather, unmoored by) metaphor. Following Lee Edelman, we could say that Crane's metaphoricity is more precisely catachrestic,[9] and that catachresis in Crane often operates at the level of the adjective. For instance, Crane writes of "tendoned loam" ("Lachrymae Christi," 20) and "inventive dust" ("For the Marriage of Faustus and Helen," 27). Loam and dust are resuscitated through adjectives that pull their respective nouns toward some new form. In the case of the former, loam acquires the taut architecture of a body; in the latter, dust acquires the potential inventiveness to become nearly anything. Whereas loam and dust are adjectivally torqued into alternate shapes, smiles are adjectivally stabilized — unyielding, frozen. Adjectives do not transform smiles into something else, or even describe their particularity, so much as insist (strangely, tautologically) on their tenacity. This tenacity, however, is itself catachrestic in an emblematically Cranian way, to the extent that a recalcitrantly frozen smile strains against the fleetingness which for smiles (conventionally speaking) is definitional. In any given situation, a smile becomes less convincing, the longer it is held.[10] Real smiles, ordinarily, are quick glimmers. Not in Crane. Ironically, the Cheshire-positivity of Crane's smiles makes them difficult to hold on to, even as they aspire, in their resilience, toward being held.

The relation between the optimism adduced in Crane's letters and the smiles littered through Crane's poetry is not self-evident. While uncontroversial to imagine optimism and smiles in each other's vicinity, extrapolating from vicinity any account of causality (e.g., one smiles if one is happy, one is happy if one is optimistic) or synecdochical identity (smiles in Crane's poetry as shorthand for optimism) presumes from the get-go that we know how Crane's smiles and optimism operate when in fact the poems present a version of smiling that is anything but transparent. For instance: ordinarily, a smile exists within a slender window of opportunity — because a smile is short-lived, it most often comes on the immediate heels of to what it is a response. Or failing that, a smile comes on the heels if not of an event, then the recollection of an event.[11] Most of Crane's smiles, by contrast, follow no such accord.

A logic of transience seems inapplicable to Crane's poetics in part because the event, as component of his lyric poems, is so much subordinated to the exigencies of his thick, catachrestic style. Crane's style *is* the event,[12] and in this regard, if smiles indicate an affective response, they are responses not to what the poems describe, but to the poems' style as such. Affect, within Crane's writing, is no more bound to protocols of intelligibility than is, for instance, speaker or narrative. These smiles are confusing because they are nominally identifiable even as their contexts are not. Their adjectival modifiers do not specify the qualities of the smiles so much as specify their nonfungibility, before the poetry has disclosed what the smiles are nonfungible or durable in relation to. Take, for example, the first stanza of "Lachrymae Christi":

> Whitely, while benzine
> Rinsings from the moon
> Dissolve all but the windows of the mills
> (Inside the sure machinery
> Is still
> And curdled only where a sill
> Sluices its one unyielding smile) (19)

Joseph Riddel's influential essay "Hart Crane's Poetics of Failure" illustrates how such smiles have otherwise been read. " 'Lachrymae Christi,' " Riddel notes, "moves from smile to smile through the agony of sacrifice and tears, and ends in the ecstatic moment of anticipated self-transcendence."[13] Indeed, the poem does move from smile to smile. Its last stanza reads,

> Thy face
> From charred and riven stakes, O
> Dionysus, Thy
> Unmangled target smile. (20)

For Riddel, Crane's poetry is caught between the insufficiency of words that could never rise beyond their worldly limits, and the impossibility of words that could do his poetic vision justice. As such, Riddel converts (I would venture yields and mangles) this poem's smiles into respective instantiations of the insufficient and the impossible. This conversion effectively wipes the smiles from the poem's face. The first smile ("its one unyielding smile"), Riddel claims, "is the blank expressionlessness of a sterile world" (487). "Unyielding," for Riddel, is equivalent to an affective obdurateness that disqualifies the smile from expression. To imagine the sterile world as blankly expressionless is to perform a personification devised to shut itself down.

By contrast, Riddel nullifies the second smile ("Thy / unmangled target smile") by deferring it as "a vision of wholeness anticipated in the moment of fragmentation" (487). Riddel later claims that the "smile of Dionysus . . . is not an achieved and communicated vision in the poem; it is the ecstasy of anticipated fulfillment" (491). In claiming this unmangled smile as "anticipated," Riddel quarantines it in some unspecified future. The smile can't be reached, in part because Riddel's Crane can't reach it without sacrificing himself on the altars of "that vision of wholeness" (477).[14] To reach wholeness, one first has to endure obliteration. Riddel directs his reader to "the crucial passage from *The Birth of Tragedy*," which underwrites this necessity of self-sacrifice: "[T]ragic myth, through the figure of the hero [i.e., the poet] delivers us from our avid thirst for earthly satisfaction and reminds us of another existence and a higher delight. For this delight the hero readies himself, not through his victories but through his undoing" (477).

Crane's Dionysus, however, is not necessarily identical to the Dionysus of *The Birth of Tragedy*. The passage that Riddel quotes from Nietzsche concludes that "[b]y virtue of this noble deception [of tragedy] it is now able to move its limbs freely in dithyrambic dance and to yield without reserve to an orgiastic abandon."[15] Orgiastic abandon or, as Crane writes in his letter to Allen Tate, "dance in proper measure"? Riddel's argument for the ecstasy of "Lachrymae Christi" depends on the poem's smiles being read in dialectical opposition, the terms of which, while importable from Nietzsche, seem less than immediate in the poem itself. Against Riddel, I read Crane not only as inclined toward the possibility of lyric smiles being purposively unyielding or unmangleable, but also himself interested in a reiterative, accumulative network of smiles, not only in this poem, but in the poems of *White Buildings* by which it is bordered. Read serially, the smiles of *White Buildings* not only ask not to be discounted or transformed, but ask, with all the contested eloquence of a writer wanting to counter Eliot's pessimistic project, what it would mean to take smiles seriously as unyielding rhetorical and affective phenomena. This isn't to say that Crane knew how to answer his own question. Riddel, in only a slightly different context, cedes as much:

> Crane's poems do often achieve a constellated structure of recurrent images — the curve and circle imagery of *The Bridge* for example — but what kind of vision these manifest patterns represent is, to say the least, ambiguous. Surely it is more something desired than something possessed and known. (476)

Riddel's account of Cranian ambiguity itself follows the rhetoric by which Riddel constrains the smiles of "Lachrymae Christi." A "constellat[ion]," a series of "recurrent images," is, for Riddel, "achieve[d]." The immanence of this "achieve[ment]," however, recedes in the face of a "vision" that is (like the smile of Dionysus), for Riddel, inflexibly futural ("something desired" rather than "something possessed or known"). But what is a constellation if not a "vision" in its own right? What, if not a "vision," is a "structure of recurrent images?" Riddel invokes in visual terms the rudiments of understanding Crane, only to claim these rudiments as not vision enough; these patterns are "manifest" and they are not. In manifesting themselves rather than manifestly pointing to something beyond themselves, these patterns cede their constellative usefulness to the abyssal confounds of a black hole.

Rather than search for meaning beyond the terms of "Lachrymae Christi," what if the poem's terms were taken on their own? "Lachrymae Christi," the poem's title, connotes both the tears Jesus weeps upon being crucified, and a brand of sweet wine of the same name. Getting drunk and getting crucified are two ways of imagining a body in throes. It may be useful to recall that intoxication often conjures the idiom of being plastered as it does being sloshed, or smashed; and that being plastered isn't just the precondition to being smashed, but its own state.[16] While the poem's title prepares a reader for some bodily crisis, the crisis of the poem's opening stanza is a far cry from the title's comparable perspicuity. The stanza's landscape (such as it might be) is not illuminated by the moon, but dissolved by it, moonlight turned not to silver but to benzine. Illumination, in this context, occasions not greater clarity, but the threat of erasure, to which the stanza seems no less vulnerable than the scene the stanza evokes.

If the poem's opening lines seem syntactically unavailable, their difficulty in part stems from their enacting as much as articulating the moon's benzine rinse. "Whitely" dissolves to "while." "Still" dissolves to "sill," as though the stanza were a repository for both antecedent terms (whitely, still) and what — under conditions beyond rhetoric or grammar but by which these antecedents rhetorically are implicated — these terms become. Even as the poem is dissolving, the dissolution is not absolute: hence the stanza's emphatic parenthetical, which seems less subordinate than saved from or impervious to what precedes it:

> (Inside the sure machinery
> Is still
> And curdled only where a sill
> Sluices its one unyielding smile)

And within this parenthetical we find another "inside" — or are the conditions of the "sure machinery" themselves those of the parenthetical? The opening stanza, contra Riddel's presumption of vision beyond vision, presents vision within vision; and even more disorientingly, vision that is ceaselessly self-referential: "while," as the effect of the stanza's own imagined moon on the stanza's opening line. This self-referentiality conjures both itself and what (under the internal conditions of the poem) it is becoming; in the same moment that a reader (resigned, exasperated) might (like Riddel) seek reference elsewhere.

The light that dissolves, however, itself figures in the poem as nondissolvable. Dissolution not only circulates across what it has dissolved, but overflows ("sluices") into itself. Dissolution becomes its own form of nondissolute abundance (or to recall an earlier section of this chapter, positivity), capable of leaving traces and marks, even as it washes the marks from what it touches. And the mark left by benzine (or left untouched by benzine?) is the sluice of the sill's "one unyielding smile."

The difficulty of discerning whether the smile is that which escapes dissolution or that which surfaces as the consolingly accretive fact of it is constitutive of the stanza's poetic concerns. These concerns attach less to speculating on what lies beyond the poem (or beyond a smile) than querying how and when the poem might be susceptible or nonsusceptible to itself.

The poem's final quatrain repeats the confusions of the first. "Thy face / From charred and riven stakes, O / Dionysus, Thy / unmangled target smile." In concert with Riddel's reading, Thomas Yingling suggests that in these lines "the dismembered body is for Crane the eroticized body carried to its logical extreme. . . . But perhaps we ought to take the poem's closing image as a figure for textuality itself, one that suggests the importance of a dismembered text."[17] Perhaps we ought to recall, however, that we are met in these lines not by a dismembered body, but by a disembodied face. And that the face signals not the dissolution of Dionysiac frenzy but rather a counterintuitively nonbachannalian "unmangled[ness]." This unmangledness forms a frame with the first stanza's "unyielding." The poem counters its dismantling energies with an intense valuation of the nondismantleable. Benzine, after all, might be capable of dissolving other solutions, but its solvency is itself comprised of bonds between carbon and hydrogen. The CH groups of benzine (and of the Cheshire cat) reappear in the CH of "lachrymae" and "christi," as well as the first stanza's "machinery," the last stanza's "charred," and elsewhere throughout the poem ("chant," "chime," "unstenched"). The poem's proliferation of CHs posits an elemental integrity inextricable from a poem otherwise read solely for its thematization of breakage. Inside the machinery of the poem lies a tacit insolubility, whose initials, as though held up to a mirror, are the initials of Crane himself. Along these lines, the poem's smiles not only evince the intransigence of CH, but are registers of intransigence. Smiling, in this poem and others, does not describe delight, or for that matter any other affect, but rather describes durability itself.

The Smile of Prufrock

Crane's first book experiments with a smile's durability in the absence of the personal relations that might produce them. These experiments are a direct response to the more personalized but (or "and therefore") degradable smiles that surprisingly litter T. S. Eliot's first book of poems. *Prufrock and Other Observations* (1917) contains twelve poems, and these poems invoke nine smiles. Eliot's smiles designate possibilities that have been either foreclosed or eschatologically deferred, and as such their grammatical mode is emphatically subjunctive. Eliot's poem, "Portrait of a Lady" ends with the question "And should I have the right to smile?" which reiterates both Prufrock's question, "Would it have been worthwhile, / To have bitten off the matter with a smile," and the futural formulation of the book's last poem, "La Figlia che Piange":

> So I would have had him leave,
> So I would have had her stand and grieve,
> So he would have left
> As the soul leaves the body torn and bruised,
> As the mind deserts the body it has used.
> I should find
> Some way incomparably light and deft,
> Some way we both should understand,
> Simple and faithless as a smile and shake of the hand.[18]

The stanza's anaphoric "so" posits the first set of actions as causal (I have him leave in order that she grieve) or analogous (in the same manner as I have him leave, I have her grieve) without specifying a preference for either. Similarly, the next anaphoric "as" describes a relation between events that is neither precisely narrative nor analogous (do soul and mind leave the body at the same time, or in the same way?). This collapse of modes converts romantic (i.e., causal/narrative) crisis into a series of poetic (i.e., analogous) relations — a conversion apparent even in the imposition within the scene of this orchestrating "I," who arranges the other two figures (him and her) as an author arranges characters.

From this series of postulations (I would have done this, and this, he would have done that) in the past, the stanza switches registers not to what the poem's "I" should have done, or what he does, but what he "should" do. That is, the second half of the stanza doesn't provide an alternative to the sets of possibilities already assembled (which is how a "should" following a "would" ordinarily operates), but introduces a separate, tangentially related, system of contingency. The stanza's system of subjunctives delineates a temporal zone of contingent past and contingent future that skips over anything like a present. In this crowd of persons that could have but do not necessarily leave, and should but do not necessarily come together, the smile and the handshake govern as liminal gestures that write themselves to the point of being unwritten.

The formulation beginning "So I would have had him leave..." worries the relation between persons by suspending accounts of how personal motivations are related (that is, narratively/causally, analogously/synchronically). The stanza's last lines, on the other hand, question neither the temporal nor rhetorical conditions of persons and their actions, but the terms of the very moment of interpersonal connection. This, even as "the very moment" is to be understood as qualified by the force of "should"—this is not a moment that is happening, but which might happen were it not for any number of unspecified intervening factors. Taken on their own, the "smile and shake of the hand" would in fact seem to designate simple ways of understanding—one thinks, for instance, of all the smiling and handshaking Eliot must have executed in 1917, the year not only of his book publication, but also of the beginning of his career at Lloyd's Bank. The "way" understanding is demonstrated, however, is as dangerous as it is simple. The smile and handshake form a contract between persons ("let's shake on it") which their ascribed faithlessness potentially if not imminently voids.

Are both persons privy to the smile's faithlessness, or is faithlessness the prerogative only of the poem's "I"? It is unclear within the stanza to whom "we both" even refers (e.g., two people, or three?), or to what understanding they are coming, or to what end this understanding is staked. What difference would it make, for example, if "I should find" or not find this way of marking mutual recognition? Eliot's smile is the simultaneous beginning and end of loyalty, emerging as reparation after the leave-taking of a lover ("As the soul leaves the body torn and bruised"), when in fact reparation counts only as the grounds for future betrayal, governed by contingencies themselves consigned to inutility, in part because the terms of understanding are so jeopardized from the start.

Within this epistemological muddle, the questions of "Prufrock" and "Portrait of a Lady" linger darkly. "Would it have been worthwhile to have bitten off the matter with a smile?" Should I have the right to smile? Even if the former Prufrockian smile weren't faithless, but could lead to a relation to the world that wasn't undermining, the question of "worth" would be unanswerable if not irrelevant, because this sort of engagement remains suspended as unexecutable possibility. Or rather, Prufrock's evaluation of action's worth displaces the more operative question as to whether Prufrock could actually have engaged the world in such a way (he cannot), and so the smile is not Prufrock's (nor even a retroactively projected version of Prufrock), but belongs more precisely to a person that Prufrock cannot imagine, let alone emulate. Eliot's "Portrait of a Lady," on the other hand, mobilizes smiles not as visible trace of the unenvisionable, but as enigmatic precipitate of the confusion of understanding, misunderstanding, and complacent ignorance. In its second section, the poem's titular lady observes a decidedly non-Prufrockian interlocutor:

> Now that lilacs are in bloom
> She has a bowl of lilacs in her room
> And twists one in her fingers while she talks.
> 'Ah, my friend, you do not know, you do not know
> What life is, you who hold it in your hands';
> (Slowly twisting the lilac stalks)
> 'You let it flow from you, you let it flow,
> And youth is cruel, and has no remorse
> And smiles at situations which it cannot see.'
> I smile, of course,
> And go on drinking tea. (9)

Like the faithless smile of "La Figlia che Piange," the smile of the cruel youth simultaneously affirms and undermines relation by making a contract out of misrecognition. Smiling, the lady's companion makes good on the lady's charge (that youth is cruel), while turning not-seeing into its own (if not only) form of understanding. In leaving unchallenged whether he in fact sees or doesn't see, the youth and his smile make indistinguishable the surfacial distinction between understanding and not caring. If the poem's final question — "should I have the right to smile" (12) — lexically echoes Prufrock, it nevertheless conjures not an unimaginable agency that might produce engagement (were agency itself less unimaginable), but rather a fantasy of ceding engagement. The right to smile, as defined by the poem, amounts to the right to contractual faithlessness — the right not only to "not knowing what to feel or if I understand" (12), but to not caring whether one knows or feels at all. Smiling, here, functions less as register of affect than as substitute for it.[19] The stakes of Eliot's smiles involve an agreement against having stakes; Eliot's smiles as often designate the abdication of possibility as they do any futural possibility (hence the uninterest, in "La Figlia che Piange," in distinguishing one form of contingency from another). The smile that ends the poem "Morning at the Window" thus can hover and vanish without even seeming like lost possibility:

> The brown waves of fog toss up to me
> Twisted faces from the bottom of the street,
> And tear from a passer-by with muddy skirts
> An aimless smile that hovers in the air
> And vanishes along the level of the roofs. (19)

Insofar as Eliot's smiles seem related to each other if only by their consistent ironizing of what a smile could or should mean, their iterations within the book acquire the energy of a compulsion to repeat.[20] In a poetry which (even at this early stage) privileges an ethics of impersonality, it isn't surprising that affect and registers of affect would be controverted as untrustable. This untrustability, of course, itself depends on affect's intelligibly operating within the domain of the personal. And indeed, within Eliot, it does. Smiles belong to persons who mis-employ them for depersonalizing or estranging ventures; or emphatically do not belong to but are longed for by persons who would use smiles correctly if they weren't ontologically unviable; or do not belong, as in the stranger of "Morning at the Window," in ways that suggest the shedding of old skin. In the velocity of Eliot's urban street, a smile and its repertoires (ironic or nonironic) grow obsolescent if not obsolete.

As we have seen, the smiles of *White Buildings* more often than not are deracinated from the axis of the personal, neither belonging nor not belonging to an individual, but rather cropping up, as it were, within the materials of the poem. Whereas the smiles of Eliot are scrutable throughout (if only as undoing the sorts of things of which a smile might otherwise be imagined capable), the smiles of Crane emphatically are not scrutable. Rather than adhere to persons, the smiles more often than not are asked to be taken as commensurate with terms with which smiles seem initially noncoincident. For all their proliferation, Eliot's smiles don't add up — because either too deferred or too disintegrated to be counted. Crane's smiles, by contrast, accumulate, take up space. Such a space is conjured at the opening of Crane's great 1923 poem, "For the Marriage of Faustus and Helen":

> Across the stacked partitions of the day—
> Across the memoranda, baseball scores,
> The stenographic smiles and stock quotations
> Smutty wings flash out equivocations. (26)

Whereas Eliot's might be understood as the smile of a banker — arbiter and conserver of value, and in turn, bureaucratic minister of the valuable and dispensable — the smile of the above lines is that of a stenographer, who writes in shorthand in an attempt to keep pace with some other person's or event's velocity. The stenograph is not an event so much as the recording of an event, just as "baseball scores" differ from — and as importantly, outlast — a game already played. Unlike the "aimless smile" that "vanishes," stenographic smiles acquire the gravity (if not, in this instance, the gravitas) of the material (specifically, of the textual), linked less to a future than to a recent past (stenographically transcribed). As in "Lachrymae Christi," the stenographic smiles do not (cannot) reach toward a metaphorical beyond, because so lashed to a lyric present (itself assertively, if searchingly, attempting to understand its relation to the lyric presents that it follows).

Cruising, Beyond Cruising

What does it mean for a smile to mean something? How to distinguish a smile's own local conditions and effects from the conditions and effects that a smile (metaphorically or otherwise) might designate beyond itself? These questions resonate with analogous, critically urgent problematics of conversion: the challenge, for instance, of distinguishing the conditions of personhood from the conditions of what personhood (within queer theory and other disciplines) has become; or hermeneutically, the difficulty of doing justice to a text without displacing the latter with one's sense of it. As I've already suggested, the perils of conversion cannot be sequestered, within Crane's poetry, from the conundra of metaphor. Taken one step further, metaphor itself serves as a metaphor for the ethical and intellectual consequences of reading, misreading, reading into.

Again: following Crane's own account of what he termed his poetry's "logic of metaphor," it would seem irresistible to read Crane's poems along metaphorical lines.[21] While this section discusses the logic of metaphor that Crane proposes, it more intently will pursue the no less important experience, within Crane's poetry, of metaphoricity's coming up short; or (as in "Lachrymae Christi") the ceding of metaphoricity's compulsions to the perplexingly nonmetaphorical. This section's subject is "Possessions," the poem immediately preceding *White Building's* "Lachrymae Christi." Like "Lachrymae Christi," "Possessions" most solicits and resists metaphoricity in the moment of a smile. Unlike "Lachrymae Christi," the smiles of "Possessions" arise (at least minimally) in relation to the poem's ambient flirtations with narrative. To the extent that the narrative of "Possessions" has been critically received as esoterically erotic picaresque, the poem's smiles in turn have been critically received as punctuation of the poem's simultaneously extravagant and elusive erotics. As the crossing of metaphorical and nonmetaphorical meaning, poetic and erotic legibility, the smiles of "Possessions" — and no less so, the critical reception of them — form a compass for queer theory's own attractions and orientations.

In his essay "General Aims and Theories," Crane singles out "Possessions" as a poem that cannot be technically explained, that must rely on its organic impact on the imagination to communicate its meaning:

> In manipulating the more imponderable phenomena of psychic motives, pure emotional crystallizations, etc., I have had to rely even more on these dynamics of inferential mention, and I am doubtless still very unconscious of having committed myself to what seems nothing but obscurities to some minds. A poem like "Possessions" really cannot be technically explained.[22]

Crane himself thus notes "Possessions" as exemplary of a poem that demands for entry an emotional (as opposed to "technical") mode of reading — that is to say, a poem that relies on the absented metaphorical tenor characteristic of what I imagine as Cranian reading-as-erotic-project.[23] "Possessions," however, is striking not only for its hermeneutic difficulty but also for its own internal reaction to this particular sort of difficulty. Within a poetics that construes desire as a rhetorical problem — that invokes emotion as the means as much as the object of understanding — "Possessions" reformulates desire as an analytic of presence, rather than absence, and conceives erotic immanence as intractable. "Possessions," that is, revises the poetry's more pervasive notion of desire as a movement toward something else — and likewise challenges any notion of desire as self-shattering — in imagining a presence-of-desire around which the poem's terms circulate:

> Witness now this trust! the rain
> That steals softly direction
> And the key, ready to hand — sifting
> One moment in sacrifice (the direst)
> Through a thousand nights the flesh
> Assaults outright for bolts that linger
> Hidden, — O undirected as the sky
> That through its black foam has no eyes
> For this fixed stone of lust . . .
>
> Accumulate such moments to an hour:
> Account the total of this trembling tabulation.
> I know the screen, the distant flying taps
> And stabbing medley that sways —
> And the mercy, feminine, that stays
> As though prepared.
>
> And I, entering, take up the stone
> As quiet as you can make a man . . .
> In Bleecker Street, still trenchant in a void,
> Wounded by apprehensions out of speech,
> I hold it up against a disk of light —
> I, turning, turning on smoked forking spires,
> The city's stubborn lives, desires.
>
> Tossed on these horns, who bleeding dies,
> Lacks all but piteous admissions to be spilt
> Upon the page whose blind sum finally burns
> Record of rage and partial appetites.
> The pure possession, the inclusive cloud
> Whose heart is fire shall come, — the white wind rase
> All but bright stones wherein our smiling plays.[24]

While the syntactical and conceptual logistics of "Possessions" remain mystifying to many of Crane's readers, there prevails among critics a consensus as to what the poem is about—as though designating the subject of the poem could somehow organize or even decode local opacities which (taken on their own or even collectively) remain indecipherable. Critics as various as R. W. B. Lewis, Warner Berthoff, and Robert Martin agree that "Possessions" is about cruising.[25] Such readings depend on an excavatory hunch whereby the cruise at hand fundamentally is Hart's own, and whereby the poem's difficulty arises (on Crane's part) as a form of self-censorship. Implied is that Crane strategically mystifies the experience within the poem so as to make it available only to those readers already in the know.[26] Such a hunch oversimplifies the subtleties of interaction and noninteraction inherent in the deceptively sleek denomination of cruising. This reading implies, unhelpfully, that difficulty within the poem is something like phobic, self-proscribing response, additive to experience rather than constitutive of it, or constitutive not of the experience, but its recounting. Against these contentions my own reading will suggest that cruising is more complicated—and more interesting—than the likes of Lewis, Berthoff, or Martin let on, and furthermore, that difficulty within the poem is as fundamental to its cruisy subject as to its style.

R. P. Blackmur claims that Crane's poetry exonerates itself of referential obligation:

> In a lesser poetry of the same order, and in poetry of different orders, words may only indicate or refer to or substitute for the feelings; then we have the poetry of vicarious statement, which takes the place of, often to the highest purpose, the actual complete presentation, such as we have here. Here there is nothing for the words to take the place of; they are their own life, and have an organic continuity, not with the poet's mind nor with the experience they represent, but with themselves.[27]

Blackmur's divorcing of words from what words might take the place of becomes increasingly difficult to imagine in the context of cruising, which, like Crane's poetry, depends on a semiotic simultaneously ornate and palimpsestic. Cruising, understood as the choreography by which two strangers end up in relation to each other, provides an interpersonal correlative to Crane's logic of metaphor. The intersection of erotic and poetic practice is evident in Crane's exposition of the latter in a 1926 letter written to Harriet Monroe, if one substitutes "cruising" for terms such as "language," and "cruiser" for "reader" (after all, a cruiser is nothing if not a reader, par excellence):

> It implies (this *inflection* of language) a previous or prepared receptivity to its stimulus on the part of the reader. The reader's sensibility simply responds by identifying this inflection of experience with some event in his own history or perceptions — or rejects it altogether. The logic of metaphor is so organically entrenched in pure sensibility that it can't be thoroughly traced or explained outside of historical sciences, like philology or anthropology. This "pseudo-statement," as I. A. Richards calls it in an admirable essay touching our contentions in last July's *Criterion,* demands completely other faculties of recognition that the pure rationalistic associations permit. . . . I don't wish to enter here defense of the particular symbols employed in my own poem, because, as I said, I may well have failed to supply the necessary emotional connectives to the content featured.[28]

Cruising, like Crane's difficult poetics, is a pseudo-statement, the reception of which depends on the supply not of any clear explication but of "emotional connectives." And "Possessions," as Crane notes in his essay "General Aims and Theories," is exemplary of his difficult poems. That is, "Possessions" is both a poem about cruising and an instantiation of a poetics nearly analogous to it.

There are many smiles involved in cruising. First comes the smile across the room, or across the street. This smile is the drop of fishing-line, a letter addressed to whomever receives it. This first smile communicates the cruiser's interest and availability; ideally, this smile meets with a smile that communicates a specular interest on the part of the other. If smile no. 1 is not met by smile no. 2, smile no. 1 may as well not have occurred. It is a tree falling in a forest without audience, and its being recognized without reciprocation perhaps results in embarrassment (but not necessarily to termination of the smiling game). If, however, smile no. 1 is reciprocated or reflected back by smile no. 2, then smiling escalates and intensifies. Faciality initially presented as politesse — in those opening cruising gambits, it is vital that interest, if not reciprocated, can slink back into polite friendliness, in case lack of interest adheres also, say, to homophobic recoil—ups its ante with cocked eyebrows and lambent lips. These smiles are bidders' sticks, a silent opera of evaluation and contingent commitment, until the auction's deal is sealed. Cruising ceases to be cruising when smiles and their gestural extensions cede to words. Once two people are talking, the cruise qua cruise (more or less) is complete.

"Possessions" suggests the stratagems of a cruise in its capacity to cover its own tracks. Erotic innuendo, intense volley of ocular exchange, depend on initial registration of a glance, what Crane, in his letter to Harriet Monroe, calls "emotional connectives." Failing these connectives, Crane cedes, the poem will remain closed to its reader. The text cannot guarantee its being understood (any more than Crane, walking the dark Brooklyn docks, can guarantee a hookup) so much as guarantee its ever potentially occluded availability. The poem signals this perpetual availability in its opening imperative, "Witness now this trust!" What trust? What is one witnessing? The object of the reader's gaze, at this point, seems less clear than the terms under which this gaze operates. First, witnessing presupposes a relation that is at least minimally dialectical—bearing witness requires he who sees, and what or who is seen. Second, witnessing presumes (for its Austinian felicitousness) the synchronicity of the act of witnessing and the event that is witnessed. It is the fact that the witness sees (as opposed to remembers or retroactively elucidates) that authorizes what has been witnessed. Each time a reader turns to "Possessions," he is bearing witness before knowing what he is seeing. As witness, he authorizes ("this trust!") before he understands. The poem might "be" about a cruise. More eerily, the poem picks up the reader faster than "this trust" becomes a tryst. Faster, indeed, than "witness now" melts into "white as snow."[29] The "he" that transforms "witness" into "w(h)it(e)ness" is both the subject and the object of Crane's cruise.[30] "He" energizes the poem by simultaneously being both possessed and fugitive.

In contrast to this flickering "he," the smiles of the poem's final line are nothing if not caught. Such is the effect of their being bound to "bright stones," although exactly how the stones and smiles relate to each other remains unclear. "Wherein," as a preposition, describes relation, but what does it mean to imagine an inside to a rock? (This is a question to which Crane will return, three years later, in "Island Quarry.") Are we talking geodes? Or a stony crypt? Or might "wherein" refer not to a literal interiority, but to a stone's reflective surface, as when one speaks of objects "in" a mirror. Regardless, these various scenarios indicate a lexical maze in which smiles are preserved at the expense of being removed. But then how can smiles in individual stones play? Does each smile live in its own stone? Are stones shared? Are the stones bright because illuminated by the smile, like a face's blush? Do smiles play with each other, or by themselves? Is playing an active enterprise, as in games, or an incessant reeling, like the play of a radio? The poem's enigmatic final line mobilizes these problems of relationality, interiority, and agency, which smiling occasions but does not itself resolve.

These smiles, clearly enough, are no longer the smiles of a cruise, cruisy as this poem begins. Most readings of "Possessions" characterize its concluding vision as one of ecstasy. Tim Dean writes that these last lines "go beyond sex to a different kind of intensity," figured as "ecstatic transcendence."[31] Such a reading is dissatisfying in part because ecstasy by definition so exceeds description that locating it in Crane's poetry practically amounts to giving up on trying to describe it. I don't yet know how to describe this poem's final smiling, or to what such smiling might refer. At very least, both the smiling and the stones seem engendered by "the pure possession" (if not the objects to be possessed). It seems plausible that Crane has this "pure possession" in mind when, in "General Aims and Theories," he writes of those "pure emotional crystallizations" that his poetry seeks to "manipulate." Manipulation itself connotes the fact of holding something, "ready to hand," as though emotions were something that could be held. Manipulation, in this context, as much suggests that emotions could be handled, as that they could be altered. Hence Crane's insistence on "pure emotional crystallizations," an exquisite petrifaction of a piece with the poem's own "pure possession." Rather than ecstasy, these last lines ruminate a nonecstatic ardor as permanent (if not as clear) as crystal.

As I suggested at this chapter's outset, for all that the practices of queer theory have opened and illuminated Crane's difficulty, the singular difficulty of smiles like those of "Possessions" corresponds to a blind spot within queer theory's own lines of sight. As an illustration of the quandary posed to queer theory by something like Crane's smiles, I turn now to a different text, which relates an uncannily similar scene:

> People can tolerate two homosexuals they see leaving together, but if the next day they're smiling, holding hands, and tenderly embracing one another, then they can't be forgiven. It is not the departure for pleasure that is intolerable, it is waking up happy.[32]

The observation is Foucault's, made in the late 1980s in the gay French magazine *Mec.* It makes its way into English, and therefore, into the annals of American queer theory, via Leo Bersani, who cites the observation in his book *Homos.* The smiles of Foucault's hypothetical happy gay men prove as untenable for Bersani as Crane's smiles do for critics such as Riddel or Dean. "There may be nothing to say," Bersani writes, "about these gays holding hands after a night of erotic play" (78). There *is* something to say, however, for both Bersani and Foucault, if only on a different register. By "nothing to say," Bersani doesn't mean nothing, per se, but nothing other than what initially is communicated. "Don't, Foucault warns us, read *their* tenderness as the exhausted aftermath of cocksucking that would 'really' be a disguised devouring of the mother's breast, or a fucking that would 'really' be the heterosexual repossession of a lost phallic woman" (78). Don't, that is, presume metaphoricity where meaning is literal. As in Crane's poetry, which reiterates smiles as the privileged site at which meaning doesn't waver, Bersani and Foucault exempt gay tenderness ("two homosexuals . . . smiling") from the equivocations of metaphorical, psychoanalytic interpretation. For both Bersani and Crane, the smile monkey-wrenches poetic practice.

Just as Riddel reads the opening smile of "Lachrymae Christi" as expressionless, Bersani reads Foucault's smiles as blanks. "No, those homosexuals gaily embracing as they go to breakfast in the Castro or somewhere off Christopher Street are blankly, superficially, radically, threateningly happy. 'There is,' Foucault says, 'no anxiety, there is no fantasy behind happiness' " (79). The redundancy of a smile's instancing nothing but a smile seems as discomfiting here as the redundancy of a gay gay. If there were not anxiety behind happiness, readings such as these wouldn't be so quick to equate happiness with nothing. "[W]ith no fantasies to fantasize about, the silenced interpreter becomes the intolerant homophobe" (79). By "silenced interpreter," Foucault refers to the average Joe on the street who can't abide that gays are happy. From a different vantage, however, Foucault and Bersani are silenced interpreters, too. Differently put, the homophobia of such a silenced interpreter poses a threat to the scene's gay couple, but is not threatening to Bersani's theorizing of it — the subject of homophobia is the site, in Bersani's account, of neither nonplussedness nor intimidation, but of the mental agility and brilliance characteristic of Bersani's writing from the very beginning. At the same time, Bersani's project seems least surefooted in its parsing of the threatening blanks of gay happiness. Why presume the vacancy of smiles? And following this, why so quickly turn vacancy into threat, as though to tender further meaning to tenderness would dilute what in tenderness is most essential? That the value of happiness should reside in its threatening disruptiveness recalls Sundquist's elision of smiles and smirks, as well as Jonathan Lear's foreclosing alignment of happiness and the death drive.

Happiness, in Bersani's analysis, is asymptotic. Claiming to "want to return to those two happy men and, without wishing to explain or interpret their happiness, at least conjecture about how they spent the night" (80), Bersani nonetheless does not return to those two happy men. He skips past them, past the morning street, to an anterior cruise and its consequent sex. (It is not the departure for pleasure that is intolerable, it is waking up happy.) Bersani wants, maybe, to return to the smiles, wants, even "to be one of those happy gays [himself]," but within his account, he cannot. He may not want to explain or interpret happiness (although the question remains why happiness remains exempt from interpretation), but in fact he does. What is conjecture, after all, if not an attempt at explanation or interpretation?

After further digression, Bersani returns, in a way, to Foucault's smiles. "Indeed, Foucault's thought is all the more appealing, to me, in that his utopian visions never include the pastoral promise — so fashionable in utopian vision in recent years — of predominantly caring and nurturing human intimacies. There are of course those two hauntingly happy and tender men" (83). I wonder to what "fashionable utopias" and "recent years" Bersani was referring when he wrote in 1995, because queer theory's most fashionable strain much more vigorously has involved the exclusion of nurturing human intimacy. Even as Bersani wants "happy and tender men" to exist unproblematically without fantasy, they return, within Bersani's essay, as what analysis cannot make sense of. Such is the force of "there are of course," which performs diffidence even as the reintroduction of these gay gays seriously challenges both Bersani's and

Foucault's accounts of homosexual threat. If these gay men, for Bersani, are no longer "blankly" happy, it is because Bersani has raised his observation's adverbial stakes. Now, the gay men are "hauntingly" happy. (As though a happy homo were a dead homo. As though not having an unconscious were equivalent to being an unconscious.) The durability of Cranian smiles emerges in Bersani's reading as the spectral smile that won't go away. It seems Bersani cannot look at the happy men without inadvertently conjuring their own retroactivity. We have moved from a happiness that is blank (which can tell us nothing beyond the tautological) to a happiness that is haunted (which might speak, but only, as it were, from the other side of the grave). And this movement, in a way, aligns Bersani with his own opposition:

> no one can stop looking. But we might wonder if AIDS, in addition to transforming gay men into infinitely fascinating taboos, has also made it *less dangerous* to look. For, our projects and our energies not withstanding, others may think of themselves as watching us disappear. The heightened visibility conferred on gay men by AIDS is the visibility of imminent death, of a promised invisibility. Straight America can rest its gaze on us, let us do our thing over and over in the media, because what our attentive fellow citizens see is the pathos and innocence of a doomed species (21).

Smiles, from this vantage, are both doomed and indefatigable. If the smiles of a cruise are singular in their capacity to undo themselves, the smiles of "Possessions" (and the smiles that hauntingly possess *Homos*) are singular in the intensity with which they are undone, undoable, ever present.

"Hard and Glad": From Stones to Quarry

Whereas Bersani under-reads the smiles of Foucault's anecdotal gay men, Crane, in "Possessions," literally encrypts smiles, as though to save them from being read at all. This is not to say that the smiles of "Possessions" are therefore unreadable. Similarly, to note their encryption is not (in the manner of Aida or Antigone) to ascribe to these smiles a living death. Crane gives no indication that these smiles could or would ever fade out: their interminability (if not anachronicity) registers in Crane's designation not of a single smile or even several smiles, but of "smiling" (in fact, "*our* smiling"). A noun (such as a smile, potentially subject to narratives of ephemerality) becomes a gerund, "smiling," which (as a verbal noun) isn't in Crane's poem subject to an extrinsic temporality so much as autonomously temporal. "Gerund," after all, etymologically denotes a carrying on, which is what these smiles do — whether read, misread, or unread altogether. That this smiling might be potentially intelligible without being immanently so frustrates the poem's ostensible interest in possessability. What does it mean to have something without access to (which is to say, understanding of) it? In this sense, Crane's "bright stones" resemble both Laplanche's enigmatic signifier and D. W. Winnicott's transitional object, imagined as a "first possession"[33] intermediately existing "between the subjective and that which is objectively perceived" (Winnicott, 3). This intermediate area (Crane's simultaneously compelling and occluding "wherein") "is an area," writes Winnicott, "that is not challenged, because no claim is made on its behalf except that it shall exist as a resting-place for the individual engaged in the perpetual human task of keeping inner and outer reality separate yet interrelated" (2).

Three years after writing "Possessions," Crane returns to a problematic of happiness and stone in "Island Quarry." The earlier poem broached the dilemma of smiling to be had if one could have it, the vicissitudes of possessability defining the terms by which satisfaction might be gained, lost, or pined. "Island Quarry," on the other hand, reconfigures happiness not in terms of an object — a stone that could be held — but as a Winnicottian space that could hold *us*; this later poem converts the hermetic emblems of "Possessions" into their own geography. The bright stones of "Possessions" seemed either identical to, extensions, or revisions of the "fixed stone of lust" which earlier circulates through the poem. "Island Quarry," by contrast reverts to a scene preceding possessability, before stone circulates at all. Differently put, "Possessions," conceives of happiness as Winnicottian intermediate object somewhere between the outside world and the self, whereas "Island Quarry" allegorizes happiness as outside world (although in the context of the exaggerated external and internal contours of a quarry, we must take "outside" with a grain of salt).

Translating happiness from object into geography suggests one poetic tactic by which happiness could be explored (the way a geography might be explored). "Island Quarry" thus furthers Crane's distinction between "positive" and "ecstatic." Whatever happiness might be found on or in this mountain, it is not obliterative, in the manner of ecstasy, but a sustainable object of exploration (suggesting Comte's philosophical positive as much as positive's vernacular). Contra theoretical conflations of happiness with pleasure, pleasure with sexual pleasure, sexual pleasure with *jouissance, jouissance* with a sort of death (etc.), "Island Quarry" produces an account of happiness not only divorced from narratives of evanescence or self-dissolution, but bound to something like geological force:

> Square sheets — they saw the marble only into
> Flat prison slabs there at the marble quarry
> At the turning of the road around the roots of the mountain
> Where the straight road would seem to ply below the stone, that fierce
> Profile of marble spiked with yonder
> Palms against the sunset's towering sea, and maybe
> Against mankind. It is at times —
>
> In dusk, as though this island lifted, floated
> In Indian baths. At Cuban dusk the eyes
> Walking the straight road toward thunder —
> This dry road silvering toward the shadow of the quarry
> — It is at times as though the eyes burned hard and glad
> And did not take the goat path quivering to the right,
> Wide of the mountain — thence to tears and sleep —
> But went on into marble that does not weep. (116)

The eyes that walk "the straight road" toward thunder are asked to differentiate between this silvering road which leads "on into marble" and the "goat path quivering to the right." The quivering goat path might sound like the way Crane might pursue, but it isn't. "Tears and sleep" sounds like another shitty night, not unlike that of the rage and partial appetite penultimate in "Possessions." The road into marble, on the other hand, does not weep. This negatively defined alternative to tears is informed by the eyes, "hard and glad," that view it. Gladness, that is, describes both the eyes' predisposition, as well as their choice. In a different context, this conjunction of hardness and gladness would be plausible enough for a poet taken by the vagaries of his and other erections. Still, the gladness of being (staying) hard risks falling out of the poem. Edward Brunner and Allen Grossman, for instance, argue that "Island Quarry" entails a choice not between dissatisfaction and gladness, but between reason and sentiment. Brunner writes that the speaker "has had enough of vulnerability, and he is drawn instead to . . . the firm marble that does not weep, that is inexpressive."[34] Grossman similarly describes the eyes as foregoing "the wavering path of sentiment . . . putting an end to monumental craving."[35] Brunner's elision of gladness for a reading privileging inexpressivity recalls the mischaracterized "inexpressiv[ity]" attributed by Riddel to the opening smile of "Lachrymae Christi." The blindspot that precludes Brunner's ability to envision the simultaneity of "hard" and "glad" depends upon the presumption that gladness could be simultaneous only with frenzy, or even the tears which the poem's eyes pass over. Choosing the "straight path" ends up seeming queerer than the bent road curving up the mountainside. So difficult is it for the poem (and us) to imagine this strange alignment of stubborn gladness (i.e., a stubbornness other than stoicism, or reason, or cadaverous nonexpression) that the poem can commit to its choice, but cannot further imagine what this choice would look like.

Choice is difficult to conceive in "Island Quarry" because agency itself has become diffuse. There is no subject of the poem who could choose durability for himself, as though durability were an object to be acquired or ethic to be cultivated. The closest the poem has to a subject is the set of eyes which saw the marble, and walk the straight road, and did not take the quivering path. The precedent for Crane's strange subjectal dusk-vision is Emerson:

> Crossing a bare common, in snow puddles, at twilight, under a clouded sky, without having in my thoughts any occurrence of special good fortune, I have enjoyed a perfect exhilaration. I am glad to the brink of fear. . . . Standing on bare ground, — my head bathed by the blithe air, and uplifted into infinite space, — all mean egotism vanishes. I become a transparent eye-ball; I am nothing; I see all; the currents of the Universal Being circulate through me.[36]

Emerson is as meticulous in describing the whereabouts of his ocular transformation as is Crane. He is crossing a bare common; he is standing on bare ground. Crane's eyes — Crane's dissipated person — is at the quarry out of which come the square sheets (of prisons, of poems), and the quarry, at this magic hour, is floating as though attendant to some new set of laws. Whereas Emerson's "I" is glad to the brink of fear, Crane's eyes are glad without brink whatsoever. Crane's brinklessness, in fact, might be the more fearful proposition.

Emerson's iconic account of auto-iconoclasm ironically resonates with queer-theoretical procedure far more than the "hard and glad" of "Island Quarry." Although it is nature and not sex that catalyzes Emerson's transcendental askesis ("perfect exhilaration"), the qualities of Emersonian transparency nonetheless mime the grandiose self-evacuation that sex, by Bersani's account, avails:

> It is possible to think of the sexual as, precisely, moving between a hyperbolic sense of self and a loss of all consciousness of self. But sex as self-hyperbole is perhaps a repression of sex as self-abolition. It inaccurately replicates self-shattering as self-swelling, as psychic tumescence.[37]

One might ask of both Emerson and Bersani if self-abolition no less represses an experience of self-hyperbole. Indeed, the commensurability of Emerson's vanished ego and his conduction of "the currents of universal being" suggests an evacuation indistinguishable in quality from Bersanian tumescence. For both Emerson and Bersani, the exhilaration of vanishing—the "loss of all consciousness of self" (itself always juggernauting into its opposite)—presupposes an anterior self one wishes (or ought wish) to lose. "Island Quarry," by contrast, cannot lose a lyric self insofar as the poem so severely takes lyric absence as its conceit. Where there might otherwise exist a self—along the lines, perhaps, of the ravishingly desirous speaker of "Possessions"—"Island Quarry" offers only "the eyes." The poem's displacement of erotic repertoire (what one wants) with ocular repertoire (what one sees) does not metonymically establish a person to whom such eyes belong, so much as displace metonymy itself with a personification of eyes. This personificatory move further erases a self from the lyric, in suggesting that the appproximation of self does not exist outside the poem (let alone has written the poem) but, rather, tenuously depends on the poem for its wavering culmination.

Again, this lyric absence is a conceit (no less so than Emersonian or Bersanian absence) on poetic and psychical registers. But as conceit, the attenuated "egotism" of "Island Quarry" cannot operate as ecstatic telos (as it does for Emerson and Bersani), to the extent that a straw-figure egotism cannot be presumed at poem's outset. If self and lack of self, in Emerson and Bersani, seem equally tumescent, self and lack of self in "Island Quarry" seem equally humble. The poem's first stanza appears, in its last line, to want to communicate something personal: "It is at times," suggesting the incipient correlation of perceived landscape and personate experience, the germ of pathetic fallacy. If pathetic fallacy describes the imposition of affective solipsism onto landscape, however, "Island Quarry" differently conjectures that perception itself could become part of the landscape: "At Cuban dusk the eyes / Walking the straight road toward thunder." The fantasy of eyes navigating the quarry's road enacts solipsism in reverse — not a world incorporated into oneself ("the currents of Universal Being circulate through me"), but perception extrojected as part of the world; an attempt to annul the estrangement between subject and object that perception requires and on the grounds of which intimacy falters. The world — "this island" — nonetheless remains as tentative as the eyes that see it: hence the poem's speculative "maybe," its twice-repeated "as though," which founders between the certainty of simile and the speculativeness of similarity.

Along these lines (and against the fictions of anterior ego on which Emerson's and Bersani's theorizations of self-emptying are predicated), it is important to note that the eyes are less sure about their gladness than they are about the marble's not weeping — the eyes don't burn hard and glad, it is as though they do. The poem's landscape — which is to say, the poem — at best serves as proxy for an approximated self and that self's attendant feelings, even as such a self proleptically learns from the marble's "not weep[ing]" as it modestly, withdrawingly conceives it. Such a claim revises my earlier suggestion that Crane's eyes are glad without brink: The eyes of "Island Quarry" are on the brink of a gladness so delicately nascent as to make self-shattering — the becoming of a transparent eye — aggressively gratuitous. Safe in marble (which is only as sepulchral as critics would make it), what might this tenous gladness (queer-optimistically) see? What might it (queer-optimistically) become?

Broken and Unbroken

There is among Crane critics an acquiescence if not tacit agreement that "The Broken Tower" is Crane's last poem. In a 1959 essay titled (straightforwardly enough) "Hart Crane's Last Poem," Marius Bewley opines that "[t]here is a literary superstition to the effect that the last work of a good artist is likely to show a deeper insight or wisdom, a last gathering of forces, as death comes on."[38] The deeper insight that the "The Broken Tower" purveys has, invariably, to do with its brokenness. For Joseph Riddel, brokenness describes the insolvent suicidal poet who can't help but write a poem that performs his own inability: "Hart Crane's last poem, 'The Broken Tower,' is so confused with the sensational events of his last days that it is hard to consider the poem apart from the man. On the whole, it seems wise not to try to, for this is a poem which dramatizes, once and for all in our time, the pathetic gesture of a man dying into his work."[39] Revamping not the fact of failure, but its theoretical fruction and the aura around it, Tim Dean more recently has noted "that Crane identifies neither with mother nor father, but with *the brokenness of relation itself.* This symbolic identification not with any positive entity but with an absence, a rupture, is suggested in Crane's final poem, 'The Broken Tower' " (Dean's italics).[40] Likewise, Lee Edelman writes that in " 'The Broken Tower,' [his] final poem . . . [Crane] identifies his poetry as a 'long-scattered score / Of broken intervals' in a stanza that refuses to evade the necessary and generative violence that marks the origin and originality of his work."[41]

These various Crane critics expound the "deeper insight" of breakage, even as such critical recursions produce a monolithic reading of Crane opposite the violence, pathos, and ruptures that such analyses advance. In disavowing Crane's identification with any "positive entity," Dean's championing of the negative takes up a suspicious amount of space. Analogously, Edelman's detection in Crane of a "poetics that embraces the necessity of discontinuity" (269) chafes, in its emphatic return throughout Edelman's study, against his argument's own unremitting incessance: such friction anticipates the tension in *No Future* between unceasing disruptiveness and Edelman's rhetorical *Always.* Recuperating the negative into something resembling a positive which itself goes unquestioned, however, forces Crane and his poetry — not to mention the persons and practices for whom Crane and his poetry always potentially, imminently stand in—into an impossible corner in which the positive/nonbroken/continuous is without explanation verboten, even as the negative/broken/discontinuous covertly acquires the former's putatively hegemonic tendencies.

Contrary to such readings, and as evinced in poems such as "Possessions" and "Island Quarry," Crane's poetry attempts a sustained broaching of "positive entities," where the positive signals persuasiveness and value in its own right. We will not know the full implications of what Edelman terms Crane's "ideology of rupture" or "poetics of negativity" [13] until Crane's poetics of positivity has itself been done justice. This latter poetics—which would accommodate cohesion, and consistency, and nondissolution, as well as nonjouissant joy that needn't travel the circuitries of pain to count not only as convincingly joyful, but as critically or poetically interesting—comprises a critical gap, which in part explains why "The Broken Tower" remains unchallenged as Crane's final poem. Although few critics are as forthright as Bewley in admitting to the superstitions of finality, the last poem of a poet nonetheless records a sort of poetic last will and testament—or in the case of a poet who kills himself, a suicide note.[42] Rather than disputing the compelling magic of a "last poem," I want to posit an alternate ending to Crane's life and career, in "The Circumstance," a poem that extends the work of "Possessions" and "Island Quarry" in a last investigation into the mysteries not of dissolution, but of a curious, oracular permanence. "The Broken Tower" was finished in March 1932 and may in fact be Crane's last published poem, but in April of that year, perhaps just days before drowning, Crane was writing "The Circumstance."

That "The Circumstance" was written (or even in the process of being written) at the same time as and subsequent to "The Broken Tower" helps to defetishize the forms of fracture that critics repeatedly locate in "The Broken Tower." More than this, however, "The Circumstance" speaks to "The Broken Tower" as an amendment of it. "The Broken Tower" invokes a bell-tower made of stone, only to dismantle it for the sake of rebuilding a dematerialized tower in (what the poem conceives as) the comparably capacious and imaginatively infinite space of "the within," the lyric poet's heart:

> And builds, within a tower that is not stone
> (Not stone can jacket heaven).

"The Circumstance" salvages stone (and, in turn, a lyric relation to stone) from the apostasis of it by "The Broken Tower" as inferior to the interior architecture by which stone is replaced. In this regard, "The Circumstance" forms a triptych with "Possessions" and "Island Quarry." This counterfactually "last poem" both recontextualizes the cryptic formulation of "Possessions" of smiles-in-stone, and resumes the contemplation of "Island Quarry" of what stone might be carved into, and what from stone one might learn:

> The anointed stone, the coruscated crown—
> The drastic throne, the
> Desperate sweet eyepit-basins of a bloody foreign clown—
> Couched on bloody basins floating bone
> Of a dismounted people....
>
> If you could buy the stones,
> Display the stumbling bones
> Urging your unsuspecting
> Shins, sus-
> Taining nothing in time but more and more of Time,
> Mercurially might add but would
> Subtract and concentrate.... If you
> Could drink the sun as did and does
> Xochipilli,—as they who've
> Gone have done, as they
> Who've done.... A god of flowers in statued
> Stone... of love—
>
> If you could die, then starve, who live
> Thereafter, stronger than death smiles in flowering stone;—
> You could stop time, give florescent
> Time a longer answer back (shave lightning,
> Possess in halo full the winds of time)
> A longer answer force, more enduring answer
> As they did—and have done.... (203).

The stone that "The Circumstance" anoints is a statue of Xochipilli, Aztec god of flowers, games, beauty, and song. So fun-loving a god might seem a suitable object of optimistic devotion. Crane's interest in Xochipilli doesn't follow so predictable a course, no more so than did his letters' theorizations of optimism as not only an insistence on the merit of joy, but the merit of insistence. Contrary to criticism's paradox of Crane and Crane's poems as monolithically fractured and dissolute, and contrary to the explorations of dissolution of "The Broken Tower," this chapter has offered an alternate account of Crane's lyric exploration of durability. This durability constellates around smiles catachrestically described as nontransient, and this nontransience in turn is literalized in Crane's lyric returns to stone. In the spirit of queer optimism (rather than optimism), "The Circumstance" does not posit Xochipilli as "anointed" for the felicities that fall under his jurisdiction. The stone Xochipilli, moreover, is not "anointed" insofar as the statue affords access to some numinous body for which it stands as proxy. Such deference depends on a religious faith, structurally identical to metaphor; both faith and metaphor, in turn, depend on a future that likewise organizes optimism, but displaces the present "circumstance" that is queer optimism's particular province. Against these hypothetical accounts of worship, Crane's relation to the stone idol is aesthetically motivated, and intently secular. This secularity is structurally identical to those nonmetaphorical phenomena I have already traced.

"The Circumstance" honors the stone Xochipilli less for being Xochipilli than for being stone — for outlasting the Aztecs ("dismounted people") ostensibly responsible for it, for presenting not a metaphor for perdurability, but a literalization of it. The poem's study of lyric durability doesn't simply recapitulate canonical fantasies of a poem existing long after poet or time of poem's writing; for one, "The Circumstance" offers itself not as Shakespearean sonnet or Horatian ode, but as a series of iambic fragments, ellipses, and attenuated repetitions ("as they who've / Gone have done, as they / Who've done"). The poem might, as critics speculate, constitute a work-in-progress, but might — in the time of *our* reading — no less be imagined as having been written as work-in-progress. Again, a poem preserved *as-being-written* amends "The Broken Tower," poem-as-brokenness. If Dean has argued that "The Broken Tower" suggests "the brokenness of relation itself," "The Circumstance" differently holds itself out — *holds out* — as a sustaining of relationality. It's not that if "[y]ou could stop time," you might master it (this poem is far removed from the unhappy binary of mastery/failure in which Crane too often has been caught). Rather, in stopping time, one could "give florescent / Time a longer answer back," a "more enduring answer."

Time stops, yet still flowers (or to note the specificity of suffix, is beginning to flower), just as stone flowers ("flowering stone"). While it is difficult adequately to parse "death smiles in flowering stone," such difficulty doesn't compromise my argument but impels it. Is "death," here, a noun or an adjective? Is "smiles" a noun or a verb? The overdeterminedness of Crane's formulation amounts to "[a] longer answer" in its own right, sustaining the poem not only as unremittingly being-written, but being-read. Even to begin to ask these questions of Crane — beyond grammatical surfeits, how might we even begin to ideate (beyond the stronghold of critical negativity) "death smiles in flowering stone?" — is to make possible if not definitive answers then "longer" ones. To begin to ask these questions is to renew a conversation that Crane has begun, and that *Queer Optimism's* subsequent chapters continue.

Chapter Two

EMILY DICKINSON'S QUEER PAIN

"One Claw Opon the Air"

> *Facing reality means, therefore, living in a state of turmoil and upset. The only way to become a realist, and for Arendt we all must do so for our mutual survival, is to cultivate a suspicion of intellectual and psychological comfort in whatever forms we find them. Arendt hated illusions about the terrible facets of human existence and wished for herself and her "co-builders" of the world to accept willingly a wounding by them. Suffering is so much a part of her notion of thinking that only by feeling pain can one know that one loves the world properly.*
>
> —Deborah Nelson, "Suffering and Thinking: The Scandal of Tone in *Eichmann in Jerusalem*"

As already should be clear, queer optimism is no more wed to queer theory's established vocabularies than it is to those of optimism. Queer optimism seeks to extend what is conceivable as the province of queer theory, as much as it seeks an extended province of optimistic thinking. In positing a set of nonequivalent but constellated terms (affirmation, coherence, happiness, smiles, etc.) as limit beyond which queer theory itself must reach, queer optimism insists, in the reaching, that queer theory can (and ought) reconfigure its understanding of itself, its lexicon, and its own ends. Along these lines, my study of Dickinson does not recapitulate the ways other Dickinson scholars have deployed queer theory, nor seek to make use of some other extant queer vocabulary that might further illuminate Dickinson's lavender tints.

My resistance to such forms of reiteration corresponds to my resistance to forms of reiteration inherent in queer scholarship itself. Crane, read alongside or through Bersani, too often surfaces from such a reading if not as confirmation of Bersani's argument then anticipation of it. Similarly, Dickinson's extravagant and often provocative lyric experiments in personae — voices of girls, of boys, of variously enabled or delimited women, of men and gods, of the living and the dead — make interlineations of Dickinson and Judith Butler, for many critics, nearly irresistible. Such readings, however, render Dickinson either a confirmation of queer theory's terms, or an avatar of them. For instance, Sandra Runzo writes that

> [t]he sense of the theatrical that informs Dickinson's poems conveys remarkable consonance with recent theories that examine gender and sexual identity in relation to performance. Theorist Judith Butler, for instance, speculates that the "self" is constituted through a "string of performances": the repeated performance creates a semblance of self-coherence and establishes and circulates one's sexual and gendered "being." (The repetition, she notes, also contests any continuity and coherence, each new performance supplanting the previous one.) Asserting that there are no fixed or "proper" gender roles and that what appears to be clear and stable "gender" is the consequence of impersonation, Butler commends the "necessary drag" of gender and sexual identity.[1]

What does this conveyance of "remarkable consonance" tell us about Judith Butler that we don't already know? Does Dickinson's consanguinity with Butler afford new insight into Dickinson's writing, or substitute for insight a kind of collusion or mutual corroboration? In the context of Dickinson's poems, what "self" could approximate a Butlerian subject, let alone "semblance of self-coherence?" More pointedly, in a body of work riddled with dashes — including fragments and epistolary excerpts as much as anything like a complete poem — might there be other means of approaching "a semblance of self-coherence" (for instance, as point of departure, rather than end)?[2]

In an earlier essay, Runzo proposes that "all the personae [of Dickinson's poems], even those that ostensibly recede or nearly disappear — ostentatiously parade in the cracks and closets of the poems, making exalted claims to power, conducting spectacular permutations, demonstrating their unlimited capacities for pretense and gestures of duplicity."[3] As *atava* of camp, Dickinson "locates value in this very effacement [of her poem's 'denied homoeroticism' or 'demeaned greatness']."[4] Runzo's essays are representative of the loci in which queer theory's radar largely detects Dickinson: as arch-destabilizer, proto-Butlerian performer, consistently inconsistent brilliant trickster. But again: if, queer theory seeks to destabilize, complicate, or challenge systems of taxonomy and valuation, are such readings of Dickinson — by queer theory's own criteria — *queer enough*?[5]

In "Amplitude of Queer Desire in Dickinson's Erotic Language," Suzanne Juhasz rehearses some of the banners under which queer readings of Dickinson have processed. "Erotic desire — sensuous, nuanced, flagrant, extreme, outlandish, and profound — is," Juhasz writes, "[Dickinson's] way of interacting with the world. Dickinson is not only sexy, she's edgy; Polymorphous Perversity! Lesbianism! Autoeroticism! Necrophilia! Cross-Dressing! Masochism!"[6] It's difficult, upon first read, to gauge Juhasz's tone in such passages: are the exclamation points to be read as equivocal (along the lines of Dickinson's dash) or trumpetingly cheerful (like the exclamatories of Frank O'Hara)? Performance of the abashed, or unabashed? Suggesting, finally, a zeal more sincere than facetious, Juhasz's multiplication of Dickinsonian red-light districts eventually magnetizes to one topic, that of masochism. "For the Dickinson subject," Juhasz writes, "desire quickens in response to a force from without, and its pleasure/pain occasions new understandings or interpretations of herself in and of the world."[7] Repeating the compression of "pleasure/pain," Juhasz later posits that "the three-part Dickinson masochistic sublime might look like this: (1) Desire quickens from a force outside the self; (2) Pleasure in pain is experienced and reaches erotic climax; (3) The result is not satiation but a new world altogether."[8]

Juhasz will go on to reference "pleasure/pain," and "pleasure in pain" several times before essay's end, concluding, in a reading of lines from "I would not paint — a picture — " (F348)[9] that "sweet torment and sumptuous despair have that customary masochistic twinge."[10] Such twinges are important to Juhasz's queer reading of Dickinson, not because evidence of Dickinson's absolutely masochistic subject position, but because so pervious with concomitant locutions of sadism.

And "[s]adomasochism," for Juhasz, "is transformed with the final image of a queer body participating in all aspects of its desire."[11] Sadomasochism — the bending of agency into passivity, the sluicing of pain/pleasure equilibria — enables the polymorphousness that heads Juhasz's initial catalogue of Dickinson's edginess. Masochism, following Juhasz, undoes sadism's privileged (authorial) claim on pain, and in so doing isn't just one of several instantiations of queer desire, but the logic that subtends queer desire itself.

It is unsurprising that queer readings of Dickinson gravitate toward masochism, in that masochism not only posits pain with a sexy twist, but outs pain as a site of parading performativity of the sort conjured by Runzo, informed by Butler. Pain's privileged position within queer readings of Dickinson differs perhaps in quality but not in kind from pain's longstanding privileged place in Dickinson criticism more generally. George Poulet's 1956 essay, "Time and American Writers" offers one of the most elegant (and operatic) assessments of Dickinsonian pain, a tack that subsequent critics variously follow:

> Such is Emily's lot: Condemned all her life to unhappiness in order to pay the price of a single instant of happiness. But what is striking is not that she is rebellious and finds her lot unjust. On the contrary, always suffering, she will the sooner repent of remembering too often the single moment free of suffering.[12]

Albert Gelpi, in 1965, ruminates Dickinson's proleptic sympathy with Yeats and Pound (and makes clear the proximity of recent masochism scholarship to canonical Dickinson criticism). "Yeats wrote in his biography," Gelpi writes, that "[w]e begin to live when we have conceived of life as tragedy. In his version of *Women of Trachis,* Ezra Pound had the dying and thwarted Herakles exclaim: 'what / SPLENDOR, IT ALL COHERES.' Emily Dickinson, who spoke of 'Confident Despair,' would have understood these expressions of tragic joy. It was knowledge of 'this brief Tragedy of Flesh' that made life precious; it was acceptance of loss and defeat that made an unexpected moment of vision in 'that bright tragic thing.'"[13]

Less operatic than soap-operatic, Jane Eberwein writes that "there can be no question that isolation intensified neurotic tendencies in Emily

Dickinson and allowed for the flowering of eccentric behavior that contributed nothing to her happiness or anyone else's."[14] Eberwein proceeds not to speculate but to assert that "[i]n her life, as in her poems, Dickinson exploited the opportunity to make negative choices, recognizing that her tendency to deny opportunities marked her off as eccentric and exclusive while exposing her to pain."[15] Eberwein's notion of Dickinson's "exploit[ation]" of negativity implies less pain's inexorability (that pain is everywhere and inevitable) than that the redemptive ends of pain make nearly irresistible Dickinson's enterprise to make pain *seem* so. This latter account of exploitation revises as choice (authorial and otherwise) what Poulet construes as fate — the "lot" to which Dickinson is "condemned." This movement within Dickinson criticism reflects a reappraisal of both pain's value and how a person or poet is able to access that value. Echoing Poulet's version of Dickinson as pain's passive object (she who endures or is condemned to something not of her own construing), Robert Weisbuch writes, "[b]oth agony and dying eliminate façade."[16] Weisbuch's observation substitutes for Dickinson's agency pain's own personified agency: we shall return to this matter of persons displaced by personified emotion. Eberwein's contrary insistence on Dickinson's agency — courting pain rather than victimized by it — bears a logic structurally equivalent to later accounts of Dickinsonian masochism. Masochism is nominally inapplicable to Dickinson's "exploit[s]" if only because the ends of Dickinsonian pain, for Eberwein, are didactic rather than erotic: "Emily Dickinson shaped her life by a startlingly consistent pattern of negative choices, in a way that intensified every limitation upon her, exaggerated every barrier. And she did so consciously, not in order to punish herself, or court discomfort, but to promote reflexive inward growth."[17]

Again, masochism differs from the relation to pain that Eberwein describes in that the former bears an assiduous relation to desire, rather than to self-reflection or perspicacity (desire's possible relations to perspicacity is a different subject altogether). Desiring pain, the masochist produces occasions for pain that undermine what I have termed pain's inexorability. On the one hand, pain (or for Weisbuch, "agony and dying") eliminates façade, but on the other, pain masochistically is façade — or at very least, arises as a series of choices and confabulations not necessarily opposed to façade.

To return to Butler's terms, is pain a series of performances, or an entity *ab ovo*? Marianne Noble's chapter on Dickinson in *The Masochistic Pleasures of Sentimental Literature* interestingly attempts to define masochism as simultaneously theatrical and veracious. Noble cites the first two lines of the following poem's second stanza as instance of Dickinsonian masochism's nongenetic, fabulated character:

I can wade Grief—
Whole Pools of it—
I'm used to that—
But the least push of Joy
Breaks up my feet—
And I tip—drunken—
Let no Pebble—smile—
'Twas the New Liquor—
That was all!

Power is only Pain—
Stranded—thro' Discipline,
Till Weights—will hang—
Give Balm—to Giants—
And they'll wilt, like Men—
Give Himmaleh—
They'll carry—Him! (F312)

Noble does not offer a reading of these two lines, perhaps because they seem so vigorously to speak for themselves. "Power is only pain stranded through discipline" has the ring of a masochist's bumper sticker, not least because it so securely situates pain within the unimpeachably Foucauldian nexus of discipline and power. Pain is conceivable as fabulous in its imbrication with power; in its utility, pain participates in wills to power that cast suspicion on formulations of pain that do not take ideological motivation into account. Returned to their poem, however, the aphoristic assertiveness of these two lines differently suggests the assertion of assertiveness, rather than assertiveness itself. The poem's traversal of the hyperbolic and hyperbolically understated makes it nearly impossible to read the "only" of "Power is only Pain" as marker of unequivocal declarative (more specifically, declaration of a particular hermeneutics of suspicion). Rather, the poem situates this declarative as one (potentially) loopy statement among others. To excerpt the two lines as dictum is to foreclose the poem's own play of facetiousness and tonal instability.

How is one to take as truth (the force of "______ is only ______") a statement about the instabilities of truth (pain isn't pain, per se, but part of larger network of persuasion), embedded in a poem insistent on its own instabilities (" 'Twas the New Liquor—/ That was all!")?

Before engaging this poem in its entirety, I wish to sketch the logic of masochism on which Noble's readings more generally depend. "In Dickinson," Noble writes, "one important, recurrent manifestation of this scenario ["in which victims willingly submit to the abusive domination of an extremely powerful male"] is the image of the female flower with her head bowed in anguished adoration before a domineering, powerful male figure, who appears as Christ, King, Duke, Master, Caesar or Sun."[18] This scenario, for Noble, is most potently figured in Dickinson's "man of noon" letter:

> you have seen flowers at morning, satisfied with dew, and those same sweet flowers at noon with their heads bowed in anguish before the mighty sun; think you these thirsty blossoms will *now* need naught but—*dew?* No, they will cry for sunlight, and pine for the burning noon, tho' it scorches them, scathes them; they have got through with peace—they know that the man of noon, is *mightier* than the morning and their life is henceforth to him.[19]

In her readings of this and related scenes of floral wilting, Noble presumes pain as inextricable from a particular "longing for presence" (155). For Noble, the flower chooses to be scorched, as though the choice were scorching or bust. That is, if the flower/woman has to choose between love and no love, she chooses the former. "The terror that also obviously characterizes the relationship of Phoebus and Daisy is another important component of this image, intensifying its capacity to express ecstatic desire. Dickinson associates both marriage and sex with a mixture of agony and ecstasy" (151). Noble implies that terror or agony, as emotional energies, might be added, recipe-like, to ecstasy—as though there were a raw form of ecstasy not already spiked with a certain bad feeling. Terror, however, does not intensify ecstatic desire—the intensity of "ecstatic desire" definitionally already involves terror. And similarly, agony is constitutive of ecstasy even before it is superfluously added. In this conceptual field, in which desire always already is ecstatic (not to mention always already routed through "marriage and sex," as though these were a person's only erotic options), masochism emerges not as the only way to love pain, but the only way to love love.

At the outset of her essay, Noble interestingly subordinates discussion of this particular kind of pain to analysis of the spaces of authorship this pain occasions. That is, Noble (correctly, I think, and salutarily) tends to the ways in which Dickinson's writing actually forges scenes of pain so as to relish the correlative power of inventing fictional mistreatment. Pain, along these lines, becomes a site of strategy and opportunity, rather than of desolation and travail. To remember the lines of Noble's epigraph, this is the difference between "stranded" as techne and as state of bereavement. Noble writes that "sentimental masochism serves three interrelated modes of expression for Dickinson: representing a vulnerable Daisy submissive before a ruthless Master is a mode of fantasizing about power and expressing anger; alluding to sentimental and religious links between pleasure and pain is a mode of expressing desire; and collapsing desire for presence with the presence of pain is a mode of addressing ontological anxieties relating to abandonment" (156). Bracketing all the various other things masochism does or can do, it's important to note the sheer fact that masochism, here, not only describes the energy of "victims [who] willingly submit to and even seek to be dominated or hurt" (147), but also serves ulterior purposes themselves inextricable from the scene of writing. Noble goes so far (though not far enough) as to claim that Dickinson's Daisy "ingeniously invents methods to perpetuate her ontological state of relatedness to [Master.] His absence is a punishment he is inflicting upon her" (155). More radically than this, Daisy ingeniously invents absence itself as the grounds for all subsequent inventions.

How is ingenious invention related, for Noble, to ontological state? If an ontological state is partly defined in terms of its perpetuity, can we accurately describe such a state in terms of ontology if its duration is non-intrinsically orchestrated? Even as masochism might seem conceptually adequate to the indeterminacies raised by such questions, the masochism of Noble's study in fact eschews indeterminacy for a demonstrativeness which, in Noble's reading, reflects pain's own demonstrativeness, and no less so, pain's capacity to expose what isn't painful as less real. Imagining pain as mode of analytical inquiry (rather than object of analysis), Noble cites Dickinson's "A nearness to Tremendousness" as "crucial in a study of Dickinson's uses of sentimental masochism" (161), but leaves unclear how either the poem or the reader could move to masochism from pain and back again. If masochism (an erotics of pain, or the elegant contractuality of pain) is only nominally distinguishable from pain as such, does this make all pain theatrical (in the manner of Butler), or all pain — even that underwritten by orchestrative agreement — non-theatrically keen? Noble suggests the latter. As a consolidation of pain's powers (even as such a consolidation undoes the persuasiveness of everything that *isn't* pain), the masochism of Noble's project recalls — if not on the level of performativity, than on the level of logic — the ways in which melancholy (within Butler's own project) eludes the acuities to which the nonmelancholic world is subjected. If "A nearness to Tremendousness" articulates a form of masochism, it is a masochism entailing less a desire of pain, than of reality:

> A nearness to Tremendousness —
> An Agony procures —
> Affliction ranges Boundlessness —
> Vicinity to Laws
>
> Contentment's quiet Suburb —
> Affliction cannot stay
> In Acres — It's Location
> Is Illocality — (F824)

Noble views this poem as "crucial in a study of Dickinson's uses of sentimental masochism" (161). "Pain destroys the peaceful illusion of coherence that is indulged by the bourgeois residents of 'Contentment's quiet Suburb.' Pain splits the illusion of identity apart, exposing the gaps that lie at its core" (161).[20] Noble cites another Dickinson critic, Christopher Benfey, for corroboration. "As [Benfey] points out, Dickinson is attracted to pain and death because one 'knows' they are true" (181). What exactly does it mean for Noble to qualify knowledge in scare quotes? What's the difference between being "attracted to pain" and "knowing it's true," or "knowing" it's true? These sorts of questions point not to the salaciousness of a Dickinson-in-furs, but rather to much broader, less sensationalist questions, concerning the reality-effects of pain-as-such. Might pain, as Noble glosses it in this poem, destroy the illusion of coherence, not because more real, but rather because more convincingly illusive?

Noble's apprehension of a pain that might in some contexts seem real without actually being so surfaces in her own writing, in a series of overemphatic testaments to pain's veraciousness. The fact that pain might be disputable, controvertible, or noninevitable resounds in Noble's litanous protests to the contrary: "Pain feels indisputably present to us" (181); "a suffering that is inevitable" (182); "her pain is indisputably present" (183); "incontrovertible fact of present suffering" (183) "traumatic separation that one must inevitably undergo" (183); "indisputable here-and-nowness of the pain" (184); "inevitability of separation" (185). Noble's own compulsions instantiate one of her essay's most challenging (if finally unrealized) claims—that pain isn't the emptiness out of which language arises, but that which language itself sustains as originary.

For Noble as well as other Dickinson critics such as Robert McClure Smith,[21] masochism discloses as theatrical the violences it presumably parodies. Subsequently, masochism becomes the means by which the ontological fluidity left in its wake is salvaged as consolingly authentic. Such is the implication of both Noble and Smith, who celebrates Dickinsonian masochism for its undoing of "stable identity" and "power hierarchies," as Judith Butler's brand of performativity undoes "sexual identity itself."[22] For all the fictive spaces enabled by masochism's theater, however, its most engrossing script construes masochism as a catechism into realism. In the equivalence drawn between what is painful and what is real, learning to desire pain acquires the ethical importance of desiring to see the world stripped of ideology, what Noble aligns with Dickinson's "contentment." Masochism in this light seems less perverse than self-righteous.

Dickinson, in the poem with which Noble begins, calls this masochism's realist bluff; as though uncannily intervening in the theories of pain that eventually would inscribe her, Dickinson concedes travail as its own kind of ease, which is to say, potentially, its own form of contentment:

> I can wade Grief—
> Whole Pools of it—
> I'm used to that—
> But the least push of Joy
> Breaks up my feet—

Dickinson's critics, like the poem's giants, wilt under the impossible pressures of balm and trip over joy's smiling pebble. They wilt like men, but also like Dickinson's flowers, "bowed in anguish before the mighty sun." This balm is both less familiar and more demanding than both grief and the masochism that teaches us to like grief — we already do. And unlike the agonies of ecstasy, which fantasize a body's dissolution, balm depends (in a literal register that might extend to the ontological) on a body's dermal surface. Some might argue that the poem is more or less flip, but that argument itself presumes that we already know how pleasure operates. If taken seriously, the poem posits joy as a field of inquiry neither Dickinson nor we entirely understand.

Querying Pain

It is in part the sheer difficulty of understanding joy or pleasure that makes masochism — telegraphically defined by Juhasz as "pleasure/pain" — inadequate an entry into Dickinson's writing. Subsequent sections of this chapter more intensively will investigate the unfamiliarities of Dickinson's lyric pleasures. This section, on the other hand, shall investigate the extraordinary strangeness — the queerness — of Dickinsonian pain itself. My insertion of queerness, here, is not desultory. Queer theory's great contribution to studies of emotion lies in its complication of the ways in which emotion and affect might be measured, experienced, navigated. Queer investigations of Dickinsonian emotion (usually pain, and usually following masochistic protocol) nonetheless have not furthered our understanding of pain (or despair, or mourning), so much as made of pain an empire. This state of affairs is all the more in need of correction, given that Dickinson's own accounts of pain are themselves so flintily inquisitive, attached less to pain's indubitability than to its solicitous openness to scrutiny.

That experience of pain might open onto something greater than it but likewise might not is suggested in the specificities of "A nearness to Tremendousness." If we take tremendousness as a sort of epistemological sublime, agony does not procure it, but a nearness to it. "A nearness to Tremendousness" produces a set of certainties about the locatability of emotion, even as certainty is constituted by the certain indeterminacy of location. Tremendousness, as such, hardly clarifies agony's contours, latitudes, longitudes. Furthermore, given the intense, sometimes vertiginous quality of Dickinson's landscapes (as in "Above me Dips Eternity"), how can one be certain of this procured region's qualities? Likewise, and more unequivocally equivocal, affliction's locality is illocality. Most available an explication of this assertion is that affliction itself is unplaceable because so unpredictable and ambiently ubiquitous (or at least potentially so). That affliction's "Location / Is Illocality," however, suggests not only that affliction is impossible to place because uncontainable — "cannot stay / in Acres," or homonymically, in achers, those who ache — but that location along such narrowly spatializing lines is unable to apprehend an affliction so exceeding the poem's disingenuous positing of real estate. Inability to "stay," after all, could reiterate Affliction's ranginess (of the first stanza), but more specifically speaks to affliction's temporal characteristics, where temporality intersects with spatial knowledge but is independent of it.

What if, for the moment, we imagined "acre" as homonymic displacement of "acher?" That affliction cannot stay in one who aches negatively advances a spatial claim (does not exist in one place, but doesn't necessarily occupy another), but simultaneously makes a constative observation about time. Affliction cannot stay: cannot stop moving. Or cannot pause. The temporal affinities of "Stay" are themselves adjacent to claims about feeling (to stay, as in to comfort) and about thinking (to stay, as in to stand one's ground, to have confidence in). In this way, the poem seems less an assertion of affliction's ontic value over contentment's quiet (to recall Noble's reading) or of affliction's spatial inclinations, than of the inability to make sense of affliction spatially, if extricated from the temporal (and other) matrices in which space itself operates.

Sharon Cameron notes that "such poems . . . often resort to the language of measurement in order to insist on the impossibility of it."[23] I agree with Cameron that "A nearness to Tremendousness" introduces a spatial enterprise to enact, finally, that project's inutility. I think also, however, that the poem introduces the language of temporal measurement as supplement (if not alternative) in the face of spatiality's failure. "A nearness to Tremendousness," in its attempt either to spatialize or temporalize pain, does not make claims about pain's veracity so much as query the difficulties intrinsic to identifying veracity at all. Affliction cannot stay, cannot stand one's ground. And here, the literal, spatial sense of ground gives way to the epistemological quandary of affliction trying to hold its own, to produce and sustain its own persuasiveness. It is helpful here to recall Dickinson's knowledge of Latin. In querying the contours of affliction's credibility, Dickinson also queries the credibility of her own dashed lines. Affliction, from the Latin verb "fligo": to dash (against), describes a textual event—the attempt to articulate if not the conditions of despair per se then the grounds by which despair might be experienced at all—as much as a phenomenological one. That Dickinson's dashes raise fundamental questions about the reading of a given poem (where to pause, how long to pause) mirrors the temporal confusions inherent to affliction, as such (where, what, if, it stays).

Such spatio-temporal challenges are illuminated by a less familiar poem, "No Man can compass a Despair—" of which I cite the opening two stanzas:

> No Man can compass a Despair—
> As round a Goalless Road
> No faster than a mile at once
> The Traveller proceed—
>
> Unconscious of the Width—
> Unconscious that the Sun
> Be Setting on His progress—
> So accurate the one.... (F714)

Again, we are presented with the impossibility of spatial measurement, albeit the exactitude of "No Man can" seems dogmatically definitive alongside the comparable blurs of "A nearness to Tremendousness," whose nearness, vicinity, and boundlessness collectively reach, only asymptotically, toward definite locus. At the same time, the latter poem at least generically is attuned to Agony's potential dimensions; we are, there, in the realm of tremendousness. More specifically, the poem's recourse to laws, suburbs, and acres describes human proportions in turn reflected in agony's own personificatory logic, by which emotions (as though to compensate for the poem's lack of persons) could function like people, inhabit (or nearly inhabit) this likewise domesticated place.

While the immediate dimensions of "No Man can compass a Despair" are those of a person (a man with a compass), the scale of despair itself is less intelligible than those of the other poem's correlative personifications and domestications. The compass might be a mathematical implement, thereby shrinking Despair to a circumference small enough to fit a page, or even smaller. The compass might as feasibly be navigatory by which Despair could fit on a page only figuratively (as on a map), but otherwise could be anywhere (and anything) capable of being mapped. The poem's subsequent lines hardly clarify how Despair is to be compassed — how we are to compass the compassing — in archly introducing a simile that potentially validates the two compasses equally. A circuitous road suggests the work of a mathematical compass, and the possible need for a navigatory one. Mathematical compass describes how the road (or blueprint of road) was planned and executed; navigatory compass describes how the road, once constructed, might be traveled, or how the road relates to the terrain around it. Despair's two compasses thus bear inverted relations to figuration. The former inscribes a figure that might then materially be executed; the latter navigates a topos that textually might be figured only after the fact.

If the simile, then, sustains Despair's possible (mathematical) minuteness as well as its possible (navigatory) tremendousness, it also throws both these forms of spatialization into confusion as it proceeds. "No faster than a mile at once / The Traveller proceed." How have we moved from questions of distance and orientation to questions of speed? If the round "goalless" road is a circle, why travel it at all? Why does the traveller's speed matter? "No faster than a mile at once": how fast is a mile? A mile per what? What are we measuring, and how? The poem at this juncture seems less a lyric than a very hard problem on a high school math test. And the problem doesn't get easier. The traveller doesn't know the width of the road. (Width, here, trumps length only because the road is circular, and the width from compass' center to outside leg defines circumference, equivalent in this instance to the road's length.) The traveller, however, likewise doesn't know the sun is setting, and at this turn in the math problem I start to feel despair of my own. If traveller is unaware of sun setting at such and such a rate along a circular road of whose width the traveller similarly is unaware, how quickly does traveller need to circle said road, to helpfully extend an analogue to some other man trying to measure Despair with an unspecified compass.

Thank goodness we have received Dickinson's text as lyrical rather than algebraic.[24] As a lyric, the mathematics of "No Man can compass a Despair" insists not that we solve for Despair, but that we reckon the difficulty of reckoning despair among so many other variables. To pursue the lyric problematic (rather than mathematical problem), the sun is setting. The setting sun importantly looks like a spatial phenomenon (slow passage from east to west, in the manner both of nonmathematical compass-points, and the arc inscribable by a mathematical compass), but likewise marks a temporal change. Or is it both, and if so to what end? The man who cannot compass Despair ends up analogous to the Traveller unaware that what looks spatial (were he aware of the sun at all) might in fact be temporal, or depend on temporal movement in nontransparent ways.

Time, within Dickinson's poems, depends on something like a pain axis, as much as pain itself depends on a temporal axis. Time therefore becomes as unreliable a marker of pain as space, insofar as pain alters how time measures or is measured at all:

> Pain — expands the Time —
> Ages coil within
> The minute Circumference
> Of a single Brain —
>
> Pain contracts — the Time —
> Occupied with Shot
> Gammuts of Eternities
> Are as they were not — (F833)

It is in this context that a vocabulary of masochism pertains to (if not ultimately explains) Dickinsonian pain. Gilles Deleuze helpfully provides an understanding of masochism more flexible than Juhasz's or Noble's formulation of "pleasure-pain," and if not transferable to Dickinson's enterprise then more enablingly conversant with it. "Material definitions of masochism based on the pleasure-pain complex," Deleuze writes, "are insufficient . . . they do not indicate the possibility of what they define, they do not show that particular conditions must follow. But worse still, they lack distinctive features. . . . Fundamentally, masochism is neither material nor moral, but essentially formal."[25] Several pages earlier, Deleuze clarifies his understanding of masochism's formalism:

> [I]t is a mistake to treat the pleasure-pain complex as raw material able intrinsically to lend itself to any transformation.... Formally speaking, masochism is a state of waiting; the masochist experiences waiting in its pure form. Pure waiting divides naturally into two simultaneous currents, the first representing what is awaited, something essentially tardy, always late and always postponed, the second representing something that is expected and on which depends the speeding up of the awaited object.[26]

"The mechanism" of masochism, for Deleuze, "remains uncomprehensible if it is not related to the form and in particular to the temporal form that makes it possible."[27] Deleuze characterizes masochism less in terms of pleasure or pain than in its particular relation to time: waiting, or the contractual, by which one waits for something "stated, promised, announced, and carefully described... [to be] accomplished."[28]

What does it mean, in the context of Dickinson's poems, to speak of "waiting in its pure form?" How—given the divagations and errancies of Dickinson's temporal experiments—can we presume in her lyrics a "pure waiting," let alone a waiting that could "divide naturally"? Or for that matter, that could produce something so reliable as "always late," or "always postponed"? Deleuze's masochism resembles Dickinsonian pain in that both rely on a temporal architecture, but differs from it in that the temporal vicissitudes of Dickinsonian pain shift too capriciously to serve as predicate for anything so noncontingent as Deleuze's "always," for anything so formalized as the contractuality that governs Deleuze's understanding of Masoch. The fidelity of time enables Deleuze's masochistic pain-contract; time, for Deleuze, contracts masochistic pain. As in the above poem, however, time does not enable the contracting of Dickinsonian pain: pain contracts time. Within Dickinson's poem, it is impossible for pain to follow a temporal logic, even as inextricable from it. This is because Dickinsonian pain calls the "shot[s]," dictates temporal terms that might only retrospectively be seen to dictate it. Recalling the tautology implicit in the earlier poem's circular, "goalless" road, Dickinsonian time is a pain as much as pain is a pain. Far from revealing some more lucid reality, the aberrant, terrible and exquisite nexus of time-in-pain (as opposed to masochism's conventional pleasure-in-pain) forfeits claims of ontic or ontological persuasiveness for a far more disorienting and vast investigation of pain no less painful for its obligatory factitiousness.

Delight's Despair

The elusiveness of the above poems complicates (already complicated) accounts of Dickinson's lyric negotiation of pain. More radically, this elusiveness unsteadies both how and what we know (or think we know) about pain qua pain. Such destabilizations, by Dickinson's own hand, render suspicious or at least severely premature any but the most qualified, local critical claims regarding pain's ethical, aesthetic or epistemological thresholds. Dickinson's copious formulations of pain amount to nothing less than a critique of pain's naturalized, preemptively embraced intractability. Dickinson's critique contributes to queer optimism's own loosening of critical and philosophical cathexes to what I've been denominating a correlative pessimistic repertoire. Equally valuable to queer optimism's commitments is Dickinson's complication of our relation to the field of optimism itself, beyond Leibnizian or Leibniz-informed models.

This section turns to a Dickinson poem, "Her smile was shaped like other smiles," that subjects happiness and merriment to the same scrutiny to which Dickinson's lyrics more familiarly subject agony and despair. The occasion for Dickinson's parsing of happiness is a smile. My reading of this poem therefore recalls my previous chapter on Crane, but importantly differs from it as well. In Crane, unlike Dickinson, lyric smiles occur at a remove from anything like happiness. I sought to argue in that previous chapter for a tenuous connection between Crane's serially repeated lyric smiles and Crane's coterminous epistolary considerations of poetic optimism. The tenuousness, for my purposes, was energizing rather than a liability: any more resilient an alignment of smiles and optimism would reproduce narratives of optimism and of smiles already familiar, narratives that hardly could do the weirdness of Crane's smiles justice.

The diegetic proximity of Dickinson's smiles and Dickinsonian positive emotion does not support a narrative any less strange than those culled from Crane. As we shall see, Dickinson's smiles are as unfamiliar as her conception of happiness and merriment is unfamiliar. Dickinson's understanding of happiness is inseparable from happiness's encroachment on pain. Dickinsonian happiness and pain, however, are not simply antonymous. That is, they do not replicate the unproductive yin-yang of happy/sad, whereby one can't have the former without the latter, or vice versa. Dickinson's poem is more exacting than this. And unsurprisingly, following the previous section, positive and negative feeling, in Dickinson's poem, are unthinkable outside a miscible and no less jarring temporal medium.

Before exploring the aberrances of "Her smile was shaped like other smiles," I want to put on the table another poem, "Delight's Despair at setting," which elucidates a personificatory logic important to "Her smile was shaped like other smiles," a logic already noted in "A nearness to Tremendousness." Unlike many Dickinson poems, these three lyrics lack a diegetic first person, an "I." More to the point, the poems bear traces of persons as at best bare minima or residuum. And in the place of persons who might weather emotions, around whom lyric circumstance might be organized, we find personified emotions. Affliction, not a person, "cannot stay." Agony, not a person, is the transitive subject of procuring.

Even more remarkable, in "Delight's Despair at setting," it is not a person who experiences despair, but Delight that experiences despair. I offer here the poem's first quatrain:

> Delight's Despair at setting
> Is that Delight is less
> Than the sufficing Longing
> That so impoverish.

To attempt a single reading of the lines is nearly impossible, given that its gerunds simultaneously signal opposite, incompatible actions. One set of actions and meanings, however, seems more immediately intelligible than others. As usually conceived, delight sets too quickly, in the manner of the sun—for instance, the setting sun of "No Man can compass a Despair."[29] Delight, in this sense, experiences despair over its own fading, sinking, diminishing. This sense of diminishment is apposite the subsequent lines' claim: in setting, Delight despairs because it is less (in a quantitative, if not material, register) than "Longing." Longing—in the manner of desire, a longing for more delight, or reprieve from despair itself—lasts longer than does delight. And to follow this tack, Despair is all the more ponderous in that this longing that outlasts delight is sufficing (a consolation or substitute for delight's loss), even as the sufficing simultaneously impoverishes.

That is, Longing's cold comfort seems sufficient only to the extent that sufficing occupies Delight's position (or to remember Dickinson's earlier insistence on "nearness," at very least a position vicinal to it). Were Delight not so quickly to have set, longing's consolation (sufficing) would seem less sustaining than gratuitous. One doesn't long for something that is present (that has not set or vanished), and so the sufficing that Longing can provide is also impoverishing because dependent on desire's logarithm of lack.

The above account is verbose to the extent that the quatrain's own lexicon is austere. With so few terms to work with, it is difficult to produce iterations and reiterations that do not pinball from one term to the next and back again. The ascetic impactions of the quatrain resist interpretation from beyond its own structure, and so the structure and its constitutive parts solicit unfolding and folding from within. Again, the above explication is verbose, but more to the point, utterly familiar. It is a reading of poetry, but equally so the most elementary of primers on the law of psychoanalytic desire.

Each term of this spare quatrain, however, is a gear. The gears can be shifted, turned to other interlocked positions which produce a quite different account of Delight's despair. What if "setting" were loosened from narratives of dimming and diminution? We might think of setting as the condition of being checked, held at standstill. Or in the manner of hardening, the setting of plaster. Literarily, the manner by which an idea is set in writing. Set, as psychological predisposition or expectation, as in being dead-set in one's way. Or to recall Judith Butler, the experience of congealment into one thing. This proliferation of variant definitions arguably should hold its own with if not eclipse the single sense of setting-as-a-sun, but it does not. That this latter setting, in the context of Dickinson's Delight, displaces or crowds out the other settings signals the impoverishing and impoverished narrative accorded to Delight more generally, a narrative which this poem redresses. "Setting" as denoted above, would indicate a hardening against which the Dickinsonian setting internally balks. If setting conjures the irrevocable setting of something in writing (set in stone), Dickinson's inscription of setting recalcitrantly resists its own (funereal) inscribing. Delight's despair, in this reading, arises not on account of Delight's evanescence, but on account of its hypostasization. More specifically, however, and a propos queer optimism's aims, delight's despair arises in its hypostasization not as hypostasized, but in its (counterintuitive and tenacious) hypostasization as fleeting.

In being set (frozen, calcified) as evanescent, Delight's setting is dispossessed of the durability that is no less its definitional due. And in being set as evanescently (as opposed to petrifyingly) setting, Delight seems foreclosingly and erroneously less. Qualitatively less, as already recounted. More despairingly, however, Delight's own capacities and faculties are rendered less: less interesting, less plangent, less responsive to questions of immanence, rigor, ethics. Less, in Delight's reduction to a narrative of fleetingness, a happy but shortlived waning (and as often, poof): to think of any "commonsensical" account of Delight (or happiness or merriment), it is fast, its pleasures best tallied after the Wordsworthian fact. But the internal ambivalence of "setting," within Dickinson, opens a space in which delight's other temporal narratives might be taken seriously.

If pain contracts the time, orchestrates the time, might pain orchestrate it to its own ends? Expand it for itself? And if so, what might be delight's own relation to time? If pain's expansion of time leaves delight in a temporal lurch, "Delight's Despair at setting" posits a compressed but aggressive form of lyric restitution. This restitution is likewise (if less transparently) the work of "Her smile was shaped like other smiles."

"Patient like a Pain": Dickinson's Queer Smile

The smiles of Crane's poetry, the previous chapter argued, are hermeneutically challenging to the extent that their ubiquity in *White Buildings* (and beyond) in no immediately available way seems correspondent to any singular or even collective intelligibility. Crane's smiles seem not only to arise without diegetic context for them, but likewise to outlast even the compressed, difficult contexts in which they nonetheless are embedded. Adjectivally appended to forms of durability ("unyielding," "unmangled") contrary to a smile's more commonly imagined celerity, this serialized durability doesn't cumulatively illuminate a logic of Crane's smiles, so much as multiply and refract any single smile's particular opacities and confusions.

This next section turns to the figure of a smile in the writing of Emily Dickinson. Dickinson's poem "Her smile was shaped like other smiles" resonates with those of Crane in several important ways. Like Crane's smiles, those of Dickinson's poem provocatively argue against their own presumed legibility or interpretability. And like Crane's smiles, the difficulty of reading Dickinson's smiles partly is attributable to a smile's deracination from both phenomenological and temporal milieux. What exactly are such lyric smiles outlasting, and what does it mean that they do so at all?

While taking these similarities to Crane as points of departure, this section will pursue the ways Dickinson's poem differently problematizes a smile's relation to figuration, temporality, and context (or lack thereof). Crane's smiles, to reiterate, are confusing insofar as they insist upon their own nontransience over and against poetic scenes unable to account for their presence. Dickinson's smiles, on the other hand, are not confusing on account of dissonance between smiles and surrounding, for the deceptively simple reason that in "Her smile was shaped like other smiles," there is no surrounding to speak of. If Crane's smiles sometimes have the effect of appearing out of nowhere, Dickinson's smiles are as intentional as specimens under glass. While the smile in "Her smile was shaped like other smiles" is clearly the poem's subject — as opposed to a poem's abruption, intrusion, or suggestively guarded telos — this clarity does not extend to the subject itself (which is to say, Dickinson's investigation of it). If Crane's smiles beg deciphering in providing so little deciphering of their own, Dickinson's smiles beg exegesis because so exhaustively and exhaustingly anatomized in Dickinson's own poem, but anatomized to so little avail. The simultaneous saturation and apparent unavailability of Dickinson's analysis asks a reader not to account for her poem's smiles (as is be the case with Crane) but to articulate and attempt to account for Dickinson's own accounting.

"Her smile was shaped like other smiles" arguably has received scant critical attention on account of its superficial remoteness from the tropes of trauma, loss, and misery that organize so much of Dickinson criticism. At the same time, the poem is far too thorny to be excerpted in the manner of "'Hope' is the thing with feathers," sold as refrigator magnets at the Dickinson Homestead. Critics perhaps presume that "Her smile was shaped like other smiles" is an easy poem to the extent that smiles seem like an easy topic; its ostensible obviousness (Dickinson can teach us about death, but what can she say about smiles that we do not already know . . .) bristles against the poem's vexing difficulties. In fact, the friction between what is reliably discernible and what is not describes the poem's own epistemological pulsions. The misbehaved smile of Dickinson's poem is a queer smile, though not in the manner of a cruisy smile at a bar. Rather, in its insistence that a smile might not tautologically explain itself, in its insistence that our vocabulary for understanding a phenomenon as ostensibly banal as smiling is terribly lacking. Queer optimism insists that queer theorizations of affect's intersection with epistemology must exceed a radius of negative affect; must not imagine affect and negative affect as synonymous; must not accept the repertoires of positive affect (inclusive of affective registrations such as a smile) as any more self-evident than correlative repertoires of negative affect. Along these lines, "Her smile was shaped like other smiles" is valuable to queer optimism not only as illuminating object of inquiry, but as instance of queer-optimistic practice in its own right.

> Her smile was shaped like other smiles—
> The Dimples ran along—
> And still it hurt you, as some Bird
> Did hoist herself, to sing,
> Then recollect a Ball, she got—
> And hold opon the Twig,—
> Convulsive, while the Music crashed—
> Like Beads—among the Bog—
>
> A happy lip—breaks sudden—
> It does'nt state you how
> It contemplated—smiling—
> Just consummated—now—
> But this one, wears it's merriment
> So patient—like a pain—
> Fresh gilded—to elude the eyes
> Unqualified, to scan—(F335, cited in full)

Dickinson's poem, at its most general, asserts that there are smiles and then there are smiles. That smiles might resemble those of a "happy lip," but bear no relation to happiness (a sardonic smile, an ominous smile, a despairing, pleading smile, etc.) is not in and of itself revelatory, but neither does such premise sufficiently recapitulate the interests of the above lines. This smile that is "shaped like other smiles" (without being one) "hurt you," but the fact of "hurt" likewise does not clarify the rhetorical proliferations and figurative strains engendered by the admission of hurt into the poem.

While the poem claims that the smile hurts, textural duress (for the poem's readers, for the poem itself), in fact arises not from the smile, but from the string of similes the smile calls into play. The poem is as much about difficult similes—similes shaped like other similes, without simile's ordinary ends — as it is about the poem's stated subject, "her smile." To whom does this opening pronoun attach? She, whoever she is, vanishes from the poem leaving only the smile in her wake. And this smile's unmoored relation to the similetic is belied by the first line's "like." The transformative work of a simile's conjecture occurs in the copulate "like" — simile turns the prepositional "like" into a sort of verb (if only figuratively speaking). In this first line, however, "like" isn't similetically operative because "shaped" demarcates this smile—her smile—as similarly shaped, similarity on a structural, nonsimiletic register. The ostensible ease of this opening similarity *between* smiles makes the poem's subsequent similes extending *from* smiles seem all the more beguilingly recalcitrant.

As already noted, "[h]er smile" invokes and absents a female subject in a single step. As with Crane (and unlike T. S. Eliot), Dickinson extricates a smile from its smiler. In Crane, however, extrication resulted in smiles putatively adrift in their immediate lyric surrounding. In Dickinson, by contrast, extrication pushes anything like surrounding or context beyond lyric periphery. Differently put, if smiles in Crane exert themselves in and against the poems in which they appear, smiles in Dickinson's poem delimit the scope of the poem itself. The radius of the poem is equivalent to the radius of the smile.

To speak of radii is to follow a geometric trope present at poem's outset. Smiles, here, are similar to each other in terms of shape rather than originating affect. The second line doesn't clarify the first (the shape of smiles invoked by both "[h]er smiles" and "other smiles" seem self-evident), so much as specify how these smiles have been shaped—"the

Dimples ran along" hardly confirms one shape or another, but rather, speculates on the manner by which smiles might be shaped in the first place. The dimples, while nearly personified in their running, have the effect of further removing "[h]er smile" from originating affective logic, from a realm of persons. Why is "she" smiling? Such a question matters much less to the poem than the question of how the smile is structurally executed. It is "shaped," transferring the phenomenon of smiling to the graph-like surface of a face, and that graph further winnowed to a mouth's arc. As though smiling, on the order of formation, were the result of surfacial dispersal: not (at least in this first stanza) the external instantiation of a mood, but a fantasy of surface without connection to interior logic. The subordination of a smile's internal (emotional, psychical, affective, sexual, etc.) origins to its registration as external shape likewise subordinates how or what the smiler feels to the smile's effect on someone else.

This particular smile's effect is to hurt. The predicament of "her smile" being shaped like other smiles but nonetheless hurting sends the poem into a rhetorical fugue. The stanza's apparent impulse is to clarify hurt's phenomenology, but the actual questions to which the subsequent similes might attempt answer themselves remain unclear: Does the simile ("as some bird") speak to why the smile hurts? Or the manner in which hurt is accomplished? Or how this particular hurt feels or would feel to "you"? Dickinson's similetic elaboration of hurt disorients, in part because the simile's terms all but lack intelligibility in their own right and seem incompatible with scenarios in which the energies of smiling, hurtedness, pleasure, or pain usually figure:

> And still it hurt you, as some Bird
> Did hoist herself, to sing,
> Then recollect a Ball, she got—
> And hold opon the Twig,—
> Convulsive, while the Music broke—
> Like Beads—among the Bog.

How does this smile hurt? As a bird on the verge of singing, who then recollects something else.[30] Singing begins as concerted—most available a gloss of the second line's "hoist" is that this bird plans to sing, and prepares for it; hoisting as intake of air, which the song will then expire.

Also, however, the bird might be hoisting herself onto her perch, a possibility whose eeriness involves the unlikely gravitas required in lifting so slight a creature. Penguins might need hoisting, or ostriches, or birds with broken wings. But songbirds (such as Keats's or Whitman's) are canonically nearly as fleet as their music; a songbird without flight — in need of "hoist[ing]" — seems as grim as a songbird without song.

In Dickinson's poem, neither bird nor song really takes off. The music that ends the stanza (yet we shall see that the difference between "song" and "music" is by no means insubstantial) breaks "Like Beads — among the Bog." Music, here, is heavy, subject to gravity in ways music (or for that matter, a bird) seldom is. Beads might make an initial plunk into the swamp, but more importantly, they are muffled and then swallowed up. The drama of the beads' absorption is put into relief by the poem immediately preceding it — preceding it not only in R. W. Franklin's reading edition, but in Dickinson's twelfth fascicle — whose subject is not the song of birds, but the "phraseless melody" of the wind,

> Whose fingers comb the Sky —
> Then quiver down, with tufts of tune — (F334)

One could also juxtapose this breaking music with the last lines of a later poem, in which "sequence raveled out of Sound — / Like Balls — opon — a Floor" (F867). Those latter balls, like these beads, are similarly land-borne. The floor, however, at least allows the possibility of velocity, and reverberation. The bog, on the other hand, terminates music as soon as music reaches it. Trying to make some initial sense of Dickinson's simile, one might align reception of the smile with reception of this strange music. Which, with further cruelty, aligns the receiver with the bog itself. The bog might also recall the face on which a smile appears; the beads that slowly sink into the former, along these lines, resemble the dimples that sink into the latter. But if beads (recalling both the ball recollected by the bird, and the dimples whose smile catalyzes this series of analogies in the first place) are like dimples, what counts, in the figurative domain of beads, as a smile? If music breaks like the beads of a necklace, then how to imagine the string on which music correlatively is strung? The peculiarity of such questions indicate the distance we have traveled from our initial querying of how one smile differs from another. This peculiarity likewise indicates the necessity of such vagabonding, if one is to do justice to the smiles that Dickinson's poem presents. The unfamiliarity of interpretation, in this instance, follows the unfamiliarity of the poem's own proceedings. To feel lost within Dickinson's poem is to inhabit the critical sweep not of optimism, but of queer optimism.

To return to our reading of the poem: recollection interferes with the bird's song by removing the bird from herself at the moment of song. Or rather, removing the bird from herself, to an interiority that neither song's breaking nor bird's own convulsings can reach. This interiority, however, doesn't, in any immediately obvious way, seem to matter, insofar as removal from self, and removal to self equally, dissolve into the stanza's last lines. Where there was bird and, imminently, song, there is only music. The bird's disappearance from the poem might signal her self-abdication (or sublimation?) from the poem's circumstances altogether. As the music breaks, is the bird most or least present, to herself or to her auditor?

The smile that hurts takes on it a life of its own, the way a song becomes music when there is no one to sing it. The smile that hurts emerges from a rigor that is both self-contained ("hold") and self-dispersing ("convulsive").[31] As music stands in for singer, the smile stands in for person. To transpose vehicle onto tenor results in a Cheshire-like looming of a smile in the branches, "grace of summer boughs."[32] Dickinson's analogies, I think, ultimately are not meant to clarify the manner in which this smile hurts. Rather, they suggest that the smile hurts in the very manner of analogy: which nearly illuminates but doesn't; which further distances (the potential exasperation of similes within similes), even as the distancing on a different register purports or even wishes to clarify.

One response to this stanza's baffling account of the exceptional smile is to wonder exactly how the "other [i.e., ordinary, non-hurting] smiles" operate. In fact, the second stanza seems to begin with such an account:

A happy lip — breaks sudden —
It doesn't state you how
It contemplated — smiling —
Just consummated — now —
But this one, wears it's merriment
So patient — like a pain —
Fresh gilded — to elude the eyes
Unqualified, to scan —

On first read, this stanza replicates the rhetorical movement of the first. There are smiles, and then there are smiles. Here, more specifically, there is a "happy lip," and then there is "this one." But is "this one" really the same as the smile that hurts? Rhetorically, perhaps, yes. But not really, insofar as Dickinson's account of a happy smile actually seems analogous to the hurtful one. "A happy lip," that is, breaks sudden, not unlike the hurtful smile of the first stanza, which (through Dickinson's similetic convolutions) is analogous to the breaking music of the bird. Furthermore, the smile that diverges from the norm of the happy lip, what Dickinson calls "this one," has very little in common with the exceptional smile aligned with that first stanza's strange birdless, breaking music. Whereas the exceptional smile of the first stanza (the smile shaped like other smiles which nonetheless differs from them) requires a simile to make sense of its capacity to hurt, the exceptional smile of the second stanza adheres to something like hurt, but only within a similetic register.

To clarify: while the first stanza's smile "hurt[s] you," and requires a series of similes to describe the way it hurts, the second stanza's smile is exceptional because it doesn't break sudden; and it's not that its not breaking is necessarily hurtful, but that this resistance to breaking is patient "like a pain." Whereas pain occurs in the first stanza on the level of the empirical (the experience of a hurting smile), pain occurs in the second stanza on the level of the figurative. The terms of the second stanza resemble the terms of the first, but exist on a different poetic register. For instance, "a happy lip . . . doesn't state you how / It contemplated — smiling." It doesn't explain itself, it just is. This implies that "this smile" (the patient one) does state how it contemplates; and while contemplation resonates, if only nominally, with the bird's recollection, the bird's contemplative energies do not attach to smiling (in the bird's case, singing), but rather to something else altogether: a ball. As contemplation putatively undermines a happy lip's sudden breaking, recollection, within the first stanza, underwrites it. The smile that hurts, which within the first stanza counts as exceptional, seems aligned in the second stanza with a lip that is unexceptionally happy. The closest Dickinson comes to describing what makes the smile hurtful — it is like music breaking — is counterintuitively in keeping with what makes a lip happy — it breaks sudden.

Despite appearances to the contrary, the second stanza does not extend the first stanza's investigation so much as reattempt that investigation from scratch, salvaging some of the first stanza's vocabulary for the sake of a different inquiral tack. This second time around, it's not that some smiles hurt while others do not. Nor that some are like song and others like music. Nor even that some smiles are happy and others are not. Nor that some smiles seem happy only when in fact steeped in pain: this, despite that the poem's mobilization of hurt makes this latter hypothesis at least nominally available — the unhappy smile as exceptional smile leads the poem's lineup of hermeneutic McGuffins. Rather, this second stanza discerns variation within smiles as a matter of duration:

> But this one, wears it's merriment
> So patient — like a pain —
> Fresh gilded — to elude the eyes
> Unqualified, to scan —

It bears repeating that differences in duration ("breaks sudden" vs. "so patient") do not sponsor affective differences, per se. That a "happy lip — breaks sudden" does not dictate that the patient, nonbreaking smile is not happy: it still "wears its merriment." A patient smile's affective suspiciousness — its presumed signification of a smile less happy than the swiftly breaking one — recalls "Delight's Despair at setting," and that poem's double bind (or perhaps single bind) of Delight's preemptively hypostasized velocity. While the patient smile might in fact be happy, that it might not be happy likewise doesn't automatically convert nonhappiness into sadness, or any other contrary affective state. In fact, among the poem's punctilious distinctions, "a happy lip" isn't juxtaposed with an unhappy one, but with one that "wears its merriment." Dickinson's analysis relies less on a comparison of affects or emotions (happiness versus unhappiness, or even happiness versus merriment), than on a comparison of grammatical registers (adjective versus noun). "Happy" adjectivally modifies lip, as though the lip might otherwise be modified — might acquire other adjectival characterizations as quickly as the lip itself breaks. "This one," however, is not merry, per se, but "wears its merriment." Wears its merriment, one might wonder, in the personified manner of wearing clothing? Or less figuratively, as a description of the lip's countenance? More important than whether the lip is personified or not personified is that the nominal status of "merriment" establishes it as a subject in its own right, a subject as much in need of analysis as the nominal smile.

A reader still wary of the patient smile's merriment might point to merriment's being worn as evidence of its affective duplicity. Following Judith Butler and other theorists of performativity, such a reader might argue that to wear merriment is to countenance an undermining of that merriment. This is the case, for instance, with a drag queen and her sundry outfits. Or of the person who slips from overalls to tea-dress to business suit to wedding dress and back again. Such notions of wearability, however, hardly speak to the case of Dickinson, who apocryphally wore white and only white. Whereas theorizations of drag have enabled queer theory to imagine the easy-on/easy-off of gender, Dickinson's white dress (contra Butler's or Marjorie Garber's paradigmatic wedding-gowns) oppositely consolidates personhood, or in the language of Butler herself, the sartorial instances not an intervention in conceptions of personate coherence, but a further congealment of it. I offer these sartorial speculations as ancillary to my argument that "wear," like "setting," can and should indicate durability as much as fictiveness. And that even as queer theory has privileged a logic of "wearing" as short-hand for other forms of mobility, "wearing" as readily denotes the wearing of being worn down, or worn out. Outing "wear," these lines mark the uncanniness of durability that exceeds an easier uncanniness that understands wearability as synonymous with the inauthentic. Merriment's wearability (in the sense of being worn down) requires that merriment last (for instance, as a noun rather than an adjective). And this merriment lasts through the working of a simile that returns us to the lyric shadowland of pain.

So patient — like a pain, Patience is what renders the smile anomalous, by granting it (less an afterlife than) a life that exceeds the sudden break by which smiles ordinarily are known. That merriment could be patient like a pain again recalls that Delight could feel despair. In the former, however, the personification of merriment (its move from an emotion worn by a lip to an emotion capable of demonstrating patience) depends on an earlier personification of pain. If pain's temporal properties are legislated by pain itself (and as earlier suggested, only retroactively made to appear the effects of time, itself), might pain's own personificatory patience be a ruse? If pain organizes time's own unfurling, then how else could one evaluate pain's ostensible endurance of waiting? Such queries do not entirely clarify the interpretive exasperations at hand: is merriment trustable or not trustable? Is patience trustable or not trustable? Rather, I am moved by the idea that pain, in demonstrating patience, endures itself. It's not that the person in pain endures suffering as a virtue, but that pain experiences its own pain (as a sort of virtue).

The poem thus returns us to a merriment that might endure itself, wear itself as much as worn. Merriment's being worn patient as a pain nonetheless does not indicate that merriment is painful (i.e., that merriment's pain is analogous to smile's hurt). In being patient in the same manner that pain (personificatorily) is patient, the poem claims that merriment and pain are temporally alike, without likeness jeopardizing either term's own affective integrity. Recall from my introduction Butler's confusion of analogousness and equivalence, a propos Freud's account of melancholy. "[W]hen it happens that a person has to give up a sexual object," Freud writes, "there quite often ensues an alteration of his ego which can only be described as a setting up of the object inside the ego, as it occurs in melancholia."[33] Whereas Butler took for granted that a process structurally analogous to that of melancholic incorporation ("as it occurs in melancholia") is itself equivalent to melancholia,[34] the process described seems most readily not melancholic; analogy, in both Freud and Dickinson, marks a structural similarity but not an affective one.

Patience purveys to the smile a longevity—and consequently, a representability—even as the poem, as though in protest, represents such a smile as inscrutable: first, by translating the visual into the auditory, and then, by designating the smile as "elud[ing] the eyes" which would otherwise scan it. The poem's last lines, however, bend into themselves, such that the smile might also be read as itself scanning an unspecifiable object. That is, the smile might elude the eyes from scanning, or might elude the eyes, so as to scan (personificatorily) without check. To scan unqualified is to scan without parameter. The intensely representable but aporetically invisible smile amounts to a sort of transparent eyeball, all-seeing and unseen. The poem posits patience as an alternative to ecstasy ("breaks sudden"), even as unable quite to articulate this patience's laws.

Patience usually evokes a passivity in the willingness of its sufferer to wait, to inhabit time as noninstrumentalizable medium. This passivity, a form of activity in its own right, reformulates relation as existing before the fruition of its possible objects. In Dickinson's terms, a patient smile doesn't signal "consummation" because it is capable of preceding the conditions of happiness out of which correlatively nonpatient smiles arise. A patient smile's merry scanning resembles the availability of a flaneur, for whom unattachment to any one particular interest makes everything potentially interesting. Does the patient smile borrow its happiness from the future or produce itself out of recollection? Does the patient smile exhibit a happiness without any immediate object other than the possibility of a future object that could retroactively justify it?

While Dickinson's storied solitudes potentially reduce the scene of writing — and in turn, of reading — to silent enterprises, this poem choreographs its reception on the anatomical order of a reader's mouth. (This choreography differs from the deeply aural experience of Dickinson's poems, most perceptible in their employment of hymn meter. This aurality, however, likewise significantly complicates any understanding of how we *read* a Dickinson poem in terms of how it is *heard.*) Enunciate (with only a bit of exaggeration) the final line's operative terms — patient, pain, unqualified, scan — and note one's own dimples running along, stretching one's lips into the sorts of smiles the poem describes. The poem, in this way, converts its readers into copies of itself. If this simileticallv ambivalent smile eludes the eyes, it nonetheless captivates whatever mouths attempt to speak its conditions. What is more "fresh gilded," after all, than a smile produced in the moments of its textual articulation? The alliterative simile, "patient like a pain," effects in its recursive *labial tenuis* a smile voided of internal qualities, whose patience perhaps accrues less to any emotional circumstance before or beyond it than to the textual event of the poem, itself.

Fruitlesser to Fling

A later poem, "Patience — has a quiet Outer — " takes patience itself out of temporal circulation. Even as patience, as mode of duration, derives its meaning from a temporal moment beyond it, Dickinson rotates this horizontal-temporal axis into a vertical-spatial one, in which patience, as a stillness, derives its meaning from the motion within it:

Patience — has a quiet Outer —
Patience — Look within —
Is an insect's futile forces
Infinites — between —

'Scaping One — against the Other
Fruitlesser to fling —
Patience — is the Smile's exertion
Through the quivering — (F842)

More relevant to "Her smile was shaped like other smiles" would be the possibility of smile as patience's exertion. Such a scenario simplifies Dickinson's patience in making it suspect — smile as patience's exertion suggests the labor of maintaining appearances of patience despite deeper impatience; the labor of producing a semblance of happiness despite quivering of sadness, frustration, etc. Along these lines, patience is never as patient as it seems, insofar as durability across time is riddled and qualified by the interior riddle of any given moment. This scenario informs Dickinson's without being identical to it. Patience does not exert a smile, but rather the smile exerts patience. As in the previous poem, the patient smile does not follow an event, but precedes it.

Within the scene of the poem itself, the patient smile is preceded by a figurative violence that troubles not only the phenomenon of a smile's patience, but the phenomenology of patience as action (or inaction). Recalling Dickinson's later poem, "Split the lark and you'll find the music," "Patience — has a quiet Outer" locates patience itself as a patient in Dickinson's surgical theater. In "Split the lark," the lark's splitting reveals the origins of song that the lark has sung ("the Music — / Bulb after Bulb, in / Silver rolled — "), and in turn, the queasy oscillation of the lark between bloodless lyric archetype and nonlyric bird for whom such explicatings potentially are fatal ("Gush after Gush, / reserved for you — / Scarlet Experiment!").[35] Unlike the lark, for whom vitality determines the poem's macabre blood-letting, the dissected interior of patience macabrely equivocates its relation to life and death. Do the insect's "futile forces" metaphorically convey teeming that is intrinsic to patience, teeming concealed by patience's "quiet outer"? Or are these insectual forces akin to flies or maggots on carrion (itself a possible pun on patience's carrying on), in turn establishing Patience's "outer" not as discontinuous with its insides, but the cadaverous extension of it?

Already attracting an insect's industry, is patience quiet because already dead, and if so, what to make of the smile whose patience is either teemingly vital or teemingly posthumous? To arrive at an answer requires a keener sense of the first stanza's "is" ("Is an insect's futile forces") than the poem allows. Metaphorical or nonmetaphorical? The overdetermination of this copula in turn problematizes the copula that organizes the smile's exertion ("Patience — is the Smile's exertion"). " 'Scaping One — against the Other" in this context describes not only the anatomical frisson of insect wings or of bodily surface and innards (a scaping that homonymically also is a scraping), but the friction of affects as they traverse figurative boundaries. The particularities of this traversal are the subject of this chapter's final section.

Dickinson treats the smile as though it were a subject of inquiry in its own right. A smile excised from face, and in turn excised from body or locale, can provide its own context (or, more acutely, not need one). "Her smile was shaped like other smiles" takes the smile out of circulation (which is to say, repeating the fantasy of the poem, out of time), so as to figure something like its constitutive properties. The poem treats the smile as though such analysis were possible, without executing the analysis. The poem wants to take the smile as a subject, without quite knowing how, as a subject, it would function. This subjectivating impulse motivates the poem's extravagant first simile, in which the smile hurts "as some Bird / Did hoist herself, to sing." The smile (not the smiler) asks to be taken as analogous to a discrete life form (a bird), but as the simile unravels, the latter form becomes less identifiable as form than as the complication of its surroundings. Subject removed from context ends up analogous to a sort of absolute contextuality.

"I Got So I Could Take His Name": Mechanics of Metaphor

Patient — like a pain. Merriment exhibits the temporal attributes of pain through a process left unspecified beyond the figurative work of personification. Personification, that is, allows an emotion to feel what a person might properly feel, but does not explain how this personificatory capacity for feeling comes about. Does merriment acquire (or to use a term from an earlier Dickinson poem, "procure") patience through an act of mimesis, and if so, what are the qualities of this mimetic transaction? Does merriment learn from pain? Does merriment actively enter patience's catechism in some other manner, or is merriment's patience essentially (though no less personificatorily) genetic?

This omission of personification's mechanics is all the more frustrating (hence captivating) held alongside the first stanza of "Her smile was shaped like other smiles," whose correlation between "her smile" and "other smiles" occasions both structural account of analogousness ("[t]he Dimples ran along — ") and figurative account; even as the latter ("as some Bird") confuses the terms of analogousness as much as it resolves them. Merriment, by contrast, simply is patient like a pain, without subsequent structural or figurative elaboration as to how this similitude has arisen.

In this final section of the chapter I further consider this hydraulic between Dickinsonian emotions: how one emotion might learn from another; what it would mean for emotions to be legible to other emotions; how such a pedagogy of feeling might further our understanding of one emotional assemblage's relation to another. "Her smile was shaped like other smiles" begins and ends with emotional similitude, the mechanics of which remain less legible than similitude itself.[36] By contrast, a more familiar Dickinson poem, "I got so I could take his name," oppositely takes as subject the mechanics of affective mimesis, but leaves obscure the dividends of the poem's recounted methodology.

The attentions of this section move away from earlier sections' analyses of Dickinson's complex figurative articulations of feeling. Earlier poems — "No Man can compass a Despair," "Delight's Despair at Setting," "A nearness to Tremendousness," "Her smile was shaped like other smiles" — explored the qualities of feeling through simile, metaphor, and personification. And as often, implied a kinship between the exhaustive confusions that attend Dickinson's analysis of feeling, and the confusions attendant the figurations by which these analyses are conducted. This section, by contrast, attempts to theorize, through the mechanics of "I got so I could take his name," how such figurations might in fact work. Attempts, that is, to imagine the work enumerated in "I got so I could take his name" as a material correlative to the figurative transformations (and deformations) already discussed.

Obliquity, in "I got so I could take his name," accrues most extravagantly to what Dickinson denominates (albeit not without qualification) "Grace," which the poem juxtaposes with "Misery." While this juxtaposition parallels juxtapositions that we have already explored — contentment/affliction, delight/despair, joy/grief, merriment/pain — Grace might or might not extend to other fields of positive feeling. I nonetheless take the grace of "I got so I could take his name" as no less powerful a term in Dickinson's pedagogy of feeling, in what I've proposed as Dickinson's own queer-optimistic vocabulary. Dickinsonian grace, in this poem, asserts the possibility of nontheological grace, extricable from an omniscient God that renders a person's own thinking beside the point. Extricable, for instance, from the sentiment offered by Leibniz in the *New Essays on Human Understanding*:

> still, we ought to judge that in those who have the true religion without having proofs of it, inward grace will be making up for the absence of rational grounds of belief. And charity leads us to judge further . . . that when people of good will are brought up amongst the deep shadows of the most dangerous errors, God will do for them everything that his goodness and justice require, even though we *may not know how*.[37]

Accommodating rather than exceeding the particularities of human thought, Dickinson's grace departs from Leibnizian grace — "upon which creatures have no claim"[38] — as queer optimism departs from Leibnizian (or more accurately, utopic) optimism.

Jane Eberwein writes that "[Dickinson's] poems posit a direct connection between grace and suffering,"[39] and notes Robert Gillespie's earlier claim that "the most successful poems on the attainment of grace are poems in which its dubious blessing, like an infection, causes [Dickinson] to suffer and without the suffering it would not be grace."[40] While no less dubiously framed, however, the grace of "I got so I could take his name" does not cause suffering; furthermore, while it might be true that without the poem's suffering there would be no grace, such is not the case on account of the Calvinist logic that governs Eberwein's and Gillespie's analyses. Rather, the idiosyncratic grace of "I got so I could take his name" learns its métier from suffering. Specifically, the poem characterizes misery in terms of near-ceaseless repetition that grace in turn might mimetically model. Repetition, in this poem, affords a more particular account of the mechanics by which pain, as Dickinson elsewhere articulates, "expands the time." If "Her smile was shaped like other smiles" posits a merriment informed by patience no less than a pain informed by patience, "I got so I could take his name" implicitly argues that such an analogous patience — a capacity for lasting (for setting, for staying . . .) — might itself be achieved through a mimetically derived practice of reiteration:

> I got so I could take his name —
> Without — Tremendous gain —
> That Stop-sensation — on my Soul —
> And Thunder — in the Room —
>
> I got so I could walk across
> That Angle in the floor,
> Where he turned so, and I turned — how —
> And all our Sinew tore —
>
> I got so I could stir the Box —
> In which his letters grew
> Without that forcing, in my breath —
> As Staples — driven through —
>
> Could dimly recollect a Grace —
> I think, they called it "God" —
> Renowned to ease Extremity —
> When Formula, had failed —
>
> And shape my Hands —
> Petition's way,
> Tho' ignorant of a word
> That Ordination — utters —
>
> My Business — with the Cloud,
> If any Power behind it, be,
> Not subject to Despair —
> It care — in some remoter way,
> For so minute affair
> As Misery —
> Itself, too vast, for interrupting — more — (F292)

Eberwein's essay, for all its thoroughness, fails to address the grace of this poem. And in the work of R. P. Blackmur and Sharon Cameron, two of Dickinson's most sensitive readers, the grace of "I got so I could take his name" isn't under-read, so much as the site of reading's (Dickinson's and their own) exhaustion.

Sharon Cameron situates "I got so I could take his name" at the beginning of her analysis of Dickinson's experiment in what Cameron calls the dialectic of rage. The poem, for Cameron, is instructive not because it instances this dialectic, but because it demonstrates what happens to a poem in that dialectic's absence; specifically, what happens to a poem in rage's failure. Rage, following Cameron's reading, emerges as "a way of preventing the convergence of sexuality and death,"[41] or differently put, averting the inexplicability of desire and disappointment. Rage interrupts inevitability by positing within the inevitable a discourse that is immune to a poem's operative dicta of narrative and circumstance. Rage, that is, becomes a way of describing that technique in Dickinson that overrides incontrovertibility of position.

The challenges of such a poetry — legible narratives that cede to unrecognizable scenarios; metaphors that fold too much into or out of themselves; metaphors that fail to distinguish one term from another; dashes that perforate utterance and convert the irresolute into its own decided avoidance of commitment on ontological, epistemological, or emotional grounds — establish enragement as a particular sort of literary event. Contrary to conceptions of rage as blind, and therefore removed from lucidity, Cameron (preceding similar if diluted observations by Noble) makes a case for rage as the very grounds for understanding. Rather than absorption in a situation, rage becomes here a rising above "the laws that ritualize life" (85) and in that freedom from ritualization, becomes the occasion for new insight. New insight, of course, is what Dickinson is best at, which makes rage (what Cameron elsewhere terms "protest") seem all the more indispensable from an analysis of such radical and unfamiliar epistemological adventures.

That Cameron's articulation of Dickinsonian rage exceeds the faculties and effects that rage ordinarily is accorded becomes all the more apparent by chapter's end, in which rage nearly coincides with presence itself. "At a distance from experience," Cameron writes, "presence comes to know its own mind. It shakes off the imperatives of past and future, self and other, sexuality and death, by learning its responses to them and by learning, too, that action, however inexorable, cannot do away with response... [presence's] wisdom consists in what it comes to know of experience once it has been freed of the compulsion for consequence" (89). Presence, then, shakes off the imperatives of sexuality and death; this sort of shaking is identical, it seems, from the tasks allotted to rage at chapter's start. "Rage is a way of preventing the convergence of sexuality and death," rage "lodge[s] its protest" between the two other points. Cameron posits rage as alternative to the acquiescence to a double bind that many of Dickinson's poems could not otherwise weather. Rage/presence asserts the management and even sublimation of phenomenal experience of which lyric poetry seems nearly constitutive.

"I got so I could take his name" belongs near this category of poems, but (as Cameron rightly notes) not in it. The voice of this poem does not, in lyrical rage, transform poetic circumstance. As an extension of Cameron's reading, I mean to argue that the poem's voice does not merely trail away from itself. "Meaning breaks off," Cameron writes, "dissolves, goes under, at the moment when it is perceived as too painful" (60). "Agony—in fact all meaning—," Cameron continues,

> goes dead on the speaker when she summons distance from her experience and in so doing, relinquishes it. The poem, though not, I suspect, intentionally, is about what it is like to trivialize feeling because, as is, feeling has become unendurable. Better to make it nothing than to die from it.[42] (60)

Rather than break meaning off, the poem, I think, extricates meaning from pain; the poem's absence of rage signals the intolerability of certain modes of meaning and feeling, but does not preclude meaning or feeling as such. In foregoing the particular forms of meaning derivable from rage, the poem proposes an alternative that might resemble abdication, but isn't. The poem proposes a circumvention of sexuality and death (desire and disappointment) that entails neither rage nor escape. The poem offers a poetics of transformation predicated on a peculiarly defined and enacted grace.

The first three stanzas describe the ends of labor that has occurred before the time of the poem proper. The dividends, even as constitutive of this poem, are by a certain logic nonlyrical; that is, these first three stanzas recount the relief of actions executed without resonance, the accretion of nonreverberative experience:

I got so I could take his name—
Without—Tremendous gain—
That Stop-sensation—on my Soul—
And Thunder—in the Room—

I got so I could walk across
That Angle in the floor,
Where he turned so, and I turned—how—
And all our Sinew tore—

I got so I could stir the Box—
In which his letters grew
Without that forcing, in my breath—
As Staples, driven through—

The anaphora with which each stanza opens signals a mastery both of and over iteration. The speaker has gotten to the point where inhabiting the sites of previous crisis no longer conjures crisis. Reiteration, along these lines, has become merely formal. The undisclosed name can be taken without anything tremendous happening, which is to say, literally, without tremor. "Tak[ing] his name" loses the incantatory resonance of taking, say, either the lord's name in vain, or another's person in marriage; instead, and as an extension of the anaphoric "I got," taking seems less oath-like than merely acquisitive, or rather reacquisitive, in reclaiming the name from its former forces—"That Stop-sensation—on my Soul—/ And Thunder—in the Room—." Such is the logic of the two stanzas that follow. The superstitious-seeming particularity of a floor's angle can be retraced, the letters saved in a box can be stirred, without these revisitations animating the travail to which they'd been attached.

Energies of attachment move simultaneously along opposite axes, insofar as attachment/detachment describes both the practice of the poem (recapitulating scenes so as to stage detachment from them) and the interior events against which the poem pulls: "he turned so, and I turned—how—/ And all our Sinew tore—." The salutary faculty of formal distance supplants some earlier somatic distance's breaching. Similarly, the magic of earlier repetitions (e.g., if a name's recitation can't conjure a lover, it can at least conjure, as consolation, the thunder of amorous malady) cedes to a different sort of incantation. Countering an earlier condition's amorous tremor of "I lost, I lost, I lost," the repetition of

"I got... I got... I got" casts a spell whose magic lies precisely in its emptiness. Or rather, in the production of its speaker as this sequence of discrete victories over her own past lyrical energy.

These three initial stanzas are striking in their mobilization of repetition and detachment as solutions to or reprieves from alternate forms of repetition and detachment. The fourth stanza, in turn, is striking in its eschewal of the preceding anaphoric formula. If the first three stanzas formulate a certain relief in executing acts divorced from recollection of their antecedents, it is counterintuitively unsurprising that this fourth stanza imagines relief in terms of recollection; unsurprising, given the poem's evident interest in a certain methodological frugality by which self-help and duress are, if only mechanically, nearly indistinguishable:

Could dimly recollect a Grace—
I think, they called it "God"—
Renowned to ease Extremity—
When Formula, had failed—

And shape my Hands—
Petition's way,
Tho' ignorant of a word
That Ordination—utters—

It is at this point of the poem that Cameron claims that we as readers are "tantalized" by the possibility of the poem's "collapse of control" (59). In lieu of tantalization, "we get a distraction from it: an appeal to God that becomes a way of avoiding feeling, and the poem ends not with passion, as we might expect, but rather with passion defended against" (59). Defense against passion becomes, via this reading, coincident with the avoidance of feeling. The poem's incontrovertibility is not, however, one of situation (as described in Cameron's subsequent treatment of other poems), but of passion itself. That is, rage surfaces not as the poem's escape from itself, but more strongly as that from which the poem must escape.

The poem does indeed voice control as "control recollected," although control's having been won in the past does not entail its having in the present been lost. The fourth stanza doesn't appeal to God, but to grace. Nor is "appeal" exactly what the speaker makes: she "dimly recollects"; dim recollection has itself been the object of the poem's previous efforts — control has been exercised precisely to the extent that dim recollection has been impossible. In a pluperfect preceding the poem's initial past tense, recollection presumably feels nonmnemonic because phenomenologically indistinguishable from its antecedents — until she gets to the beginning of the poem, reliving the scene of denouement *feels like denouement.* Not only do these stanzas feel the sting of present absence; pain issues in the claustrophobia of a past forever encroaching the present's boundaries. Writing, as usually theorized, preserves loss as an archive or renders it as supplement evaluatively equal to the fiction of an original. Dickinson's opening stanzas cede this grammatology and lament it. The eternal return of crisis will not go away. Nor does pleasure exist in the governing of the recursive crisis. The task of the poem is not to animate language as substitute for something otherwise irrecoverable (it's recoverable, the poem says — that sort of poetry is easy and dreadful), nor to produce a crypt that the Abrahamian object might then haunt.[43] Rather, the task is to document the exhausting of its own nearly limitless resuscitative capacities. Grace delivers recollection-as-dim: following the poem's opening travails, it is as though grace could come on the scene in no other way. Grace, in this context, has less to do with transformational magic than a kind of antimelancholic exorcising.

The poem's dim recollection of grace furthermore can be read not as disingenuous (insofar as dim recollection describes precisely what the speaker, at poem's outset, is unable to author), but more generally descriptive of what Allen Tate recounts as Dickinson's peculiar, reliquary inheritance of New England puritanism. Of Dickinson, Tate writes that "she had all the elements of a culture that has broken up, a culture that on the religious side takes its place in the museum of spiritual antiquities. Puritanism, as a unified version of the world, is dead; only a remnant of it in trade may be said to survive."[44] Following Tate, the poem's grace mightn't signal merely an "appeal to God that becomes a way of avoiding feeling." To take Tate's observation seriously (an observation supplemented, if not supported, by Dickinson's own refusal to follow the suit of her childhood's Northampton revival) is to reckon grace as the site of "certain disintegrating obsessions,"[45] the meanings of which are no longer immediately at hand — no more for Dickinson, I think, than for her comparably secular constellation of contemporary readers and scholars.[46]

In his essay "Emily Dickinson: Notes on Prejudice and Fact," R. P. Blackmur (riffing off of Tate) conceives of Dickinson's puritanism as the only "machinery" available to support her poetry's observations.[47] Blackmur's machines sometimes seem to resonate with the pathos of Tate's "museum of spiritual antiquities" — that is, with the pathos of machines that no longer work; or that obsolesce in the undesirability of their product; or that have ceded use-value as such, to the play of contemplation and speculation catalyzed in their retiring. More to the point, however, Blackmur's machinery effects an extravagant supply of objects in flux between established and novel use:

> There is the advantage of the existing machinery of meaning in the specific culture, which is still able to carry any weight and which is universally understood; and there is the advantage of a new and personal plasticity in the meanings themselves. Faith, in the agonized hands of the individual, becomes an imaginative experiment of which all the elements are open to new and even blasphemous combinations, and which is subject to the addition of new insights. It is no longer enough to repeat prayers and to rehearse Mass or its protestant equivalent. The great advantage for a poet to come at a time of disintegrating culture is, then, to sum up, just this: the actuality of what we are and what we believe is suddenly seen to be nearly meaningless as habit, and must, to be adequately known, be transformed to the terms and modes of the imagination. Nothing can be taken for granted but the machinery, which is there, all available, and which indeed cannot help being taken for granted.[48]

Dickinson's grace exists between meaninglessness of habit and "imaginative experiment." Given Blackmur's interest in a poetics teased from defunct machinery, it is not surprising that his essay on Dickinson concludes with a reading of "I got so I could take his name." The poem recuperates grace not as a formula, but as that which emerges "When Formula, Had failed." This failure of formula, this shaping of hands (what Blackmur and Deleuze both might call a prayer-machine) occurs even as "ignorant of a word / That ordination — utters," which is to say that "it is no longer enough to repeat prayers and to rehearse Mass." Grace, in this context, adheres to form without prior commitment to form's meanings. Blackmur recalls this Dickinsonian distinction between the formal and the formulaic in "Language as Gesture," an essay written several years after his essay on Dickinson. In poetry, Blackmur writes, "what is wanted cannot be articulated in a formula, but on the other hand it cannot be articulated at all except when delivered within a form" (13). With an ear to my earlier discussion of Dickinson's soliciting of masochistic analysis, grace describes an experience of bondage without pain, of contractuality as carte blanche. For Cameron, Dickinson forestalls the collapse of death into sexuality through a poetics of rage. In "I got so I could take his name," rage is supplanted by grace, which likewise adjudicates between the poles of ecstasy/collapse and comportment/removal. Dickinson posits grace as the possibility of formalized (which isn't to say formulaic) emotion, as alternative to passional intensity and anhedonia.

As I said, it makes sense that Blackmur concludes his Dickinson essay with a reading of a poem that illuminates not only his particular account of Dickinson, but the more general discussion of poetry he would publish several years later. What is surprising is that Blackmur does not claim the poem as exemplary in any fashion beyond its "technical and moral confusion." Following his citation of the poem in full, Blackmur continues his (uncharacteristically blithe) critique:

> Nothing is more remarkable than the variety of inconsistency this effort displays. The first three stanzas are at one level of sensibility and of language and are as good verse as Emily Dickinson ever wrote. The next two stanzas are on a different and fatigued level of sensibility, are bad verse and flat language, and have only a serial connection with the first three. The last stanza, if it is a stanza, is on a still different level of sensibility and not on a recognizable level of language at all: the level of desperate inarticulateness to which no complete response can be articulated in return. One knows from the strength of the first three stanzas what might have been meant to come after and one feels like writing the poem oneself — the basest of all critical temptations. We feel that Emily Dickinson let herself go. The accidents that provided her ability here made a contrivance that was not a poem but a private mixture of first-rate verse, bad verse, and something that is not verse at all. Yet — and this is the point — this contrivance represents in epitome the whole of her work; and whatever judgment you bring upon the epitome you will, I think, be compelled to bring upon the whole. (49)

What Blackmur, *con brio,* suggests "is not verse at all" in fact seems a strange retelling of Dickinson's recycling of machines. Grace, like faith, has become an experiment "in the agonized hands of the individual." Blackmur's agony, however, points to a different sort of machine in Dickinson's poem, a machine that likewise (but in different ways) "cannot help being taken for granted." That is, the poem describes the breakdown of a pain-machine:

> My Business — with the Cloud,
> If any Power behind it, be,
> Not subject to Despair —
> It care — in some remoter way,
> For so minute affair
> As Misery —
> Itself, too vast, for interrupting — more —

Before the time of the poem, pain could reproduce itself indefinitely. The "minute affair" — of invoking a name, of walking across the floor's angle, of stirring the letter-box — becomes a factory-line when that minuteness can repeat itself beyond duration. Hence the mechanization even of the third stanza's "staples," as though mechanically iterated pain could hallucinate even breathing as extension of its industry. (It bears recalling that Dickinson's own relation to collation did not involve staples, but the comparably less efficient intimacy of needle and thread.) The victory of these first stanzas involves the monkey-wrenching of a pain that has turned grief into an automaton.

The cessation of this industry — with the perversely financial ring of loss, recalled in the second line's pecuniarily resonant "tremendous gain" — provides the terms by which the last stanza might conceive a different sort of "business." The pain-machine — what I have in other contexts described as the persuasions of queer pessimism — cedes to grace as nonreplicative moment. This is not to say that the poem harbors a categorical suspicion of replicativeness. The poem, on the contrary, seems fascinated with the mobilization of single events into serial narrative. This fascination culminates in the final stanza; if pain or misery can exceed their original moments, then why, the stanza opaquely wonders, can't grace? Grace, theologically, does exceed its original moment, but Dickinson's grace, as Tate and Blackmur note, is not straightforwardly theological. If anything, the poem's ambition is to replicate the interminability of theological grace, in the absence of that theology's faith. In trying to animate a secular grace, the poem turns not to God (maybe there's a power behind the cloud, and maybe there isn't), but rather to the magic of pain itself.

Along these lines, the penultimate line's "as" operates by way of analogy. Dickinson's new business ("not subject to despair") cares for "so minute affair / As Misery," but also (and much more provocatively), it cares for so minute an affair the way that misery cares. The poem takes misery as a heuristic structure, the way the patient smile of "Her smile was shaped like other Smiles" takes pain as a heuristic structure. Patient like a pain. It cares as Misery cares. In both formulations, reprieves from or alternatives to despair turn to despair for the secret of durability that despair might itself impart. "Not subject to despair," but learning from it, Dickinson's grace dreams of a vastness that could in turn make misery seem minute; misery, that is, that fills minutes rather than machinic interminability. And machinic interminability, in turn, might become the métier of a grace whose "more" juts—as some new ordination—from the poem's surface.

I have suggested that the poem's first three stanzas push iteration to the point where reenactment of earlier scenes of crisis no longer produces crisis. What I have described as the pure formalism of this venture likewise is describable in terms of the salubriousness of tautology. The reparative faculties of Dickinsonian iteration will provide one context in which to understand the restorative seriality of Jack Spicer's poetics. Before moving from Dickinson to Spicer, however, it behooves repeating that this reparative iteration differs from the iterability of queer theory's performative precisely in its therapeutic capacities. The formulaic, in the context of queer performativity, inevitably betrays its own underlying factitiousness, as though such discovery were an end unto itself. The tautological movements of "I got so I could take his name" on the other hand, do not empty gesture of its value, but restore value of a different sort.

In Paul de Man's terms, Dickinsonian iteration underwrites the aesthetic's inextricability from knowledge—in contrast to queer-theoretical epistemologies that identify iteration as epistemological object on which knowledge, from some extrinsic vantage, might speculate. Knowledge, for de Man, is precisely what secures the aesthetic's practical and political relevance. "What gives the aesthetic its power and hence its practical, political impact, is its intimate link with knowledge, the epistemological implications that are always in play when the aesthetic appears over the horizon of discourses."[49] And this link to knowledge depends for de Man — and in many instances, I think, for Dickinson — on the aesthetic's "reference to systems of formalization and notation rigorous enough to be patterned on the model of mathematical language."[50] This model of "mathematical language" pertains to the repeatable angle of "I got so I could take his name," but no less so, to the Dickinson poems earlier examined — the Cartesian graph on which is charted the smile's dimples, the compass that tries to measure feeling.

Mathematics obliquely affords an alternate way to understand the grace that the poem's speaker "dimly recollect[s]," and which "they" (correctly or incorrectly) denominate "God." In the realm of de Manian aesthetics, after all, it is grace — on a choreographic rather than theistic register — that rescues tautology from itself, that makes available within iteration the secular relief of singularity. Of Schiller's dancers and Kleist's marionettes, de Man writes that "the perpetually repeated figures — so highly formalized that they can be recorded in notation — admit of only as much individuality in their successive execution by the different dancers as can be expressed through the grace of bodily movement."[51] Grace, in this context, indicates the unyielding élan of personhood, impersonality's inevitable, sublimated residuum; rather than (as it would theistically) the abdication of personality for some higher principle. Grace becomes the way in which one might inhabit structures contrarily devised, the proof of aesthetic power at the moment at which the iterability constitutive of that power is most vulnerable (insofar as verging, in singularity, on a nonmathematical interruption of repetitiveness as such).

Queer optimism, then, operates not only as a meta-optimism, but as an aesthetics of optimism. This particular sense of the aesthetic will inform the next chapter's account of what I call aesthetic persons. More specifically, the category of aesthetic personhood (or synonymously, for my purposes, lyric personhood) posits an alternative to queer-theoretical incoherence. Rather than having to choose between being an incoherent (psychoanalytic) subject or a coherent one, aesthetics allows one to differently reckon the choices one could or could not make. "[W]e shall find grace at its purest," Kleist writes, "in a body which is entirely devoid of consciousness or which possesses it in an infinite degree; that is, in the marionette or in the god."[52] What is understood, de Man continues, "is that the increased formalization of consciousness, as in a machine [for instance, what I have called the machinic interminability of "I got so I could take his name"], far from destroying aesthetic effect, enhances it; consciousness's loss is aesthetic's gain."[53] If we are willing to wager aesthetics as consolation for the loss of consciousness, it indubitably is in our own interests to understand, as inventively as possible, what we gain in such a turn to aesthetics. All the more so, in this turn to an aesthetic optimism, which necessarily derives its persuasiveness through forms of knowledge maintained both through and in spite of a queer grace that is knowledge's simultaneous margin and center of gravity.

Chapter Three

JACK SPICER'S *BILLY THE KID*

Beyond the Singular Personal

> *Fate set a stage. Out of nowhere into the drama stepped this unknown boy. Opposite him played Death. It was a drama of Death and the Boy. Death dogged his trail relentlessly. . . . It lay in ambush for him. . . . By bullets, conflagration, stratagems, every lethal trick, it sought to compass his destruction. But the boy was not to be trapped. He escaped by apparent miracles; he was saved as if by necromancy. He laughed at Death. Death was a joke. He waved Death a jaunty good-bye and was off to new adventures.*
>
> —Burns, *The Saga of Billy the Kid* (53–54)

Death and the Boy

My preceding chapters on Crane and Dickinson imported a vocabulary of seriality to describe forms of iterability — of smiles, of affect variably attached and detached from action — attendant to those poets' own queer-optimistic explorations. This chapter elaborates the theoretical and poetic implications of Cranian and Dickinsonian seriality through the poetry of Jack Spicer, who (along with George Oppen) often is credited with first imagining a poetics in explicitly serial terms. Even as Spicer's understanding of seriality cannot entirely describe corresponding phenomena in Crane's and Dickinson's poetry, Spicer's comparably more developed account of the serial nevertheless invites consideration of what such accounts particular to Crane and Dickinson would entail and encourages future readers of Crane and Dickinson to think about the repetitions that inform their poetry with something like Spicer's seriality in mind. As argued in my examination of Crane's *White Buildings* as response to T. S. Eliot's *Prufrock and Other Poems*, seriality introduces a mode of iterability substantively distinct from repetition as such, a mode that is productively removed from the psychoanalytically derived narratives of trauma and loss on which so many accounts of repetition lean. Seriality's additive, accretive effects depart from the negative stall — one step forward two steps back — attributable to many accounts of repetition. Seriality likewise differs from performativity, whose iterations and accretions (at least in theory) so often repeat themselves for the sake of exposing their own seams and cracks. Seriality's singular additiveness reflects just one way in which a theory of seriality informs *Queer Optimism's* enterprise.

My analysis of Spicer most clearly veers from my analyses of Crane and Dickinson in that it concerns not the field of positive feelings, but the no less beleaguered field (within queer theory) of positive persons. Positive persons is a coinage in which I am invested only as shorthand, demarcating an interest in coherent, noncorrosive, nonperformative persons — against queer theory's own demotion of such possible categories in favor of persons conceived as performative, shattered, shattering, shameful, traumatized, traumatizing, or death-driven. As with my insistence on a queer optimism stranger than and in excess of conventional optimisms, my understanding of positive personhood (or more succinctly, personhood) does not seek to reinstate the sorts of persons that queer theory, deconstruction, or psychoanalysis has aimed and aims to dismantle. In speaking of persons, I am not speaking of subjects, nor subjectivity, nor ontology. The sort of personhood at stake in my analysis of Jack Spicer more specifically involves an aesthetic person — conceivable within the space of Spicer's 1958 serial poem, *Billy The Kid,* and not manifestly extendible, as such, to a predestined phenomenological, material, or political order. Rather, the aesthetic particularities of Spicer's text must be investigated scrupulously, before ceding to applicabilities beyond themselves.

My interest in recuperating persons — in the loving, nonideological recuperability of aesthetic persons — is itself a response to and echo of Spicer's own interest in the loving recuperability of persons. In this sense, to speak of recuperation is (if only obliquely) to speak of positive feeling — Spicer's toward his subject, Billy the Kid. The dialectical space, in *Billy The Kid,* between Billy and Spicer is a personal one, although more specifically, an aesthetically personal one. On one level, Spicer's poem is an elegy for Billy the Kid: the poem opens with an announcement of Billy's death:

> The radio that told me about the death of Billy The Kid
> (And the day, a hot summer day, with birds in the sky)
> Let us fake out a frontier—a poem somebody could hide in....

The poem's penultimate lines diapasonically insist, in the face of this death, "Billy The Kid / I love you." Again, on one level, such a frame suggests elegy, but the poem's innovative and extravagant pulsions beyond the elegiac both produce (and in turn require) a vocabulary for understanding persons loved and lost that exceeds a vocabulary of elegy. Far exceeds, that is, a vocabulary of melancholy that might initially seem pertinent to the elegiac mode.

Judith Butler, in one of her many considerations of melancholy, writes that

> If the object can no longer exist in the external world, it will then exist internally, and that internalization will be a way to disavow the loss...to stay or postpone the recognition and suffering of loss.[1]

Spicer's Billy crosses the death sentence ("that told me about the death of Billy The Kid") with which the poem opens into a fractured picaresque that the death sentence forecloses. This traversal might in fact seem borne of melancholic suspension, were it not so indifferent to the fact of loss. This indifference — on the part of Billy and of the poem — surely requires subsequent theorization, albeit even this possibility of indifference is at odds with Butler's observations. "If this...then this" posits nearly any response to "no longer exist[ing] in the external world" as "disavow[al]," such that indifference—taken nonsuspiciously as the radical loosening of loss as lynch-pin—could only unfold as disavowal unaware of its own ulterior motivations.

Spicer's poem, no less than the mechanically reproduced aura of Billy,[2] evidences the conceptual limitations of externalization and internalization, on which this hydraulic of loss/melancholy depends. Does a poem (as surfacial as a painting) exist simultaneously as externalization and internalization? To consider a poem as internalization gone external itself conjures an eerie moebius void, as when pulling a knot tighter sometimes results in the knot's undoing. Even as the structure of melancholy — dependent, for Butler as for Freud, on the diacritical fidelity of inside and outside — strains against the arguably generic conditions of poetry,[3] melancholy's essential coefficients — love and loss — are nonetheless essential to *Billy The Kid*. They are essential, even as the mathematics informing Spicer's poetics departs from melancholy's demonstratively clipped "if this . . . then this." One might say that Spicer's poem eludes melancholy as dexterously as Billy eludes death.

If Spicer's poem is itself on the run from melancholy, this is due not only to the captivation of shared terms (love and loss), but to the fact that Spicer's relation to Billy so alluringly recapitulates one of queer theory's most recurrent melancholic scripts: a gay man in love with and mourning a heterosexual paradigm, the (heterosexual) man he himself will never be. After all, unlike Milton's mourning of Lycidas and Shelley's mourning of Keats, Spicer is mourning a cowboy, infamous for killing twenty-one people in as many years.

Is Spicer's love for Billy, then, an aggression against himself? Might we find in Spicer's cowboy love the kernel of some internalized homophobia? Such questions — raised both in Butler's accounts of melancholy and Bersani's accounts of masculinity, in "Is the Rectum a Grave?"[4] — might be generative within properly psychoanalytic or political registers, but are too broad to speak to the fact that Billy's own status as person (not to mention cowboy, straight man, etc.) is so exorbitantly equivocal. Which Billy does Spicer, in his poem, have in mind? A historical Billy, visually available from a series of nineteenth-century daguerreotypes? Billy as killer and/or killed? How to conceive of internalization of an "object" whose external existence, properly speaking, precedes Spicer's by nearly a century? Or are there other forms of external existence? What would it mean to love and lose (or in the order of Spicer's serial poem, lose and love) a person always already saturated with and riddled by his own dubiousness? Butler, again, broaches such a problematic, though in terms inadequate to Spicer's poem:

> is it regarded as a "true" love, a "true" loss, a love and loss worthy and capable of being grieved, and thus worthy and capable of having been lived? Or is it a love and a loss haunted by the specter of a certain unreality, a certain unthinkability, the double-disavowal of the "I never loved her, and I never lost her," uttered by a woman, the "I never loved him, I never lost him," uttered by a man? Is this the "never-never" that supports the naturalized surface of heterosexual

> life as well as its pervasive melancholia? Is it the disavowal of loss by which sexual formation, including gay sexual formation, proceeds?[5]

For Butler, the value of both love and loss depends on ontic validation extrinsic to them. Equally so, the value of loss depends on the antecedent value of love; even as the veracious intensity of grieving likewise retroactively could render love itself more persuasive. Successful mourning, along these lines, depends not only on a correlative ontic appraisal of the loss at hand, but on an anterior privileging of truth's adjudicative faculty. Mourning chokes and stutters into melancholic bloom if veracity comes up short. But what if the persuasiveness of veracity itself came up short? As we saw in Dickinson, what seems truthful as often is an effect of something else. Following Dickinson, we might conjecture not only that loss retroactively shores up the eloquence of dolorous love, but that loss, behind the scenes (internal? external?), shapes the gauge of truth by which it disingenously asks to be measured.

Spicer's *Billy The Kid* arguably does present a love haunted by a "certain unreality," but this love is not melancholic in part because this unreality is not the verso of the "true"; Billy's unreality, freed from the binary of "is it this . . . or is it this" (the melancholia of "if this, then this"), is the poem's starting point. This chapter, in fact, suggests that there never is or was a Billy separable from "unreality." Spicer's poem might at a distance resemble Butler's never-never, but the ranginess of Billy leaves never-never in the dust. So succinct an equation presumes with stunningly little leeway that we understand what never means, or that one's choice is as stark as truth or nontruth.

Several years after my beginning of this chapter, Leo Bersani published an essay titled "Psychoanalysis and the Aesthetic Subject." Bersani's account of an aesthetic subject, grounded in a reading of Pierre Michon's novel *La Grande Beune,* advances the possibility (against opposing, psychoanalytically prevailing tendencies) that "interiority in *La Grande Beune,* far from refashioning the world into the structure of a psychic obsession, is actually produced by the world."[6] In querying the direction of creative transactions between subject and world, Bersani's essay potentially redresses his own earlier assertions of erotic aggression.[7] More than its capacity to redress his own earlier formative claims, however, the propositions of "Psychoanalysis and the Aesthetic Subject" (in a register

I would like to think not dissimilar from my own) keenly problematize melancholy's underlying structure. "We are neither present in the world nor absent from it,"[8] Bersani's essay begins. If we are neither present nor absent, how adequately to distinguish melancholic loss, structurally (not to mention affectively), from living itself? Neither present nor absent in the world reiterates my own reservation with melancholy's preemptive discrimination between external and internal.

Bersani's account of the aesthetic, furthermore, raises the possibility that where melancholy might otherwise dominate scenes of loss, the imagination as such might flourish. The realm of the imaginary might be melancholic, but melancholy's particular emotional energies, within the parameters of Bersani's essay, remain subordinate to the faculties of the imaginary; Bersani posits the imaginary as a topos of which melancholy's repertoire constitutes just one locality. "[T]o remember events," Bersani writes, "is to recognize ourselves in their imaginary presence. From this perspective, the past is what has passed from the phenomenological to the virtuality of the imaginary."[9] My account of aesthetic persons most differs from Bersani's account of aesthetic subjects in that my analysis of Spicer's *Billy The Kid* attends to the pervious boundaries between Spicer and his text, whereas Bersani's account of *La Grande Beune* locates such perviousness but only within the sequestered space of Michon's novel. Bersani's analysis, then, is attuned to the transactions between persons and worlds calibrated to the same order, whereas my analysis broaches the perviousness of persons — both Spicer and Billy the Kid, the subject of Spicer's poem — in relation to worlds equally various (the biosphere of Spicer's poem, and as we shall see, the world of Billy's own archive).

Billy The Kid, a serial poem in ten parts, serially reproduces some form of Billy, although more specifically serially contemplates what it means or entails to attempt such reproducibility.[10] The Billy of each of Spicer's ten sections is related to that of the others, but neither chronologically nor genetically. Billy appears (or nearly appears) as though following a logic extrinsic to poem or poet, and in this manner recalls the ubiquitous but exegetically confounding smiles of Crane's *White Buildings.* Before turning to the vagaries of Spicer's Billy, however, it behooves us to address the vagaries preceding Spicer's Billy, vagaries constitutive of Billy the Kid, himself — "self" taken as openly as possible.

Even on a nominal level, Billy the Kid was just one name among many. As Walter Burns writes (in a biography published a year before Crane's *White Buildings*):

> [T]hroughout his life of lurid adventure, Billy the Kid's name was lost in his pseudonym. His name really doesn't matter much; by any other, he would have shot as straight; but it happened to be William H. Bonney, and he was born in New York City, November 23, 1859. William H. and Kathleen Bonney, his parents, both of unknown antecedents, emigrated in 1862 to Coffeyville, Kansas, taking with them three-year-old Billy and a baby brother named Edward.[11]

A rose by any other name might smell as sweet, a boy by any other name might shoot as straight, but Billy's name (or rather, the pseudonym in which he "was lost") really does matter, to the extent that all stories of this person accrue to the name. The name — or rather, the pseudonym — becomes synecdochical for a vast archive of narratively rich and theoretically complicated material.

As this chapter's epigraph by Burns indicates, Billy was as notorious for eluding death as he was for bringing it to others. Billy's slippery (or "jaunty") relation to death reaches beyond nineteenth-century apocrypha or sheriff reports. Billy returns as Billy (and something far more vexing and magnificent than Billy) in countless early-twentieth-century radio-plays and films. Spicer himself noted Arthur Penn's 1958 release, *Left-Handed Gun* as one of his favorite films.[12] Written by Gore Vidal, Penn's film starred Paul Newman as the Kid, albeit only due to chance: James Dean had already been cast as the Kid, and would have been the film's star were it not for Dean's September 1955 death. This filmic Billy (adumbrated or back-lit by James Dean's ghost) is only one of myriad iterations of Billy. Penn's film, along with dozens that precede it, treats Billy's dodging of death as exemplary exploit, inseparable from but also transcending Billy's more cowboyish exploits of killing, gambling, stealing. Billy's own seriality — his infamously industrious auto-iterability — becomes the alluring and felicitous heart of a burgeoning serial film industry. Billy's apocryphal nonmelancholic relation to his own death anticipates the logic of the films' serializations of his death-defying adventures. I shall return to this observation again, specifically as this serial logic informs Spicer's understanding of Penn's film, and more broadly, his poetic returns to a Billy as elusively allusive as elusive.

In 1938, in *Billy the Kid Returns,* Roy Rogers plays not Billy, but a Billy the Kid look-a-like. As though Billy's replicability were as irresistible a conceit as that of Euripides' Helen. The 1949 film *Son of Billy the Kid,* posits that Billy has survived not only those deaths he'd famously eluded, but even the death that ostensibly really claimed him (however "really," in this context, might be taken); twenty years after supposedly being shot by Pat Garrett, Billy surfaces in the 1949 film as a respected banker. Surfacings and resurfacings of Billy *eideloi* and Billy bankers diegetically literalize a dazzling proliferation of film-Billies in circulation throughout Spicer's own adolescence and early adulthood: *Billy the Kid in Texas* (1940); *Billy the Kid in Santa Fe* (1940); *Billy the Kid's Fighting Pals* (1941); *The Law vs. Billy the Kid* (1954). The 1950 film *I Shot Billy the Kid* uncannily rehearses the 1996 film about Valerie Solanos, *I Shot Andy Warhol,* a spectrum of iterability beginning with Billy's silver-screen saturations, reaching toward Warhol's saturated silkscreens, and with Spicer dead center.

This short list of Billy films doesn't include Howard Hughes's 1943 *The Outlaw,* in which Jack Beutel's Billy the Kid resembles, according to one ardent online fan, "a fey Johnny Depp." Nor does it include the Billy films starring Buster Crabbe, a former Olympic-swimming hunk along the lines less of Depp than Matthew McConaughey. Crabbe also starred in the 1936 *Flash Gordon* and 1939 *Buck Rogers,* suggesting an intersection between science-fiction and cowboy lore no less pertinent, as we shall see, to Spicer's own poetic practice. Crabbe's 1933 leading role in *Tarzan the Fearless* commends to Spicer and others the ravishing photoshoot of Crabbe in leopard loincloth. Moving from loincloth to chaps, we find Crabbe as Billy in *Billy the Kid Wanted* (1941); *Billy the Kid's Round-up* (1941); *Billy the Kid Trapped* (1942); *Billy the Kid's Smoking Guns* (1942); *Law and Order* (1942); *Sheriff of Sage Valley* (1942); *The Mysterious Rider* (1942); *The Kid Rides Again* (1943); *Fugitive of the Plains* (1943); *Western Cyclone* (1943); *Cattle Stampede* (1943); *The Renegade* (1943); *Blazing Frontier* (1943).

A 1946 film, *Alias Billy the Kid,* titularly describes the translation of a person with an alias to a person equivalent to an alias. Ghost of Billy as ghost of James Dean, ghost of Billy as Tarzan in loin-cloth. Although again, to speak at this point of ghosts hardly does justice to the nonmelancholic "never-lost" of Billy's particular posthumousness.

Billy's own orchestrations of and refractions as serial person are inseparable from his primary vocation (not as banker or loinclothed swinger, but) as serial killer or, at very least, proto-serial killer. Billy's twenty-one murders themselves serially invoke a mortality in direct opposition to Billy's mediated immortality. Following the important scholarship of Mark Seltzer, however, a serial killer might nurse fantasies of immortality, but more acutely is characterizable by a kind of nonmortality, an impersonality that looks back to that of T. S. Eliot and ahead to that of Leo Bersani. In a subsequent section I shall address Bersani's conception of impersonality as it relates to Spicer's poetry. I wish, here, to invoke Seltzer for the ways his account of serial killers seems so little to describe the serialized energies of Billy. Seltzer writes that "one refrain in coverage of serial killing is just this dead average and look-alike character of the killer." Seltzer continues:

> The forensic psychiatrist Helen Morrison, who has done thousands of hours of interviews with serial killers, puts it this way: "These are basically cookie-cutter people, so much alike psychologically I could close my eyes and be talking to any one of them." There is something uncanny about how these killers are so much alike, living composites, how easily they blend in. The serial killer, as one prosecutor of these cases expressed it, is "abnormally normal": "just like you or me."[13]

Without explanation, Morrison's observations slip from the indistinguishability of serial killers from each other to the indistinguishability of serial killers from the populations into which they blend. I doubt that Billy the Kid is "like you or me." Morrison's collapse of "you or me," in fact, enacts a violence of its own kind, in presuming that "you" is equivalent in some fashion to "me" (an equivalence already punctuated in Morrison's demonstrative and vague "just like"). Not only are serial killers, in Morrison's analysis, rendered impersonal in their similarity to each other; all persons — signalled in shorthand by "you or me" — are rendered impersonal. Morrison's claims for serial killers uncannily end up seeming applicable to everyone. Morrison's observations, furthermore, ostensibly forget those "thousands of hours of interviews" conducted with serial killers, who characteristically read as much literature about serial killers as anyone else — and likely more. In this context, why might not the "you" — the reader — whom Morrison addresses be a serial killer? Even as Morrison's serial killer catalyzes the indistinguishability of "other people" who are not serial killers, the violence of her final "or" — or rather, a single prosecutor's "or," which in turn bleeds into Morrison's (and in turn Seltzer's) voice — cannot rule out that "we" (whoever this group includes) not only look like serial killers, but include them within our (unconvincingly) removed ranks.

Even as resurrections of Billy as Buster Crabbe or Paul Newman (and simultaneously, resurrections of Crabbe or Newman as Billy) perhaps bear the salaciously saccharine pleasure of a cookie jar, these "cookie-cutter people" differ from those tallied by Morrison, if only because Buster Crabbe and Paul Newman are asked to be taken not only as the same type of cookie (one gingery snap after another), but as the same cookie, in constant, arch interplay with the obvious and pleasant fact that they are only playing the same cookie. Seltzer inadvertently follow's Morrison's troping of serial persons as consumable goods, in characterizing the crime scene as nothing so much as devouring force — as though cultural and intellectual appetites for serial violence could absent the bodies of killers no less than the bodies of victims:

> The devouring force of the scene of the crime makes visible, in the spectral outline of the white shape, the sheer transparency of body to scene. It figures the violent becoming-transparent of the subject (criminal or victim) to his or her milieu. It figures the subject of violence melting into the city scene — absorbed, or eaten up, by space.[14]

We shall see to what extent Billy is "eaten up" by the "white shape" of Spicer's poem, and to what extent the poem (if not Billy himself) spits Billy back up. Seltzer's tableau suggests the possibility of a telos beyond ingestion — in the always ominous threat of the serial killer striking again. In this way, Seltzer's account of a serial person's body itself complicates the gastronomics of melancholy, which rest in the psychical discomfitures of ingestion and indigestion. At the same time, however, the proliferation of Billies I've recounted already suggests that something other than impersonalization is at work in Billy's serial instantiations. That Billy's seriality does not follow a logic of impersonality — "becoming-transparent" — is all the more intriguing insofar as Spicer, as we shall see, himself speaks of poetic seriality in explicit relation to impersonality. Nevertheless, in the case of Billy, seriality doesn't effect personal dissolution, but refraction that exceeds — diffuses without defusing — the boundaries of personate singularity.

Spicer in New England: Dickinson, Whitman, O'Hara

Billy's nonsingular personhood recalls less Spicer's own explicit accounts of seriality (to which the next section turns), than Dickinson scholars' articulations of lyric variance, which does not undo a given Dickinson poem so much as further intensify that poem's textually magnetic hold. That Dickinson scholarship resembles Spicer's own poetry is perhaps unsurprising, given Spicer's own hand in Dickinson scholarship. Difficult as it might initially be to imagine any consanguinity between the "belle of Amherst" and the beast of Berkeley — Spicer, caricaturable as much as a bull in poetry's china shop, as Dickinson might be caricatured as poetry's china. Spicer, however, for all his affiliation with the 1950s Berkeley Renaissance, spent a formative year in the middle of that decade between New York and Boston. His time on the East Coast is documented as full of outrage and disappointment. After the close California friendships of fellow gay poets Robert Duncan and Robin Blaser, Spicer found the gay poetic culture of the East nearly unbearable. Frank O'Hara and John Ashbery struck Spicer, biography suggests, as both erotically and poetically insouciant. Spicer, famous for his ugliness and sexual nervousness, as much as for aforementioned cantankerousness, maybe felt intimidated, maybe felt unqualified (poetically, erotically) to participate in this East Coast poetic culture. For all the East Coast poets, however, who turned Spicer off, Dickinson was one of the few for whom he expressed kinship and deference. Spicer was as sensitive and fastidious a reader of Dickinson as any established Dickinson scholar — as evidenced in a review by a certain "John L. Spicer" for the *Boston Public Library Quarterly,* on the occasion of the publication of Thomas H. Johnson's variorium edition of *The Poems of Emily Dickinson.*

Years before Susan Howe's material accounts of Dickinson's texts, Spicer's own analyses seem no less exacting: "Her dashes slant downward right; her periods, even if lengthened, do not slant; her commas slant downward to the left."[15] It is important that the terms of Spicer's admiration for Dickinson echo throughout the following pages, not only because the relation between Spicer and Dickinson has yet adequately to be parsed, but because Dickinson's poetics, no less than Spicer's, depends on the phenomenon of singularity and multiplicity not being incompatible or opposites. This phenomenon surfaces, in the vast and difficult Dickinson corpus, fundamentally as a material issue (albeit a materiality, as Virginia Jackson recently argues, not without poetic, epistemological consequences). As Spicer writes, in a register uncannily similar to that of Sharon Cameron's *Choosing Not Choosing,* "Perhaps for no other modern poet would a variorum edition be so necessary":

> It is difficult to tell which of the existing versions is the earlier, and it is usually impossible to decide which version, if any, she rejected. One is confronted with a number of forms of the same poem — fair copies, draft copies, work copies, and even copies written as prose in the bodies of letters. They differ from each other in varying degrees, and often it is apparent that the poet had never made up her mind as to which version she preferred.[16]

Dickinson dazzles Spicer in part for her profferal of poetic variants without specification of a preference for any single variant. In the pages that follow, I want to posit this phenomenon of textual variability as an important model for the variability that is Spicer's interest in Billy The Kid. A single poem? A serial poem? A single person, or several? These are questions introduced by Dickinson without answers. I take *Billy The Kid* as an expansion of the critical field to which such questions might be relevant.

In the years since Spicer wrote his ten-section poem, much if not most of the Kid's aura has been lost. If my project, in part, seeks to restore some of the legendary to the Billy the Kid legend, this restoration is for the sake of better understanding what Billy might have meant to Spicer as ideal, poetic subject, matinee idol, and/or anything in between. I hear Billy the Kid and I think cowboy, and to the extent that Spicer was a gay poet, I imagine Spicer's cowboy attachment as potentially analogous to my own. A poem, then, about a straight hunk; a poem about a nonviable love object. For all my differences with Spicer, attraction to implausible boys surely counts among our strongest affinities. There are, to be certain, as many ways for a hunk to end up in a gay poem as there are gay responses to that hunkiness: at least (and I half-apologize for this facetiousness) two. The first version of the gay poem about a hunk resembles the sorts of macho utopias Whitman sometimes invokes and over which he more frequently gets caricatured as obsessing. Within this type of poem, wrestling (or, say, calf-roping) marks not the limits of poetic understanding, but its apotheosis. Sexual desire, at its most apparent, circulates if not through utter identity with the cowboy, then in the frisson of such an identificatory claim: "Now I tell what I knew in Texas in my early youth," Long Islander Whitman begins the thirty-fourth section of *Song of Myself*. Whitman is one of them, and he is not:

> They were the glory of the race of rangers....
> Large, turbulent, generous, handsome, proud, and affectionate,
> Bearded, sunburnt, drest in the free costume of hunters,
> Not a single one over thirty years of age.[17]

In a line-up, it would be difficult to pick Whitman out among the sunburnt toughs. But still, in the time internal to the poem, Whitman's extrinsicality from the spectacle of turbulent handsomeness is what saves his hide. The stanza immediately following the lines quoted begins "The second First-day morning they were brought out in squads / and massacred, it was beautiful early summer" (69). And so we have in this little Whitman story an erotics founded on similarity (even if that similarity gives way to all the cowboys getting massacred). In a manner of speaking, Whitman's lines reverse the aggressions mapped by Bersani, in which vulnerability and threat accrue not to "the glory of the race of rangers," but to the queer interloper of that "race." More precisely, however, the tenderness of Whitman's lines — the fantasy of a "Lycidas" writ large, the poetic equivalent of a war memorial — delectates over these Texas toughs so as to controvert the poem's subsequent massacre as reportive rather than solely poetic. The poet disappears from the poem no less than the other bearded men in a double-erasure of criminal/poet and victim that is structurally if not psychically analogous to Seltzer's omnivorous crime scene. Psychically, the grim finitudes of this Whitmanian scene — "The maim'd and mangled dug in the dirt, the new-comers saw them there, / Some half-kill'd attempted to crawl away" — posit melancholic amorousness as the only solution to amorousness so miscarried (and carried away). Crawling away — out of the poem as much as off of the Texas field — the toughs inevitably crawl into Whitman's heart. What, after all, is Whitman's signature declaration, "I contain multitudes," if not

(Freudian or Butlerian) melancholy at its most nonambivalently, sexily democratic?

By contrast, we have version two of the gay poem about a hunk, and as representative I offer Frank O'Hara (albeit Warhol's treatment of cowboys in his film *Lonesome Cowboys* is no less illustratory), for whom the erotic is founded on utter a priori exclusion, the cowboy as horizon the poet could never reach, and in O'Hara's case, good heavens why would you want to. Hence the cowboy as object of a particular species of camp, the spectacle of O'Hara's blithe ease with guys who, in their ordinary registers, are totally incompatible with that O'Haran blitheness:

> (The western mountain ranges were sneaking along[. . .]
> like a pack of dogies and is there much
> tapping under the desert moon? Does it look magical
> or realistic, that landing?[. . .]
> In Pasadena they are calling
> "Higho, Silver!" but in the High Sierras they just shoot
> movie after movie. Who is "they?" The Westerners, of course,
> the tans. Didn't you ever want to be a cowboy, buster?) Big-
> town papers, you see, and this great-coated tour of the teens
> in (oh bless me!) imagination. That's what the snow said,
> "and doesn't your penis look funny today?" I jacked "off."[18]

Spicer and O'Hara, as already noted, "rubbed each other the wrong way" (65), and O'Hara's jacking off at the close of the above poem's sequence seems a far cry from Spicer's "jacking" of Billy the Kid. At the same time, neither O'Hara nor Spicer can help but view Whitman's cowboy optic through the 1940s and 1950s proliferation of Western movies. To this extent, as John Vincent has noted regarding Spicer's vituperation of O'Hara's friend John Ashbery, Spicer's disdain might itself signal the extent to which his poetry isn't so different, in ways, from that of a "faggot poet" like O'Hara.[19]

O'Hara's poem — recalling Buster Crabbe's inhabiting of both pioneer and science-fictional locales — moves swiftly from Western to lunar landscape. The poem's question, "does it look magical/or realistic" helpfully shifts the terms that govern Butler's account of melancholy, earlier cited. What looks magical (O'Hara's moon, or Butler's melancholy) might not be magical, and at the same time its not really being magical does not rule out its appearing so, a form of magic in its own right: that is, a shifting of the criteria of magical or realistic from the position of an object to someone perceiving the object. O'Hara's conflation of Pasadena cowboys and "the tans" renders both flavors of cowboy equivalently equivocal in regard to "magical or realistic" status. This equivocation, within the velocity of O'Hara's poetic personhood, no less renders both forms of cowboys equivalently ridiculous. Spicer, within *Billy The Kid,* cultivates a version of Whitmanian cowboy intimacy (itself predicated on what O'Hara's poem would term the "realistic") within the cultural factitiousness that makes such intimacy, for O'Hara, one hoot among others. The recuperative success of Spicer's venture depends on a poetics in collusion with the seriality O'Hara invokes ("movie after movie"). This collusion is to be distinguished (even as it seems a hybrid of) a poetics conceived as transparent to an original West (Whitman), or spurred (as in O'Hara) by a transparency of factititiousness over which it skims. Spicer, that is, takes O'Haran factitiousness as seriously as Whitman takes his dream of fact.

Spicer's Impersonality: The Vancouver Lectures

In the June of 1965, just weeks before his death, Jack Spicer gave a series of lectures in the Vancouver home of Warren and Ellen Tallman. These lectures were published as a volume, edited by Peter Gizzi, in 1998, and while Susan Howe's book-blurb calls them a "vital articulation of the poet's profound and necessary calling," they are, as a discussion of the poet's poetics, often relatively boring and incoherent material. Not that one necessarily ought to expect coherence from a poet (let alone a drunk poet)[20] discussing his own work. As Spicer admits at the outset of the second lecture, "I am never going to give you brilliant answers,"[21] and he pretty much doesn't. The lectures are nonetheless important for Spicer scholarship in their explication of Spicer's sense of dictation and seriality, practices by which Spicer imagined his own most important poetry as governed. "I think the problem of poetic dictation," Spicer says in his first lecture, "is perhaps the first problem a poet has. The second problem — one you can't 'get' too well without understanding what poetic dictation is or isn't — is a serial poem" (4).

The "problem" of dictation, for Spicer, amounts to the problem of a poet sufficiently excluding his thoughts and emotions from the practice of poetry-writing, so that the poem — the dictation — can be written with as little "personal" interference as possible. The impersonality upon which Spicer insists is not his own innovation; Spicer admits as much, in citing Blake, Yeats, and Eliot as earlier poets who took "poetry as coming from the outside rather than from the inside" (5, 88). Particular to Spicer's poetic impersonality (as adduced from the lectures), however, is the extent to which impersonality aspires toward a specifically erotic abdication, and concomitantly, the erotically neutered metaphors (as we shall see: the radio, the Martian, the building block —) through which Spicer imagines impersonally dictative poetic practice. Insofar as Spicer deems his poetic impersonality implicitly nonerotic, it is perhaps expected that Spicer's lectures seem most confused (if not ambivalent) when crossing erotic lines. Just minutes, for instance, into his first lecture, Spicer so contorts "want" with litotes that it is difficult to say exactly how or what a poet should want or not want to want: "You have to not really want not what you don't want to say" (7). Contrary to T. S. Eliot, who likens the moment of impersonalization to a chemical experiment,[22] Spicer describes the act of "empt[ying] yourself" as a kind of athletic Whitmanian auto-eroticism.[23] The aim of this kenotic grappling, contra Whitman, is the conversion of a poet from a desiring, wanting, person, into a poetic conduit. This (near-Deleuzian) conversion amounts to redesign of the poet-machine. "Instead of the poet being a beautiful machine which manufactured the current for itself... almost a perpetual motion machine of emotion until the heart broke... instead there was something coming from the Outside" (5).

Spicer insists that opposite the "perpetual motion machine of emotion," the poet imagine himself, machinically, as a radio. The space otherwise occupied by personal emotion or thought is emptied so as best to transmit the outside radio signal:

> The point is that you're not the thing which is broadcasting. You're the receiver. If you're good enough, you can get so much out of yourself that you're almost as empty as a radio tube or a transistor or whatever you're using, and the message comes through. The message may not be important, or at least doesn't seem important to me. But if it's really coming through, I read it again and again and see whether it is. The

> fact that you don't have anything to do with it, that you aren't doing anything more than relaying something, doesn't seem to me anything to be particularly disturbed about. At least I'm not. (77)

Spicer's ideal poet, transformed into radio, is further extricated from the domain of the personal, in that this radio communicates not the songs or broadcasts of other persons,[24] but the unintelligible message of Martians.[25] And what do the Martians care about? Lord knows. What matters is that the poet absent himself so the Martians can say what they want. Although "want," even in this case, seems a misnomer, insofar as Spicer precludes the possibility even of Martian desire, by replacing the language of wants with a rudimentary, quasi-Wittgensteinian lexicon of blocks:

> But the more building blocks, the more you have to arrange your building blocks, and say to the Martian, "Oh no, Mr. Martian, it doesn't go this way" . . . the more building blocks you have, the more temptation. The more you know, in a university sense, the more temptation there is to say, oh yes — yes, yes, yes — I remember this has to do with the Trojan War, or this has to do with this . . . and so forth. (8–9)

Again, even as Spicer seeks to exempt desire from his poetics, the vocabulary of Spicer's lectures bends, almost in spite of itself, to a poet's "wants," "impulses," or (as in the passage above) "temptation[s]." While temptation emerges twice in the above statement, it occurs, Spicer qualifies, "in the university sense." "Yes — yes, yes, yes" might suggest in some contexts the locutions of orgasm. Spicer, however, attaches this iteration to a scholar's tedious recognition of allusion to the Trojan war. The poet, catachrestically, constructs with building blocks whatever the Martians tell him to construct, even as Spicer flirts with a sexier version of writing in which temptation might cede to yeses, in which negation of want might be enough negated to proffer (as if accidentally) a negative negative of wanting. For all Spicer's insistence on a poetry dependent on the exclusion of persons and personal desire, it is not surprising that the lectures, on a rhetorical register, oscillate between erotic proscription, transcription, and blazon. Not surprising, since Spicer's poetry is so egregiously and often brilliantly a register of what seem to be his own desires.[26]

The first problem a poet has, Spicer opines, is that of poetic dictation. "The second . . . is a serial poem." Seriality, as delineated in the lectures, is a multiplication of dictative practice, rather than a distinct practice, per se. "Of course, it's dictation of form, you realize. It's not the same thing as dictation of lines, but it follows more or less the same laws" (53). Those laws, needless to say, involve the expulsion of personality from the poem, "emptying yourself as a vessel" (85); or as Spicer describes in explicit relation to seriality, "You have to go into a serial poem not knowing what the hell you're doing" (52); "[You can't say] this path isn't going anywhere; it looks like it's going to be a big chasm and I obviously can't go down a chasm" (74). Is the poet in the poem, but lost? Or is he out of the poem altogether? Is being lost in the poem tantamount to achieving dictative impersonality? Is being a radio equivalent to following paths one would otherwise know better than to take? How to be a radio and a poet at the same time? How to disavow desire in a poetry saturated with desire? Or more to the point, how to undermine one's own disavowals? Such are the questions with which Spicer's 1958 serial poem, *Billy The Kid,* begins:

> The radio that told me about the death of Billy The Kid
> (And the day, a hot summer day, with birds in the sky)
> Let us fake out a frontier — a poem somebody could hide in with a sheriff's posse after him — a thousand miles of it if it is necessary for him to go a thousand miles — a poem with no hard corners, no houses to get lost in, no underwebbing of customary magic, no New York Jew salesmen of amethyst pajamas, only a place where Billy The Kid can hide when he shoots people.[27] (79)

As a poet following the directives of his own eventual lectures (to wit, the poetics by which Spicer's poetry retroactively, by criticism, largely is inscribed) what the radio says must be honored, must become the poem. *Billy The Kid,* however, eschews the radio as quickly as it introduces it. The radio, here, is less the means of a poem's delivery than what amounts to the first of a poem's several false starts. The poem's second attempted beginning — "(And the day, a hot summer day, with birds in the sky)" — disposes of the radio and the figure of poet to which Spicer's radios are connected. The line's parentheticals suggest both a sort of stage direction, as well as the discreteness with which the line itself is imported, and importable. The day described, "a hot summer day, with birds in the sky," might pertain to the weather either of the scene of writing or of Billy's death. More saliently, however, it registers (especially in view of this first section's subsequent movements) as a cliché. "The day, a hot summer day," has all the specificity of a "dark and stormy night." Even the line's birds seem less to particularize the sky than to augment the sky's generic ideality.

The third line's exhortation ("Let us") ostensibly learns from the factitiousness of the line that precedes it. The cliché of a "hot summer day" cedes to an invitation to an unspecified "us," to participate in correlative cliché-making, albeit cliché deployed toward emphatically nonclichéd ends. That is, if cliché, at best, operates as a sort of shorthand, a ready-made in the non-Dadaist sense, then Spicer's reversion to cliché insists (in a manner consonant with Duchamp) that the ready-made be made. Cliché doesn't save poetic labor in Spicer's poem so much as become its own mode of important production. "Let us fake out a frontier" has the formulaic ring of T. S. Eliot and Marvell ("Let us go" and "Let us sport," respectively), which is to say, of the antielegiac terrain of what Susan Stewart calls the carpe diem tradition.[28] In Eliot's and Marvell's poems, "let us" relocates "us" outside the poem, where time is finite. The exhortation asks that real action (i.e., romantic action) be taken, because beyond the infinity of writing there are (as Catullus writes) only so many more days and nights. By contrast, the crisis in Spicer isn't temporal, because Spicer's "us" doesn't exactly occupy an outside where time could matter. The crisis, in Spicer, is less temporal than spatial: how to reconcile the outside of a text with its inside, which amounts, in this poem, to marking the effects of danger as it crosses the poem's exclusionary and inclusionary erotics.

By danger, I mean to invoke the poem's diegetical dangers, as they pertain both to Billy (on the lam from the law) and to the law (ever approaching Billy's trigger-finger). Beyond the dangers intrinsic to the poem's commencing premise, however, I mean also to invoke the dangers subject to the poet, negotiating his own entrance into or withdrawal from the poem at hand. Following poetic dicta of impersonality, the poet is no less at risk (if only on a theoretical or aesthetic level) in writing the poem, than are the poem's fugitive and sheriff. Not that the latter risks don't themselves operate on the level of the theoretical and aesthetic.

How, then, is the aesthetic status of the poet different from the aesthetic status of Billy, the poem's subject? How might the aesthetic death of the former learn from or inform that of the latter, and vice versa? Put more optimistically, how might one learn from the other how to elude one's own death sentence and, in so doing, learn how to preserve persons (by extension, the desires a person has and attracts) in spaces a priori defined as threatening to them?

We shall return to this first section's many gorgeous difficulties. For the time being, I want to note that this poem is at the service not of Martians, but of Billy the Kid. This substitution, on one level, is conventional—a poem written on behalf of some beautiful boy.[29] More specifically, the poem is being written for a beautiful boy to hide in. More specifically still, and introducing a whole range of motivations which Spicer's lectures cannot address, a poem for a beautiful boy to hide in when he shoots people. But are the Martians really the ones that want to hide Billy? An analogous set-up might involve a science teacher assigning as your lab assistant the beautiful, dangerous boy in the class. That the teacher has made the assignment conveniently renders beside the point any desire you may have for the boy. You might thank the teacher, secretly, for making your desire look like the following of orders. But this doesn't change the fact that you have the cute boy, and how to negotiate your desires and attractions within this prefab, and pretty fabulous scenario, in which bureaucracy occupies the place of ruse.

Spicer's outrageous claim for the poem-at-hand — a place "where Billy . . . can hide when he / shoots people" — conjures a poetic space that is simultaneously shelter and threat. Shelter for Billy, as the poem keeps him from the posse. Threat to the posse (and by extension the reader? the poet himself?), for whom the moment of capture coincides with moment of greatest peril. Threat, even, to Billy, to the extent that the reprieve of a hideout also potentially intensifies the peril of being found (as analogue, the giddy, half-real terror of a child playing hide-and-seek). Spicer, in aligning his poem with the Western, vernacularizes an account of poetry that Neil Hertz traces within the writings of de Man. "What is clear," Hertz writes, "is that the 'region' [of poetry] is sometimes registered as a 'shelter,' sometimes as a 'threat'; and, as de Man points out, it is common to confuse the two: 'The strategy of denegation which calls a threat a shelter in the hope of laying it to rest is all too familiar.' "[30]

Contra Spicer's lectures, the serial poem as evinced in *Billy The Kid* is not just about the poet getting lost, but about Billy getting lost. Or seeming lost. The poetics that *Billy The Kid* introduces takes as its point of departure that Billy, in some fashion, is still alive—which would seem the gravest of cardinal sins in the poetics laid out by Spicer's lectures: to take as point of departure the opposite of what the radio says. *Billy The Kid* enacts a rejection of the radio, and in the dangerous space of rule-breaking, Spicer imagines himself as accomplice to Billy's subsequent crimes.

The Poem and the Bathhouse

Despite their indubitable influence on criticism's reception of Spicer's poetry, the Vancouver lectures admittedly do not constitute Spicer's sole account of poetics — his poetry itself is often garrulous (sometimes deceptively transparent) about its sundry motivations and ambitions. One of the most anthologized of Spicer's accounts of poetry (and more specifically, the seriality that is my chapter's concern) appears in Spicer's *Admonitions,* a book of poems nearly coterminous with *Billy The Kid.* This account, in contrast to that of the lectures, describes poetry-making in explicitly erotic terms. These terms are illuminating to my study of *Billy The Kid* and, more generally, to a study of queer poetics as such. Nonetheless, the averred poetics of *Admonitions* do not clarify the stakes of dictation or seriality, so much as further complicate them. In a letter included in *Admonitions* to Robin Blaser, Spicer writes:

> There is really no single poem.
>
> That is why all my stuff from the past...looks foul to me. The poems belong nowhere. They are one night stands filled (the best of them) with their own emotions, but pointing nowhere, as meaningless as sex in a Turkish bath. It was not my anger or my frustration that got in the way of my poetry but the fact that I viewed each anger and each frustration as unique — something to be converted into poetry as one would exchange foreign money. I learned this from the English Department (and from the English Department of the spirit — that great quagmire that lurks at the bottom of all of us).... Look at those other poems. Admire them if you like. They are beautiful but dumb.
>
> Poems should echo and reecho against each other. They should create resonances. They cannot live alone any more than we can. (61)

Spicer renounces his earlier singular poems for the delights and solaces intrinsic to serial writing. While the renouncing seems clear enough, the terms by which singularity (and in turn seriality) is defined are themselves far from self-evident. Even as Spicer apostatizes singularity, he can't imagine singularity as such without inscribing discrete poems into a recursive structure. "They are one-night stands . . . as meaningless as sex in a Turkish bath." What begins as a rebuke of *the* "single poem" becomes a rebuke of "one-night stands." The single one-night stand, however, is nearly impossible to imagine: one-night stands being relatively easy to orchestrate, and potentially addictive, if not definitionally serializable. A poem might be like a one-night stand insofar as the poet writes it and moves on to another poem; or conversely, insofar as the poem seduces the poet for the duration of its lyric, then leaves by morning. The singularity to which Spicer's frustrations attach, however, becomes meaningless only after the fact, only diachronically extended — which is to say, only when singularity is temporalized into a particular form of multiplicity. Spicer aligns this multiplicity with a Turkish bath. A Turkish bath visited once (like a one-night stand attempted once) might be delightful, or harrowing, or at the very least narrativizable. Its "meaningless[ness]," however, acquires intensity (which is also to say, meaning) only in its animation into habitual practice.

This epistolary interplay of poetry and sex says as much about sexual relations as it does poetic ones, and is all the more timely now, in the context of queer theory's recent ballyhoo over certain forms of sexual serialization. With lubricious cuteness, Leo Bersani writes in a 2002 article that

> [t]he gay bathhouse is especially favorable to ideal cruising because, in addition to the opportunity anonymous sex offers its practitioners of shedding much of the personality that individuates them psychologically, the common bathhouse uniform — a towel — communicates very little (although there are of course ways of wearing a towel . . .) about our social personality (economic privilege, class status, taste, and so on).[31]

Bersani advocates the bathhouse as site of radical depersonalization: "It is as if there were a happiness inherent in not being entirely ourselves, in being 'reduced' to an impersonal rhythm."[32] Spicer, by contrast, rebuffs the bathhouse because it is meaningless not only in the manner Bersani advocates, but because its flaneuring vagary is irreconcilable with the possibility of uniqueness Spicer brings to it:

> It was not my anger or my frustration that got in the way of my poetry but the fact that I viewed each anger and each frustration as unique.

Spicer brings more and sheds less to the bathhouse-poem than Bersani's lyric account of serial sex can accommodate. It's not that the bathhouse, or for that matter, the single poem, is depersonalizing—even as Spicer would claim that all poems require, in Bersani's terms, "an intransitive pleasure intrinsic to a certain mode of existence, to self-subtracted being."

Here, as elsewhere, Bersani is glossing Georg Simmel's sociability, but may as well be glossing the dicta of Eliot's poetic impersonality. Curiously, Bersani's account of a bathhouse's propensities toward depersonalization registers as the exact opposite of Bersani's earlier description of bathhouse hierarchies, in "Is the Rectum a Grave?" Contra his later fantasy of nonregulated anonymity, Bersani earlier writes that "[a]nyone who has ever spent one night in a gay bathhouse knows that it is (or was) one of the most ruthlessly ranked, hierarchized, and competitive environments imaginable. Your looks, muscles, hair distribution, size of cock, and shape of ass determined exactly how happy you were going to be during those few hours."[33] If, that is, in 2002, Bersani's bathhouse promises a happiness predicated on "not being entirely ourselves," the bathhouse happiness of 1987 explicitly depends not only on being one's self, but being something nearly beyond one's self, a sort of hypersingularity founded on the inventory of attributes that makes one distinguishable (and hopefully sexier) than others. Potentially audible within Bersani's earlier litany of bathhouse "vital statistics" is the idea that such hierarchies are most salient that first time ("spent one night in a gay bathhouse"), as though the difference between spending "one night," for Bersani, and cruising the baths on a regular basis, were one's decreasing sensitivity to such bodily differences. I note the stark differences between Bersani's earlier and more recent positions to suggest that for Bersani, like Spicer, the vicissitudes of anonymity or habituality are not merely always already given, but themselves the object of work, the labors of inurement; an appreciation of a bathhouse's anonymity, far from originary (as Bersani's later article would have it), requires a desensitization to its constitutive insistent singularities. As in Spicer, bathhouses acquire their meaningful meaninglessness, for Bersani, only over time—as quite literally suggested in the juxtaposition of these two divergent Bersani essays.

To repeat: it's not that the bathhouse, or for that matter, the single poem, is depersonalizing. Rather: uniqueness of feeling, in the depersonalizing space of bathhouse poetry, has no place to go. The single poem, as Spicer imagines it, is a dead-letter office for anger and frustration (the calling cards of amorous unrequitedness) not because it is singular, but because, in the call for impersonality, the poem already is a sort of bathhouse. The singular poem, as recounted in *Admonitions,* already looks a lot like the serial poem, as usually conceived. If the serial poem isn't about the proscription of unique feeling, isn't correlative to bathhouse or cruise, then what is it?

"Poems should echo and reecho each other. They should create resonances. They cannot live alone any more than we can." If a single poem, for Spicer, is meaningless as bathhouse sex, it's not exactly that a serial poem is meaningful like some other sort of sex. Rather, the serial poem proposes a solution to the problem of a loneliness whose needs exceed the erotic. One could detect in this seriality a poetics modeled on a long-term relationship. Not a single one-night stand, nor a proliferation of one-night stands, but the proliferation of nights (and days) held together by the resonances between them: which is also to say, for the sake of rescuing this long-term seriality from the utopic (what Bersani calls "the dangers attached to the pastoralizing of any form of sexual relation"[34]), held together by the angers and frustrations unique to those particular resonances.[35] But what does it mean to attribute to poems a set of needs equivalent to persons ("They can't live alone any more than we can"), within a poetics that more generally, prima facie, disowns personal need? In a poetics that from the outset demands personal decathexis (a decathexis which, in his letters to Lorca, Spicer identifies as a kind of loneliness[36]), the poems, not wanting to be lonely, seem to function more like people than poets do.

This implicit conception of seriality posits the long-term relationship as middle ground between utter solitude and utterly extravagant "self-subtracted" sociability. Somewhere between a single person—inimical both to a poetics that claims personal need as distraction, and to queer theories such as Bersani's, suspicious of subjectivity as such—and a sexy gaggle, we have the intimacy of poems that "echo and reecho each other." In the move from single lyrics to seriality, we have implicitly moved not only from "sex" to "liv[ing]," but from bodies (in a bathhouse) to sounds (that reverberate). These sounds, to be sure, are different from the sounds transmitted by poet-as-radio. These sounds come not from Mars, but from the pleasures and aggressions (and consolations) of love, stretched across time.

"For Billy": Nonchronological Persons

The concerns of Spicer's letter to Blaser in *Admonitions* are inextricable, I think, from Spicer's investment in Billy the Kid. As much is suggested by the poem in *Admonitions* immediately preceding that letter, a poem titled "For Billy." With the exception of "For Billy," each of *Admonitions*'s other sections is addressed to a specific person in (or at least in some relation to) Spicer's circle—Robert Duncan, Joe Dunn, Russ Fitzgerald, etc. "For Billy," on the other hand, is most feasibly addressed to Billy the Kid himself. As such, the poem raises precisely the sorts of questions provoked by Spicer's letter to Blaser. Who or what counts as a single person? What does it mean to address an iconic (and iconically historical) figure as though he were an intimate? More radically, "For Billy" literalizes the subsequent bathhouse letter's difficulty in distinguishing the properties of a singular entity (whether a poem metaphorized as a person, or vice versa) from a multiple one. All the more relevant to Spicer's serial experiments in *Billy The Kid,* "For Billy" doesn't oppose singularity and multiplicity, but advances a multiplicity that itself expresses, even intensifies, identity, even as identity ordinarily operates through the channels of the singular:

> That old equalizer
> Called time by some
> Love by others
> Cock by a few
> Will come to meet you at the door
> When you go
> (Knowing that death is as near to you as water)
> Go to fuck and say goodbye to your Mexican whore.

> They will be waiting in the same room for you:
> Time with his big jeans
> Love with his embarrassed laugh
> Cock with his throat cut wearing a bandana.
> They can equalize anybody
> January, February, March,
> April, May, June, July, August, September,
> October,
> November,
> December,
> I love you, I love you,
> Scream when you come.
> There is not another room to go into
> But hell, Billy,
> It was hell when they shot you. (59–60)

While the poem's emotional attachments are to the singular figure of Billy, the presence of Billy, within the poem, is crowded out by the metastasis of Billy's putative adversary. The poem, even as an elegy to Billy's singularity — a singularity conjured by the poem's iterated "you," as though the specificity of Billy as addressee didn't require explication, in literally going without saying — is simultaneously fascinated by an opposite conceit, by which "that old equalizer," known by several names and several disguises, magically splinters into the convergent simultaneity of its various aliases, even as Billy The Kid (alias William Antrim, alias William Bonney) is himself the infamous boy of many names. Spicer's fascination with a specifically nonchronological simultaneity of entities precipitates the poem's litany of months; grammatically, each month potentially registers as one of the equalizer's potential victims (each month, a specification of the previous line's "anybody"), as much as the months might ordinarily signal the mensal regularity with which such equalizations could occur. The poem converts months from temporal demarcations to time's targets, which is to say, subjects a specifically chronological seriality to the poem's own nonchronological seriality. On a formal level, this conversion is evident in the apparent desultoriness of line breaks, which organize months not (for instance) along the logic of seasons, or even by any readily available internal logic or regularity. Why, for instance, the long span from April to September? Why do October, November, and December occupy their own lines if not to signal a gravity beyond the mundane movement from one month to the next? This gravity implies the extent to which an emotional-spatial logic governs the months more than a temporal one. If the months are targets of the "old equalizer," it is because the equalizer's manifestation, within the poem, demands a deracination from the chronology that months otherwise organize.

Each name for Billy's adversary becomes a figure who could kill, just as each month becomes one in a list of the equalizer's victims; the time/love/cock posse "can equalize anybody," not "anytime." All persons are rendered equivalent in the equalizing clutch of love, time, desire, or death. As the equalizer levels particular differences (in a manner not dissimilar to the leveling of Bersanian sociability), it hypostasizes its own, to the fabulous point where each alternate name arrives in a different outfit, a different affect. (Billy might even wonder, in the moment before being shot, how Cock scored the Kid's bandana, how Time fit into his jeans.) Still, Billy's singularity underwrites the poem's own doubled "I love you, I love you." This claim, despite the equalizer's equalizings, depends on the fact that "you" refers to Billy and Billy alone; just as the "I" refers to none other than the speaker. *Billy The Kid* will trouble the stability of such denominations and search for a way in which "I love you" might not require the singularity that likewise dooms Billy, in this earlier poem, to singular death.[37]

Recalling Spicer's attachment in *Billy The Kid* to a poetics of fakery, the radical temporal inventiveness of "For Billy" theoretically resonates with what Deleuze, in a section of *The Time-Image* called "The Powers of the False," describes as the "crystalline . . . (or) chronic regime" evidenced in new wave film. "We no longer have," Deleuze writes, "a chronological time which can be overturned by movements which are contingently abnormal; we have a chronic nonchronological time which produces movements necessarily 'abnormal,' essentially 'false.' "[38] Deleuze's study of temporal innovation in film illuminates Spicer's study of temporal innovation in poetry; for both Deleuze and Spicer, the unmooring of chronology, the "losing . . . (of) legal connections and laws of extremum"[39] produces newly invigorated powers of the false, "the nonproblematic coexistence of entities which, chronologically speaking, would be impossible." Deleuze argues that in new wave film "the forger becomes *the character* of the cinema: not the criminal, the cowboy, the psycho-social man." In Spicer's *Billy The Kid* (and as we shall see, in Irving Penn's filmic account of Billy the Kid), however, Billy is every bit as much a forger as he is a cowboy.

Generosities of the False: Seriality and the Aesthetic

The literal creativeness of Spicer's "great equalizer" (what Deleuze, in *The Time-Image,* might align with the generosities of the false[40]) returns in *Billy The Kid,* a serial poem in ten parts. It returns in the poem's literalizing insistence of Billy as an aesthetic object, which is to say, as an object of the poem's (or Spicer's) creativeness. Seriality, imagined (contrary to the crisis of "For Billy") as more rooms to go into, provides one mode by which Spicer preserves Billy from the poetic recapitulation of a sheriff's manhunt. Seriality is one mode, and this explicit aestheticization is another. More precisely, serialization and aestheticization are different manifestations of the same creative impulse—the former takes as its object the body of the poem, constantly subjected to new forms. The latter takes as its object Billy himself, whereby fictionalization or aestheticization isn't countered by the notion of a true Billy (for instance, a historic William Antrim, killed in 1881). Within the logic of Spicer's poem (specifically, Spicer's serial poem), the foregrounding of aestheticization is the grounds not for critiquing personhood, but for personhood itself. In this way, if I earlier claimed that Spicer's poems seem to act more like persons than poets do, then Billy, as a person, takes his cues (on what being a person is) from the possibilities of poetic form of which he is subject.

The conjunction of multiplicity and aestheticization as grounds for person-making (as opposed to grounds for doubting or obviating personhood) is most acutely suggested in the second section of *Billy The Kid,* whose initial subject is not Billy as such, but the process of collage.[41] Collage, like the seriality of *Billy The Kid* more generally, posits a form of multiplicity that doesn't diffuse singularity into sociability or variousness, but actually produces an intensified kind of singularity. Midway through *Billy The Kid's* second section, Spicer retracts his earlier claim. "No, it is not a collage. Hell flowers / Fall from the hands of heroes / fall from all of our hands / flat / As if we were not ever able quite to include them" (79). This overt move from aesthetic fastidiousness to lyric plangence approaches ekphrasis without reaching it. Spicer's ambivalent flirtation with collage argues for a medial space between the aesthetic (as distinct from qualities of life) and the animate (as distinct from qualities of art).

Billy The Kid most directly signals its commitments to aestheticization in alluding to the Western genre it cribs without recapitulating the repertoire by which that genre is most recognizable. It meditates on scenes of cowboy action without delivering any familiar form of them. Again, Deleuze's account of film provides a useful analogy to Spicer's poetics. "In neo-realism and the new wave" — forms, perhaps not surprisingly, contemporary with Spicer's poetry — "vision is no longer even a supposition added to action, a preliminary which presents itself as a condition; it occupies all the room and takes the place of action."[42] Alluding to Henri Bergson, Deleuze earlier writes that "if movement is taken from the moving body, there is no longer any distinction between image and object."[43] In this sense, one can think of Spicer's poem as a new-wave Western. Exemplary of the poem's preference for meditation over action is its decommission of Billy's gun, which in section II "does not shoot real bullets" and in section VI is termed "a false clue." "Not [being] real," like being "false," preempts the poem's objects from behaving as bullets and clues might ordinarily behave (respectively, killing and informing — the distortable relation between these two categories is never far from Spicer's poetic concern).

Ontological dubiousness transforms even Billy from picaresque hero to object of compositional fastidiousness, as literalized in section V:

> Billy The Kid in a field of poplars with just one touch of
> moonlight
> His shadow is carefully
> distinguished from all of their shadows
> Delicate
> as perception is
> No one will get his gun or obliterate
> Their shadows (81)

The lines register as aesthetic, as opposed to scenic. "Just one touch of / moonlight" flirts with what could be Billy's own tactility,[44] but then enjambment cedes touch to the domain of a painter, for whom moonlight could be an effect of touches or dabs. As a painting, however, and given, even, as "delicate / as perception is,"[45] section V's composition doesn't offer a vision of Billy so much as an obfuscation of one. We as readers are left less with Billy than with Billy's shadow, and even if his shadow were distinguished from "all of their shadows" (and whose shadows? those of the poplars, or those, punningly, of other peoples?), what does this distinguishability disclose of Billy? If composition implies the contemplation of possible action, shadows, in turn, imply the contemplation of composition itself. We are at least twice removed here from Billy doing anything.[46] Such an observation would be less interesting were Billy the Kid (and more generally, the cowboy) not usually so implicated in a filmic genre of action — gunslingings and horse-chases.

For Spicer, it is precisely in Billy's fakeness — which is to say, both his elaboration as an aesthetic person and his being multiple without one unit within that multiplicity being granted higher ontological standing than the others — that he averts the death to which singularity is vulnerable. Hence the poem's paradoxical flirtation with the elegiac mode, the poem's beginning with the possibility of Billy's death. Let's return to that first section:

> The radio that told me about the death of Billy the Kid
> (And the day, a hot summer day, with birds in the sky)
> Let us fake out a frontier — a poem somebody could hide in with a sheriff's posse after him — a thousand miles of it if it is necessary for him to go a thousand miles — a poem with no hard corners, no houses to get lost in, no underwebbing of customary magic, no New York Jew salesmen of amethyst pajamas, only a place where Billy The Kid can hide when he shoots people. (79)

Billy has died, and he hasn't. At the very least, the poet has heard that Billy has died; which isn't (not within this poem) equivalent to Billy's being dead. To the extent that Spicer's poem sort of takes Billy's death as point of departure, it's sort of an elegy. Several years later, Spicer would call a series of poems "A Fake Novel about the Life of Arthur Rimbaud," and in that spirit one might call *Billy The Kid* a fake elegy.

"Fake," in this section's third line, designates a domain belonging neither to the poet's phenomenal world (e.g., of the first line's radio) nor the poem proper. The frontier that is faked (as opposed to staked) has less in common with historical frontier (in a "real" territory such as Lincoln County) or even poetic frontier (in a poem about Lincoln County) as it does the stage-sets and backdrops of a Western. The dash that connects "a frontier" and "a poem" approximates metaphoricity without executing it, because the poem takes invention and discovery as nonalchemical endeavors, as though the imagination's resources were (imagined as being) limited as a body's. The poem could stake a frontier if it chose to, but rather takes limitation as its conceit, even as limitation could extend nearly indefinitely: "a thousand miles of it if it is necessary for him to go a thousand miles . . . [but with] no underwebbing of customary magic." The fake frontier's expandability might seem in some sense magical, but the contingencies upon which expansion depends (a poem somebody *could* hide in . . . if it is necessary . . .) actually underwrite a significant aspect of the poem's motivated divergence from realism. Counterintuitive though it may initially sound, it is what Spicer calls customary magic that enables poetry's usual reality-effects. This magic, as suspension of disbelief, transforms words into "real" places; whereas Spicer's rejection of magic leaves us only with "fakes."[47]

Indeed, the poem aspires toward fakeness as the ground for its own inventions; not only being fake, but honoring that fakeness, is the poem's desideratum. To be real, or to be taken for real, is to confine Billy to the sort of living for which death is ineluctable. If Billy can't die, then what's the point of elaborating a poem for him as hideout? The possibility of Billy's death energizes Spicer's poem not because it could actually happen, but because its ubiquitous threat (the dangerous other side of hiding out, again, is being found) underwrites the fiction of Billy's subsequent occasions for spectacular poetic escape.

In this regard, *Billy The Kid* is less like Keats's "Ode on a Grecian Urn" (as Clayton Eshleman claims[48]) than like "Endymion," less ekphrastic, that is, than antiekphrastic translation of beautiful boy into a series of tableaus. Tableaus of boys — for instance, Endymion's Adonis, with his "tenting swerve of knee from knee," and "slumbery pout"[49] — can usually compensate for their inertia in their potential for voyeurist titillation. Billy the Kid, who seems so ripe for that sexiness (even before being dreamily embodied by Paul Newman in Arthur Penn's *Left-Handed Gun*), nonetheless does not exactly come to this fruition in Spicer's poem. Sexiness remains imminent in the way action remains imminent. Section III might be the closest the poem gets to the sort of titillation implied by a gay poet's treatment of a cowboy-hunk such as Billy the Kid:

> There was nothing at the edge of the river
> But dry grass and cotton candy.
> "Alias," I said to him, "Alias,
> Somebody there makes us want to drink the river
> Somebody wants to thirst us."
> "Kid," he said. "No river
> Wants to trap men. There ain't no malice in it. Try
> To understand."
> We stood there by that little river and Alias took off his shirt
> and I took off my shirt
> I was never real. Alias was never real.
> Or that big cotton tree or the ground.
> Or the little river. (80)

This half-strip is a tease and a puzzle in several registers. The Kid, like any good fugitive, is rightly suspicious of his surroundings, but the object of his suspicion seems less sheriff or other bandit than someone like Spicer himself, the "somebody" who plants cotton candy in the dry grass. Frothily pink, and a pun on what otherwise should be there (and what, by the penultimate line, returns nonpunnily as "that big cotton tree"), the Kid might be wise to this poetic intrusion, and wise not to drink just because the poet wants him to. (Or for that matter, strip all the way down and bathe: getting Billy naked in a river, as the sort of poetic license of which Billy might be wary.) His seeming comprehension of being not by a river but in a poem (and even, maybe, vis-à-vis the campiness of cotton candy, in a *gay* poem) makes Billy as much as Spicer an arbiter of the poem's realness or falseness. As soon as Billy and his camerado take their shirts off, Billy—not Spicer—dissolves the section's constitutive parts:

> I was never real. Alias was never real.
> Or that big cotton tree or the ground.
> Or the little river.

Billy effectively voids both himself and the poem he inhabits. Or rather, like cotton candy too close to a little river, deliquesces.

Billy's deliquescing caution—borne of a perspicacity afforded *by* the scene, which by section's end registers as perspicacity *of* it—is opposite the sort of abandonment advocated in Spicer's lectures (i.e., the poet is supposed to empty himself out of the poem, not the poem's own material). Opposite, also, the brio with which the poet exhorts Section I's fake landscape into being. Fakery, from the poet's vantage, occasions the poem's place-making but, from Billy's vantage, forecloses it. If this riverside Billy doesn't believe in himself, let alone his comrade, let alone the landscape, then he hardly can be expected to believe that he is being pursued by a sheriff's posse any more convincingly real.

If the poem doesn't provide the sort of reality Billy requires, however, it (over)compensates in realizing Alias as partner in the section's *pas de* (if not *folie à*) *deux*. As noted in *The Saga of Billy the Kid,* Billy, around six years before his capture and putative death, did have a bandit-companion by the name of Alias:

> While hanging about Fort Bowie in southeastern Arizona . . . dealing monte and living precariously, he picked up a partner of unknown name but who, doubtless in dodging the law here and there about the country, had borne many names and who at this time passed under the suggestive nickname of "Alias." Alias steps out of the story here; Billy remained in Tucson for an undetermined period, living by his wits and his nimble fingers at cards.[50]

Here, even the reality from which Billy might distinguish his poetic milieu operates like a poem. What, after all, could be stranger (within either the saga or Spicer's poem) than Billy (as renowned for his polynomialism as for any set of crimes or misdemeanors) fraternizing with another alias? Spicer, cagily, plays with the history of Billy as it (if sometimes wobbily) stands and simultaneously recounts it (and the play intrinsic to it). Stranger than an alias literalized is such an alias coterminous with his own pseudonym. ("Kid," after all, is as much an alias for William Antrim/William Bonney as "Alias" is.) Spicer here introduces a simultaneity analogous to that found in "For Billy," in which Love, Cock, and Time — three names for the same entity ("that old equalizer") — wait for Billy collectively. More than a breach of realness as Billy might conceive it, this sort of simultaneity hints at a nonchronological capaciousness to which Spicer's poem is prone. A person, ordinarily, can be only one person at any given moment. In these instances, however, a person can (nonphantasmatically) keep company with himself. Looking back to Spicer's letter to Blaser, if a person, in his discrete singularity, usually operates like a lyric, he can also, under certain circumstances, embody the nondiachronic multiplicity of a serial poem. The Kid's multiplicity is exemplary. Spicer doesn't make poetry out of the Kid's life so much as learn from it a certain formal poetic possibility.

"¿Quién es?" *The Billy Archives*

To trawl the archive that wavers between history and pop-culture is to discover, as I have argued, that the mythology of Billy, as Spicer would have received it, hardly varies from the Billy of Spicer's poem. The archive — with its relish of Billy's serial lives, escapes and near-escapes, Keatsian posthumousness — is captivating as a literalizing of the poem's own ambitions. Put a little differently, for all the poem's interest in fakes, the archive argues that this gorgeous fake escapade really happened. This observation goes beyond Baudrillardian simulacra; for Spicer, the discovery of his poetics in the life of an outlaw underwrites the simultaneous (and otherwise aporetic) yearning for real (which is to say personal, if not exactly singular) desire under conditions uncongenial to authenticity and its concomitant (lyric) singularity.

One such account of Billy's death that bears an especial shine of authenticity (for whatever that's worth) is that told by John Poe, deputy sheriff under Pat Garrett and present at the Kid's putative killing. Poe's narrative, published in 1933, would have been available to Spicer and all other consumers of cowboy culture. As will become apparent, the particular terms of Poe's story resonate with those of Spicer's poetry and illuminate how the trigger-happy scapegrace might lend his figure to a poetics more various and unfamiliar than the Orphic poetics to which Spicer usually is attached. John Poe titles his testimony of Billy's death "Strange Sequence of Happenings during the Night of July 14, 1881." Even titularly, we find ourselves beyond the Western genre as commonly conceived. Where in gun-slinging is there room for strangeness? Where, indeed, in the velocity of horse-theft and revenge, is there room for the discreteness of sequence? The strange and the sequential more familiarly surface in the genres through which Spicer reads Billy, those of the ghost story or detective novel. On the night of Billy's putative death, Poe and company are ghosts in shadow, or detectives without clues.

Walter Noble Burns, in an account published in 1925 (and reviewed by none other than Charles Olson, four years before Spicer would write

Billy The Kid), sets the scene of that night with an attention to the crepuscular eeriness of Poe's "strange":

> They set off from Fort Sumner through the four-mile avenue of the cottonwoods. A quarter of a mile from town, they hid their horses in a grove of trees on the Pecos and took a position in the old peach orchard at the north edge of the village. . . . A full moon was in the sky, making the landscape as bright as day, but the peach trees were in full leaf, and in the deep shadows they were safe from chance discovery. For two hours they remained there silently watching the Bowdre door like three cats at a mousehole. But no sign of Kid rewarded their patience.[51]

Poe, among peach trees, rightly describes the watch as "fruitless."[52] After those two hours, Poe and Garrett decide as last resort to visit the home of Peter Maxwell, who, "by reason of his being a leading citizen and having large property interests, should, according to [Poe's] reasoning, be glad to furnish such information as he might have to aid us in ridding the country of a man who was looked on as a scourge and curse."[53] Garrett, upon arrival, enters Maxwell's bedroom, while Poe waits in the bedroom's adjacent porch. "It should be mentioned here," Poe writes, "that up to this moment I had never seen Billy the Kid."[54] And so when a man approaches the porch fence, "only partially dressed . . . both bareheaded and barefooted . . . fastening his trousers as he came toward." Poe has no way of knowing that this is Billy.

But it is. Billy, "butcher knife in his right hand and, naturally enough, as he was left-handed, his forty-one caliber double-action revolver in its scabbard at his left side."[55] Billy, barefoot and maybe shirtless ("divesting himself of . . . garments superfluous on a July night to a man seeking relaxation"[56]), looking for a late-night snack. Billy, upon seeing Poe, draws "his six-shooter as quick as lightning, sprang onto the porch, calling out in Spanish, '*¿Quién es?*'(Who is it?) — at the same time backing away from me toward the door through which Garrett only a few seconds before had passed, repeating his query, 'Who it it?' in Spanish several times."[57]

¿Quién es? Billy, startled, disappears into Maxwell's bedroom. Billy repeats his question to Maxwell, unaware, in the bedroom's dark, of Garrett beside Maxwell's bed. Garrett can't see Billy through the dark, but he recognizes his voice, and shoots. This, for at least some intents and purposes, is the death of Billy the Kid. So sure, however, is Poe that Billy would not have come to Maxwell's that he tells Garrett, soon after

the fact, that he has shot the wrong man. And of course, in the years that follow, such suppositions flourish. Like Elvis, Billy seems to crop up under different names, in different locales, for years thereafter. On that July night of 1881, at least, Billy almost escapes detection altogether. Staring Billy right in the face and not knowing it, Poe might be a detective in that other Poe's "Purloined Letter."

Billy doesn't expect Poe's presence any more than Poe expects his. "¿Quién es?" as a query, hovers between the two men, the vocalization of a mutual nonrecognition. The uncanniness of standing face-to-face, unknowingly, with the man for whom one had been searching all along (and conversely, the man from whom one should have been hiding) differently describes Spicer's cultivation of a poetics suspended between ekphrasis and antiekphrasis, between loneliness and intimacy, and in turn between particularity and infinite possibility. Spicer's *Billy The Kid* circles the adversarial moment, suspends it, but never delivers the actual shooting, the money-shot of Billy's myth. And as a serial poem, suspension itself becomes a serial venture, thirteen (or in Spicer's case, ten) ways of not looking at a blackguard. The sorts of confrontation Spicer's poem escapes differ from the forestalled confrontation, say, between Orpheus and Eurydice. When Orpheus turns to Eurydice, she is lost to him, forever. Poe (or, say, Spicer) can look Billy right in the face without realizing it. Were recognition possible, it would not portend Billy's vanishing; rather, Billy and Spicer seeing who could draw a gun faster. At its starkest, *Billy The Kid* rewrites Spicer's Orpheus-fascination as a duel. At its most generous, *Billy The Kid* rewrites intimacy as existing somewhere between Spicer's "I love you," Billy's "¿Quién es?" and Rimbaud's "Je est un autre."

The experience of a serial poem, Spicer suggests, is "as if you go into a room, a dark room. A light is turned on for a minute, and then it's turned off again and you go into a different room where a light is turned on and turned off."[58] To imagine Maxwell's bedroom as one section of a serial poem is likewise to imagine the light, turned on and off, as the terrible light of Garrett's own six-shooter:

> *¿Quién es?* [Billy] demanded sharply.
>
> Dropping over sideways from the chair toward the floor in a tricky, dodging movement, Garrett answered the question with a shot. A flare of lurid flame lighted up the darkness for an instant, the room shook

> with a sudden crashing explosion, and Billy the Kid fell dead with a bullet through his heart.[59]

In the final analysis, Poe's and Burns's accounts resonate less with Spicer's strange sequence than with the terrible claustrophobia of "For Billy." The hell of there being no other room after Maxwell's bedroom inscribes the outlaw as emphatically trapped (and poetically speaking, nonserial).[60] The face-to-faceness of Poe's narrative, facial recognition notwithstanding, suggests the intersection of Billy and Orpheus myths. To be face to face, for Billy and Orpheus both, is to be in trouble (but also, for the new intimacies Spicer imagines, nearly gratuitous). *Billy The Kid* flirts with this facial catastrophe asymptotically.

Persons without Faces

Like Billy's death, Billy's face is potentially immanent in Spicer's serial poem without being so. The first section ends with the face suspended in subjunctive mode: "The poem. In all that distance who could recognize his face." A rhetorical question in the form of a statement, the lines seem at once to force Billy's face to the poem's surface and locate that surface somewhere else altogether.[61] Billy is Orpheus and Eurydice at once. Billy's face returns at the end of the poem's sixth section, with similarly violent abruptness:

> The gun
> A false clue
>   Nothing can kill
> Anybody.
> Not a poem or a fat penis. Bang.
> Bang, bang. A false
> Clue.
> Nor immortality either (though why immortality should occur to me
>   with somebody who was as mortal as Billy The Kid or his gun
>   which is now rusted in some rubbish heap or shined up properly
>   in some New York museum) A
>   False clue
> Nothing
> Can kill anybody. Your gun, Billy,
> And your fresh
> Face. (81)

The section's logic is admittedly difficult to follow. The gun seems a false clue to the extent that it looks like a murder weapon but is not. Is it not a murder weapon because, as in section II, "his gun / does not shoot real bullets?" Is it presumptuous to equate "his gun" with "the gun" with which the sixth section begins? Is this latter gun, for that matter, the same as Billy's gun, at section's end? The difference between "the gun" and "his gun" potentially involves questions of action itself: are we discussing the gun that doesn't kill Billy, or the gun with which Billy doesn't kill? (Billy is Orpheus and Eurydice at once—hence the volatility of an elegy for a killer, a person on both sides of death.) While the section's various guns constellate around the poem's sustained examination of falseness/fakery, the face at section's end is neither false nor fake nor even real, but fresh. Freshness implies the sassy attitude of an outlaw, but also (and not necessarily incommensurately) a vivacity in distinction to the gun, which, if real, "is now rusted in some rubbish heap or shined up properly in some New York museum." The face emerges as a correlative to Billy's gun, but in an entirely different register. A different register, even, than that earlier "fat penis." Nothing can kill a fat penis, or nothing, including "a poem or a fat penis" can kill anybody. Either way, the fat penis seems assimilable to the poem's syntax, if in simultaneously opposite ways. The "fresh face," by contrast, seems less an extension of the logic delineated than the surfacing of an object without grammar. The freshness of Billy's face, in the end, is the freshness of a coat of paint. The freshness of something newly produced, if at all: uncannily, in the 1959 publication of *Billy The Kid,* by Spicer's own Enkidu Surrogate Press, the word "face" is missing altogether:

> Nothing
> Can kill anybody. Your gun, Billy,
> And your fresh[62]

The section ends with an ostensible error that actually performs the ambition of the poem as hideout. Where is that face, and what exists in its place? Through the thin, now-yellowed pages, where "face" should be, one can discern (almost too perfectly aligned to be accidental) the "pain" of section IV's "I will tell you about his pain," printed on the previous sheet of paper. Billy's pain haunts the page, has an afterlife—

in the thinness of paper, beyond its particular section. The word literally echoes from one poem to the next, as though typographically instantiating Spicer's own serial ambitions. The mysterious disappearance of the manuscript's "face," on the other hand, introduces a poetry that is positively anti-Orphic (without faces, there is no threat of loss, at least not as set under the terms of Eurydice). In the place of an Orphic machine (incessantly losing and retrieving the loved one from ghostliness), we have the possibility of a sort of Warhol silkscreen — the face of Billy freshly applied and reapplied to canvas, with varying intensity, sometimes (not harrowingly, but exhilaratingly) not there at all.

Screening Rooms: Spicer, Penn, Warhol

> Billy the Kid's smile was almost as famous as his trigger finger. He smiled in victory, he smiled in defeat. His cool, daredevil smile was a part of him. He smiled still in the shadow of the gallows. With death closing in, his smile was as light-hearted and boyish as in his days of freedom. . . . He seemed less a man about to die than a youth anticipating happy years.[63]

Arthur Penn's film, *Left-Handed Gun* proffers Billy the Kid as both self-serializing and impervious to the depersonalization to which end seriality, as a theoretical practice, usually is deployed. Whereas Poe fixates on the damning finitude of Maxwell's bedroom, Penn fixates on a room preceding that final showdown, a ramshackle hut in a town auspiciously called Stinking Springs. Billy and two comrades, Charlie Bowdre and Tom Folliard, have ridden there to hide out from Pat Garrett. The house, as Walter Noble Burns writes, "had no windows and only one door; within was profound stillness" (210). In Penn's version, however, the Stinking Springs hideout isn't *so* profoundly still, but festooned with Billy's own *Wanted* posters. The hideout's walls, placarded as a teenager's, suggest Billy as his own number-one fan.

Stinking Springs' proliferation of *Wanted* posters — in tandem with the outlaw those posters *want* — demonstrates the film's concern with Billy's seriality as a specifically textual issue. The myriad posters want Billy dead, and the French theory underwriting (if not undermining) most early Spicer criticism — not to mention the more practical logic of small-town law — might argue that the posters not only want that death, but portend it; under ordinary circumstances, wouldn't a signifier rule out the simultaneous presence of its signified? More to the point, wouldn't an outlaw stay as far from his own *Wanted* posters as possible? In Penn's film, however, Billy's lavishly tacked hideout implies not just the perverse coexistence of signifiers (a situation reprised by Spicer in Kid's fraternizing with Alias) but a relationship between them borne out of a self-love far stranger (and funnier, and more dangerous) than narcissism.

Although Billy's *Wanted* posters lack what has become the form's canonical mug-shot (cameras exist in Penn's film, but only [and by contrast, ironically?] to document Pat Garrett's wedding), there are indubitable parallels between Billy's den of auto-aggrandizements and Andy Warhol's contribution to the 1964 World's Fair, *Thirteen Most Wanted Men.* And, furthermore, to Warhol's 1963 installation of *Double Elvis,* whose Los Angeles installation figures a (left-handed) gun-slinging Elvis not just as a couple, "but [as] a serial, seemingly unlimited progression of Presley clones."[64] Richard Meyer's account of Warhol's serializing of dangerous men provides a useful optic through which to read Billy's Stinking Springs hut. Meyer, however, moves too quickly from investigation of an explicitly gay practice of serialization to the phenomena of 1970s gay macho clones:

> The clone's performance of butch as a kind of self-conscious dress-up, even a form of drag, distinguishes his brand of machismo from its more earnest and tyrannical straight counterpart. We need only to recall that most celebrated example of the clone aesthetic, the Village People, to confirm that gay masculinism of the late 1970s was frequently in dialogue with its own deconstruction.[65]

Serialization, in the context of Penn (and even more to the point, in Spicer), doesn't move toward deconstruction, but a more complicated ontological reconstruction. Seriality, as it relates to Billy the Kid, doesn't dissolve singularity for the sake of a community: contra Meyer's claim (echoing that earlier Spicer letter to Blaser) that "the dream of the clone was that gay sex would be constituted collectively rather than monogamously, serially rather than singularly."[66] It's not that a multiplication of Billies, like Warhol's multiplication of Elvises, voids the integrity of an original Billy, but that Billy's disseminative magic is inimitable.

Multiplicity constitutes precisely Billy's claim to uniqueness: in Spicer, and in Penn, and in those earlier Buster Crabbe films.

The spectacle of Stinking Springs reprises an earlier sequence in the film that plays out the semiotic snafu those *Wanted* posters elude, namely, Billy's uncanny ability to coincide with a textual system that by most accounts would endanger if not foreclose him. Billy, early in the film, is thought erroneously to have died in a house-fire. When Billy's sidekicks visit the bed where Billy is recuperating from burns, they deliver a mock eulogy, and lay on his coverletted chest, like flowers on a grave, a horny toad. How not to imagine Spicer as the horny toad on the pretend-post-mortem chest of Billy, as played by a gorgeous and chiseled Paul Newman, as though in the expert chisel of those cheekbones, Billy's template were itself some funeral sculpture.

Billy's death notice circulates as quickly as those eventual *Wanted* posters, culminating in the sublime moment of Billy holding his own death notice in his hand. Within Penn's film, the death notice constitutes the exclusive domain of a certain Southern dandy journalist named Moultrie, played (appropriately enough) by Hurd Hatfield, star of the 1945 *Picture of Dorian Gray*. Moultrie, from what I can glean, is Vidal's invention and, structurally, does not participate in events so much as bears witness to them. After Billy shoots his first two targeted men, Moultrie scrutinizes the bodies, not with any intelligible affect beyond the intensity of a gourmand sniffing something subtle. Moultrie returns to scrutinize aforementioned burnt house. And finally, Moultrie appears to bear witness to Billy's own, actual death. Only this time does Moultrie respond affectively, holding a handkerchief to his mouth in dainty horror. Moultrie, as voyeur to the Western within the Western, acts within the film as a parergon, separate from the homoerotic scenes he frames—Charlie kicking his legs over the side of a tub, as Billy (putatively oblivious to the nudity) plots a set of gunnings. Early in Penn's film, just after aforementioned house fire, Moultrie searches out Billy at a party, offering him a newspaper clipping that might, Moultrie speculates, be of some interest. Billy, illiterate but sombreroed, nods his head in Dubya-like mime of reading. Moultrie, with a laugh like Maggie the Cat, informs Billy that the clipping is his death notice.

The death notice likewise makes its way into the final section of Spicer's poem:

Billy The Kid
I love you
Billy The Kid
I back anything you say
And there was the desert
And the mouth of the river
Billy The Kid
(In spite of your death notices)
There is honey in the groin
Billy (83)

"I love you, Billy," despite your outliving yourself,[67] despite your "you" being diffuse, if locatable at all, though for that diffuseness no less particular to Billy, hence the incantatory pulsiveness of Billy's name, thrice repeated in full. Billy is both as vast as the desert, and seductively specific as honey in the groin of a tree — both the vagaries of a map, and the map's treasure-X, all at once. Whatever Billy says, the speaker, in love, will back. Backing, here, itself becomes a kind of duplication. Whatever you say, I will say in echo. Backing also, however, refuses to distinguish along the lines of true or false, real or fictive. The speaker doesn't specify if he backs Billy because what Billy says is true, or because Billy says it. In Spicer's context, "anything you say" amounts to love at its most aberrantly unconditional. Despite the death notices, so long as you say anything (and in the blur of 1940s and 1950s Billy movies, Billy invariably says a lot), I love you and you alone, even as your proliferations cozen me into loving anyone like you — this latter, the fantasy of Meyer and Bersani, of the Turkish bathhouse and of cruising, fantasies of seriality against which Spicer, here, has admonished. *Billy The Kid* begins, with the radio, as a potential elegy, and ends as a paean to an unfamiliarly singular serial love not undone by, but drawn from the multiplicities emerging from personality, and vice versa.

Chapter Four

ELIZABETH BISHOP'S CRANE, AND THE GOOD-ENOUGH POEM

> *To this universal address that faith, or pure subjectivation, does not constitute on its own Paul gives the name "love," agape—translated for a long time as "charity," a term that no longer means much to us.*
>
> *Its principle is this: when the subject as thought accords with the grace of the event—this is subjectivation (faith, conviction)—he, who was dead, returns to the place of life.*
>
> —Alain Badiou, *Saint Paul* (88)

Billy The Kid's penultimate declaration, "I love you, Billy," restates an amorous logic that governs Spicer's serial poem more generally: amorous logic, opposed to erotic logic, insofar as *Billy The Kid* idiosyncratically aspires to save Billy from a death that both history and the poem's own opening would render unavoidable if not already executed. I mean to distinguish love's reparative, resuscitative energies from the oppositely and variously destructive, undoing energies of desire. Such distinctions—the potentially salutary distances between love and desire, love and sex, the romantic and the more literally amorous—have proved difficult, within queer theory, to maintain. As often, queer theory has depended on the elisiveness between love and desire. This elision, Diana Fuss argues, originates in Freudian psychoanalysis's own elision of the two:

> In fact, love appears to issue from the same "energy" source as sexual desire, and indeed, Freud concludes, they are wholly coincident: "the 'Eros' of the philosopher Plato coincides exactly with the love-force, the libido of psychoanalysis." To clinch the point, he notes that "the Greek word 'Eros' . . . is in the end nothing more than a translation of our German word *Liebe* [love]."[1]

Desire's colonization of love is in part an effect of love's own comparably under-elaborated theoretical vocabulary. Desire's particular narratives—under the name if not of desire then of eros or *jouissance*—jostle and smother whatever love, taken independently, might itself contribute to both queer theory and theory more broadly understood.

As at this point should be unsurprising, *Queer Optimism* insists that love speak for itself, that love's resuscitative faculties not be subordinated to, eclipsed by, or converted to desire's own empire of danger, thrill, and threat. This final chapter looks to the poetry of Elizabeth Bishop for its extraordinarily meticulous investigation and articulation of love. That Bishop's investigation and articulation of anything could be characterized as extraordinarily meticulous seems nearly to go without saying. That Bishop's passionate and complicated long-term relationship with Lota de Macedo Soares would inform Bishop's poetic articulations of queer love likewise seems noncontroversial.[2] The subject of my chapter, however, averredly is not Bishop's relationship with Soares, nor those poems illuminated by it. My chapter's subject is the queer love mobilized in Bishop's poetry for Hart Crane.

The presence in Bishop's poetry of Crane has gone nearly unremarked, and those critical instances that have brought the two poets together as often juxtapose the two for the sake of differently describing their removal from each other.[3] Given how tenuously (and minimally) Crane's relation to Bishop thus far has been conceived, Crane's inseparability within Bishop's poetry from the lyrical work of love may well strike readers of either poet as news. That Bishop and Crane could exist at so estranged a critical remove itself strains against the ways Bishop's poetry and life so often are read relationally—alongside the poetry and life of Robert Lowell and, even more so, the poetry and life of Marianne Moore.[4] Moore's mothering and Lowell's wooing mark two opposed emotional regions from which Bishop (and Bishop's poetry) pendulates. But what of Crane? Crane's 1932 suicide would perhaps straightforwardly account for the absence of Crane in Bishop biographies. If Crane's death, however, removes him from a circle of poets (including Bishop) of which he might have been a part, his death wouldn't necessarily preclude Crane (biographically, critically) as poetic influence. George Herbert's being dead, for instance, hardly rules out criticism addressing Bishop's poetic attachment to Herbert.[5] Contra Herbert, Crane's possible meaning to both Bishop and Bishop's poetry has been jeopardized by how nearly Crane might have been part of Bishop's circle, by the extent to which Crane was lost to history, for Bishop, only aleatorily.[6]

Crane's hinterland — lost to history but with such ravishing recentness as to lack the intelligibility of the historical, per se — recalls the hinterland of Billy the Kid, simultaneously lost and not lost in Spicer's poetry. Billy's inventive posthumousness at very least acquires from queer theory some form of traction: that Spicer is a gay poet and Billy a cowboy renders Spicer's poem if not absolutely congenial to models of queer relationality then no less productively at odds with them. Queer theory, along only slightly different lines, has afforded all manner of fulcra to the parsings of Bishop's attachments to Marianne Moore.[7] Crane's hinterland, on the contrary, belies the risks and limitations of a queer theory that privileges homoerotics or same-sex desire over queer love. Queer theory, that is, is ill equipped to illuminate the potentially vast field of nonerotic love potentially shared between a gay man (Crane) and a gay woman (Bishop) — let alone such a love, poetically transmuted. Let alone when such a love collects around a gay man suspended between the living and the dead.

Doing justice to Bishop's poetic affiliations with Crane requires a more assiduous vocabulary for understanding Crane's threshold status — between living and dead, empirical and imaginary, the moment of writing and an anterior poetic tradition. No less necessary is as assiduous a vocabulary for queer love unassimilable to queer erotics. The extent to which Bishop criticism (no less than queer theory) has elided love and desire delimits consideration of love within Bishop's poetry as either celebratorily homosexual (between two women) or subversively heterosexual. So depleted a set of critical options leaves critically unaddressable the various forms of love that are not erotically organized. Despite their many keen insights into Bishop's poetry, Mutlu Blasing and Susan McCabe remain exemplary of Bishop critics' nonaccomodation of nonerotic love between a woman and a man, of criticism for which a lesbian poet's relation to such love necessarily would be disparaging; a disparagement, videlicet, that the criticism takes for granted and therefore descriptively repeats.

Blasing argues that Bishop both inhabits and dismantles the patriarchal symbolic order. Bishop's participation in preconstituted forms is less, for Blasing, "a matter of anxiety of influence" than of "entering a traditional narrative framework." Blasing's distinction between a Bloomian model of influence and a Lacanian model of linguistic initiation amounts most saliently to a distinction between a dialectical relationship and the impossibility of such a relationship's specificities, as countermanded by the symbolic order as such.[8] Blasing's dismissal of Bloom is blithe, as most recent dismissals of Bloom are blithe. Nonetheless, while I partly agree with Blasing on Bloom's irrelevance in regard to Bishop's connection to Crane, I agree on substantially different grounds.

Blasing implies that Bloom is wrong because he localizes a poetic interrelation that more precisely (symbolically speaking) is generic. I, on the other hand, think Bloom is wrong in so attenuating how localized poetic interrelation might be described: "a battle between strong equals, father and son as mighty opposites, Laius and Oedipus at the crossroads."[9] "Only this," pronounces Bloom, "is my subject here."[10] Bloom's theorization of influence seems to have little to say about the poetic relationship between Crane and Bishop: not only because Bishop is a woman, but because Bishop is so nearly Crane's contemporary. Blasing, however, doesn't correct Bloom so much as reject him altogether, and in so doing, inadvertently recapitulates a version of the much-maligned heteronormativity underwriting Bloom's Oedipal model. This inadvertent repetition of the heteronormative counterintuitively occurs in the insistence with which Blasing construes Bishop's relation to patriarchal convention as ironic. The extent, that is, to which any such system can be infiltrated requires that the system be maintained (such that ironic insinuation be at least minimally perceptible). Heterosexuality, no less than patriarchy, is thus resuscitated by Blasing's sense of irony as much as it is injured.

Writing outside of Blasing's Lacanian framework, Susan McCabe similarly claims that Bishop "both parodies traditional heterosexual relationships and refigures eroticism in her language."[11] Just a few pages following, McCabe continues: "[Bishop] often inserts herself into the male tradition, camouflaging her identity and exchanging hats, to show its limitations and liabilities for the woman practitioner."[12] Bishop ventriloquizes the discourse of heterosexual love (so McCabe's argument goes), just as she ventriloquizes "the male tradition." As evidence of the former, McCabe cites "While Someone Telephones," the third section of a four-part poem that Bishop titles, simply, "Four Poems":

> Wasted, wasted minutes that couldn't be worse,
> minutes of barbaric condescension.
> —Stare out the bathroom window at the fir-trees,
> at their dark needles, accretions to no purpose
> woodenly crystallized, and where two fireflies
> are only lost.
> Hear nothing but a train that goes by, must go by, like tension:
> *nothing*. And wait:
> maybe even now these minutes' host
> emerges, some relaxed uncondescending stranger,
> the heart's release.
> And while the fireflies
> are failing to illuminate these nightmare trees
> might they not be his green gay eyes. (78)

As McCabe would have it, this poem either parodies (heterosexual) desire or refigures (lesbian) desire, depending on how one reads the final line's "his." McCabe suggests that were one to substitute "her" for "his"—imagine, that is, the fireflies as some unspecified woman's green eyes—then the poem could count as a sincere love poem. Otherwise, for McCabe, the poem's "he" designates a mask "donned to mock heterosexual romance."[13] The presumed incompatibility between the poem's "he" and Bishop's own purported homosexuality operates on an a priori reduction of the possible affective energies between persons of opposite sexes. To recapitulate: to imagine a bond between the poem's (presumably) lesbian speaker and its (presumably heterosexual, presumably patriarchally inscribed) male object that isn't ironic jeopardizes the irrefutability of the speaker's homosexuality (which is to say, subversive position within the male symbolic). To rule out that Bishop's is a love poem for a gay man is to rule out the countless lover's discourses that aren't reductively sexual (regardless of orientations around which that sexuality is seen to circulate).[14]

Bloom's attachment to Oedipus and Laius as paradigmatic does not in and of itself illuminate how one might think about Bishop alongside Crane. As a heuristic model, however, Bloom's account of influence nonetheless gestures toward the potential productivity of imagining correlatives for any given authors at hand. For Bloom, characters from Greek tragedy personalize a relationship between poets that would otherwise remain, strictly speaking, historical. That is, poets separated by centuries (for instance, Milton and Wordsworth) are imagined as familial; and by extension, the poems of such poets speak to each other, misrecognize and rewrite each other, with an intensity correlative to that between father and son. Poetry evidences a site, for Bloom, not of personal abdication (as it would for T. S. Eliot), but rather personal intensification; poetry becomes the stage on which familially unrelated persons enact the aggressions, envies, affections, or obligations of a family. To make such an observation is tantamount to imagining (despite Bloom's putative intentions otherwise) poetry as a destabilization of the categorically nuclear family as such. Poetry, along Bloomian lines, posits a queer family in which the roles of parents or children aren't delegated by bloodline, but by the very vicissitudes that make phantasmatic relations between two poets seem familial in the first place.

There are, of course, plenty of poets whose relation to each other does not suggest the patrifilial, let alone anything familial at all. Having said that, however, what if Bishop and Crane were imagined in the context of some archetypal queer family? What if, for instance, Bishop and Crane related to each other not as female within a male symbolic matrix, or lesbian mocking the norms of heterosexual desire, but as brother and sister? Which is to say, for instance, as Antigone and Polyneices? And what if the incest taboo that haunts most critical retellings of the Antigone story[15] were de facto ruled out by the simple fact that in this retelling, both brother and sister are gay?

Queer Love

Kaja Silverman has perhaps come closest to delineating the conditions if not of a queer love then a psychoanalytically informed love from which queer love might learn, from which we, in turn, might learn to distinguish it from no less psychoanalytically informed models of queer desire by which it too often is displaced. Published a year after Fuss's 1995 *Identification Papers*, Silverman's *Threshold of the Visible World* calls for an articulation of love qua love, against Fuss's valuation of the nondifference between Platonic Eros and Freudian *Liebe*:

> Sexuality, desire, and aggressivity have all been much discussed, both within psychoanalysis proper, and within the many debates which have drawn upon it in recent years. But love has not figured prominently within either context. It has always seemed to lack respectability, as an object of intellectual inquiry — to represent the quintessence of kitsch.[16]

Love's "lack [of] respectability, as an object of intellectual inquiry," its consignation to the flea market of kitsch, indubitably and not coincidentally resonates with my own account of optimism's dustbin. In this sense, Silverman's project represents an important precursor to my own in its attempt to confer on love an intellectual viability against past decades' derogations of it. Silverman's work tries to rescue love—as Spicer tries to rescue Billy, as Bishop (as I shall argue) tries to rescue Crane.

The psychoanalytic chassis of Silverman's inquiry into love interestingly most illuminates Bishop's queer love — and for that matter, queer optimism — in those moments where psychoanalysis itself falls short. Uncannily (but again, not coincidentally), Silverman's account of Freudian love seems least responsive to queer love and queer optimism in its rigorous attachment to idealization. "All that emerged with absolute clarity from the pages of Freud's writings," Silverman writes, "was that love is intimately bound up with the function of idealization."[17] Inevitably, idealization (vis-à-vis Silverman) differs (at least in terms of technology) from idealization in the vernacular. Even within psychoanalysis's argot, however, I am struck by idealization's imbrication with philosophies of optimism. To return to optimism's most clipped cliché (a "quintessence of kitsch" in its own right), what is more expansively idealizing (psychoanalytically or vernacularly) than the mandate of Voltaire's Pangloss, "all things for the best in the best of all possible worlds"?

Following Freud, Silverman doesn't seek to dislodge love from idealization. On the contrary, Silverman insists that "idealization ... is the precondition for every loving access to the other, whether identificatory or erotic."[18] Silverman's theoretical resuscitation of love depends on a resuscitation of idealization, in terms equivalent to Freud's own. This is to say that Silverman's resuscitation of idealization seeks to revitalize idealization without conceptually altering the ways idealization itself is understood. *Queer Optimism,* in contrast, argues not for the revitalization of optimism (or ideality) as we know it, but of optimism as we do not.

Silverman's study posits a love triangle whose vertices, besides love itself, are idealization and identification. "Idealization," Silverman suggests, "is the single most powerful inducement for identification."[19] We might well ask to what extent idealization itself pertains to the queer love poetically enacted between Bishop and Crane. (We shall turn to the matter of identification anon.) Beyond the poems to which this chapter turns, Bishop's regard for Crane is most lucidly gleaned from letters Bishop wrote in 1934 to Donald Stanford. The correspondence between Bishop and Stanford (a poet and Harvard graduate student) was suggested to Stanford by Yvor Winters.[20] Winters, one of Crane's first admirers, himself engaged in an important and often intellectually thrilling epistolary correspondence with Crane, from 1926 to 1930.[21] And just months after Crane's suicide, Winters spurs this correspondence between Bishop and Stanford. Crane's appearance in Bishop's letters only partly is explicable by Crane's recent and sensationalized death.

While the death's recentness might account for Crane's epistolary presence, it cannot account for the particular manner in which Crane epistolarily appears. While Stanford's side of the correspondence (neither included in nor located by Giroux's edited volume of Bishop letters) remains to be seen, it seems plausible that Bishop's own references to Crane were solicited by Stanford himself, who, as Winters's protégé, surely figured in the margins of a posthumous Crane circle. Such a possibility might explain Crane's appearance in Bishop's letters, though it hardly accounts for the complicated attachment for Crane that these appearances signal.

But is this attachment one of idealization? In a letter to Stanford dated March 5, 1934, Bishop writes of Crane in terms that approach idealization, only in the next breath to withdraw from it:

> You know I am fairly well-read! I have studied *The Bridge* rather carefully, and I have also read [Robert] Bridges and Shakespeare. I dislike [Hart] Crane's romanticism.[22]

Even as Bishop communicates dislike for Crane's romanticism, this dislike doesn't preclude her inclusion of Crane in a literary triad including Shakespeare.[23] Studying *The Bridge,* Crane's final book of poems, is exemplary for Bishop of being well-read. How to account for Crane's seeming simultaneously paradigmatic and insufficient? Lest one think Bishop's ambivalent appraisal of Crane is particular to a single letter, this ambivalence, in nearly identical terms, returns in another letter from Bishop to Stanford, written six months later:

> I am reading, reading all the time now, but rather illogically, I guess. I went through *The Bridge* all very carefully again, and like it less.[24]

Bishop "guess[es]" that her reading is illogical, even as the logic of her reading replicates that adduced in the earlier March letter. Bishop, again, invokes Crane's *The Bridge* as paradigm *and* as insufficient. This is to distinguish Bishop's assessment from usual critical accounts of *The Bridge* as paradigmatically insufficient: in the words of Edward Brunner, a splendid failure. Or as Yvor Winters writes in an excoriating review of *The Bridge* — a review, needless to say, that marked the end of Crane's and Winter's friendship — "the flaws in Mr. Crane's genius [were] so great as to partake . . . almost of a public catastrophe."[25]

Bishop's Hiccup

Despite her resistance to *The Bridge,* Bishop at very least did not indict it as public catastrophe, even as public catastrophe might well describe, for nearly anyone in the world of 1930s poetry, Crane's ship-deck suicide. Bracketing Brian Reed's glib claim that Crane "is currently 'the' gay white male American modernist poet,"[26] the devastating reception of Crane's final book, his humiliating, destructive, and self-destructive alcoholic careens, his terrifying last hours aboard the ship *Orizaba* hardly seem to recommend Crane as object of idealization.[27] And if not a viable object of idealization, then how to conceive of Crane as object of identification? Silverman insists that "idealization is something we cannot do without because under the right circumstances it facilitates not so much rivalrous as *loving* identifications — because it alone makes possible a genuine *relation* to the other."[28] Love, let alone loving identification, surely differs from Bishop's symptomatic characterization of Crane's writing as exemplary. Bishop's queer love for (or with an ear to the genitive's double-jointedness, of) Crane is present not in these letters to Stanford, but in Bishop's poetry. The letters' negotiations of idealization and identification nonetheless importantly contextualize the queer love at stake in this chapter's study and help to clarify exactly how such love differs from that examined by Silverman, one of few queer theorists to have taken love seriously as "object of intellectual inquiry."

(One needn't be trained in psychoanalysis to realize the myriad forms of identification that are not loving). But what of Silverman's related claim that idealization "alone makes possible a genuine *relation* to the other"? What is intended in the italicization of "relation," as opposed to "genuine"? The question of what counts as a genuine relationship recalls Butler's consideration of what feels like (and is acknowledged as) true or not true love, and loss. I return to Silverman's rigid conjoining of idealization and identification because identification between Bishop and Crane is in fact detectable in Bishop's letters, although it is an identification pointedly removed from any idealizational directive.

In the March 5 letter already cited, just a paragraph before her professed dislike for Crane's romanticism, Bishop (Romantically) ruminates on the "sudden sensation" of being inside another person's body:

> Have you ever noticed that you can often learn more about other people — more about how they feel, how it would feel to be them — by hearing them cough or make one of the innumerable inner noises, than by watching them for hours? Sometimes if another person hiccups, particularly if you haven't been paying attention to him, why you get a sudden sensation as if you were inside him — you know how he feels in the little aspects he never mentions, aspects which are, really, indescribable to another person and must be realized by that kind of intuition. Do you know what I am driving at? Well if you can follow those rather hazy sentences — that's what I quite often want to get into poetry . . . [ellipses in original letter, as quoted by Giroux].
>
> You know I really am fairly well-read! I have studied *The Bridge* rather carefully.[29]

Bishop's "rather hazy sentences" suggest an account of identification substantially different from Silverman's. Following Bishop, "how it would feel to be" another person arises not out of idealization of that person (or out of some alternate affective or sympathetic channel). Rather, "how it would feel to be" someone else occurs in hearing that person cough, in the interruptive moment of a hiccup. What might begin as "one of those innumerable inner noises" surfaces in a cough, a hiccup—sudden and banal interruptions of that person's bodily unity. For Bishop, to find one's self most aligned with another person ("as if you were inside him") involves a mode of identification not just different from Silverman's, but within Silverman's framework conceptually unimaginable. Invoking Lacan's mirror stage, Silverman writes that "[w]hereas the impossibility of approximating an ideal image is apprehended by the subject through the fantasy of bodily disintegration, the successful imaginary alignment with an image evokes values like 'wholeness' and 'unity.'"[30] The incompatibility of Bishop's and Silverman's respective accounts of identification largely arises in Silverman's Lacanian commitment to the scopic perception of bodies: hence Silverman's titular insistence on a *visual* world's threshold, hence the photographs and films that comprise her book's solely visual archive. A propos the Lacanian mirror stage, a subject does not approximate an ideal person, but an ideal image (of a person). The idealizational primal scene of the mirror—an infant staring at his own reflection—depends not only on unity, but specifically visual unity: the sort of unity that a cough or hiccup would interrupt.

Bishop, in this March letter to Stanford, falls into the hiccup—needs a hiccup as much as a hiccup might jeopardize Silverman's opposite account. On a visual level, a hiccup disrupts a person's unity (imagine the frustration of a portraitist attempting to paint a person in hiccup-fits), but auditorily makes that person intensely, newly present; present enough to "know how he feels in the little aspects he never mentions." Bishop, that is, displaces the psychical and epistemological force of the visual with that of the auditory; one could watch someone "for hours" and still feel less attached to that person than in the jarring, slightly silly, spastic moment of a hiccup.

Such bodily disruptions, originating as "inner noises" but perceptible as external ones, imply that in the cough or hiccup interiority itself might be rendered external: that response to something as seemingly ordinary as a hiccup might somehow make interiority (rendered audible) differently accessible. As Bishop makes explicit, "that's what I quite often want to get into poetry." Bishop's conjuring of interiors and exteriors reprises the language, already addressed, in Butler's account of melancholy. Immediately preceding her mention of Hart Crane, however, Bishop's hiccup — in the context of Crane — reverses melancholy's architecture. Whereas the person loved and lost is internalized by the person living — that is, the melancholy person as the one who psychically incorporates someone else — Bishop, living, imagines herself as incorporatable and incorporated.

In the aforementioned March 5th letter, Bishop proffers a fantasy of being incorporated rather than incorporating (even as the former would then be reabsorbed "into" poetry). This process occurs under explicitly nonvisual conditions. In the aforementioned September letter — in which Bishop professes to have gone "through *The Bridge* all very carefully again, and [to] like it less" — Bishop does in fact invoke the realm of the visual in relation to identification, although Bishop's version of ocularly mediated identification departs from Silverman's as much as Bishop's earlier subordination of "watching" to "hearing." In the March letter, Bishop's account of "the innumerable inner noises" occurs just one paragraph before mention of Crane. In the later September letter, the subject of identification arises in the same paragraph as the subject of Crane. Bishop does not manifestly note the possibility of identifying with Crane, albeit the proximity of the two thoughts — the seamlessness with which one thought moves into the next — argues for the possibility (if not likelihood) of the two thoughts in fact being one:

> I went through *The Bridge* all very carefully again, and like it less — particularly with the addition of his other poems which I had not read. I also rather disliked the appeal to Mr. [Otto] Kahn. My former roommate and her mother [the Millers] are taking an apartment way downtown right beside Brooklyn Bridge, so that they can see it and another bridge and all the traffic on the river. It's a wonderful view. I go walking across it every now and then.[31]

Crane himself, during his romance with Emil Opffer, lived in the shadow of Brooklyn Bridge. As Crane writes to his mother, Grace, in 1924, "Just imagine looking out your window directly on the East River with nothing intervening between your view of the Statue of Liberty, way down the harbour, and the marvelous beauty of Brooklyn Bridge close above you on the right."[32] The view Crane exhorts his mother to imagine is the very one Bishop herself enjoys ("It's a wonderful view," or in Crane's words, a view "never to be forgotten").

Arguably analogous to her earlier inversion of melancholic structure, Bishop's identificatory capaciousness breaks from a subject's unilateral perception of an other, to accommodate (if not rely on) the phenomenon of seeing what another sees. Bishop's admiration of "the view" articulates identification as a parallax, whereby the bridge (and the Cranian lyric energies from which the bridge is inextricable) might psychically, if not literally, serve as bridge between the two poets. Unlike Lacan's model of identification, in which object of identification is to be seen, Bishop's account of the bridge insists that he with whom she identifies sees — has seen — no less than she. Freed from the mirror, Bishop's identificatory affiliation with Crane likewise is freed from the coercions of idealization.

A mirror, or a mirror-in-pieces? A mirror, or a bridge? Silverman, following Lacan, asserts that "the fantasy of bodily disintegration" underwrites "the impossibility of approximating an ideal image," an approximation that would otherwise facilitate identification, make possible "a genuine relation to the other." What if love, contra Silverman and the psychoanalysts from which her work extends, was not "intimately bound up with the function of idealization?" What if bodily disintegration were the occasion for identification, rather than the grounds for identificatory miscarriage? Bishop raises precisely these questions in a letter to her friend, Loren MacIver, written fifteen years after her correspondence with Stanford. Raises these questions not in proximity to considerations of Crane, but astonishingly and movingly, explictly in regard to him:

> I'm afraid I'm really disintegrating, just like Hart Crane, only without his gifts to make it all plausible.[33]

This is a form of disintegration that has very little to do with Lacanian disintegration, and a form of identification that has very little to do with Lacanian identification. And yet, Bishop's poetry tenders a response to the experience of disintegrative identification that is absolutely inseparable from the work of love. Leaving Lacan's mirror in pieces — leaving the scopic domain of the specular for differently auditory circuits — the queer love of Bishop's poetry makes good on that first March letter to Stanford: "if you can follow these rather hazy sentences — that's what I quite often want to get into poetry. . . . You know I really am fairly well-read! I have studied *The Bridge* rather carefully." Not only, however, does poetry provide the landscape in which loving identifications are figured. Poetry and its own particular capacities are themselves instrumental in the love these poems articulate.

Putting Love into Action

None of the poems I shall treat present an intimacy between Bishop and Crane so explicit as that cited in Bishop's letter to MacIver. Indeed, were Bishop's ties to Crane more poetically explicit, my argument for these ties might well be gratuitous. That love for Crane, in the Bishop poems that follow, is at best obliquely stated — that these poems might be about Crane or might not — accords with the difficulty of discerning (let alone describing) such love in the first place. Love's absence from critical conversations recalls the mystique that once gathered around homosexual love — *nefandum libidinem*[34] — in the salad days of gay and lesbian literary criticism. "The love that dare not speak its name" incited critical efforts to articulate that love, which more often than not amounted to articulations of gay desire for which love itself was euphemism or misnomer. If gay and lesbian studies (as well as queer theory) sought to give voice to particular loves kept under wraps, the putative vociferousness of these inquiries gives a very false impression that love, as theoretical entity, belongs to queer-theoretical discourse, let alone has a discourse of its own. *Queer Optimism,* following Bishop's lead, seeks to give voice to love that has been spoken for, been the occasion for sundry other speech acts, and yet itself remains unspoken.

At the opening of *Threshold of the Visible World,* Silverman writes, "I realized . . . that those of us writing deconstructively about gender, race, class, and other forms of 'difference,' have made a tragic mistake. We have consistently argued against idealization, that psychic activity at the heart of love, rather than imagining new uses to which it might be put."[35] I mean to suggest that we have consistently argued against love, and the uses to which love might be put. "Chemin de Fer," a poem from Bishop's first book, *North and South* (1946), literally calls for love's being put into action in terms removed from idealization, but entirely cognate with Bishop's earlier articulations of identification routed through auditory interruption:

Alone on the railroad track
  I walked with pounding heart.
The ties were too close together
  or maybe too far apart.

The scenery was impoverished:
  scrub-pine and oak; beyond
its mingled gray-green foliage
  I saw the little pond

where the dirty hermit lives,
  lie like an old tear
holding onto its injuries
  lucidly year after year.

The hermit shot off his shot-gun
  and the tree by his cabin shook.
Over the pond went a ripple.
  The pet hen went chook-chook.

"Love should be put into action!"
  screamed the old hermit.
Across the pond an echo
  tried and tried to confirm it.[36]

As in Bishop's March letter to Stanford, auditory perspicacity outdoes visual spectacle. "The scenery was impoverished," but the poem itself sings: not only in its rhymed quatrains, but in the auditory predilections of the poem's speaker. The poem's speaker is alone, but walks "with pounding heart." The systoles and diastoles of the pounding heart might be counted among a body's "innumerable inner noises," even as the second line's syntax no less suggests that the speaker is alone and not alone. The poem does not — or cannot — quite accede to the alone-ness with which it begins; the poem's subsequent line complicates solitude with a clause that might or might not present "pounding heart" as personification. Does "pounding heart" describe the nervousness of being alone, or the exhilaration of being alone and not alone, through personification's lyric alchemy? Given the poem's intense auditory commitments, the pounding heart, personified, might be heard as "Hart." I'm less interested, however, in arguing for Hart Crane's presence in this particular poem than in delineating how this poem's logic (akin to the previous section's epistolary logic) more generally informs the conditions of nonmelancholic love between two poets at once lost and not lost.

Just as the pounding heart oscillates between the literal and the personificatory, the railroad track oscillates between the literal and what might be called the "transpersonificatory." That is, if the speaker's heart potentially is pounding insofar as her initial perception of alone-ness cannot be sustained without equivocation, this equivocation — alone or not alone, personal or not personal, literal or figurative — recurs in the stanza's closing couplet. "The ties were too close together / or maybe too far apart." How, within the hydraulics of transpersonification, to gauge one's ties to someone else, especially when immanence and estrangement seem in the moment indistinguishable? The speaker's commitment to equivocation is crucial to an understanding of love in "Chemin de Fer," and to my own understanding, in other poems, of Bishop's love for Crane. The latter either is breathtakingly apparent or it is not. The plausibility of both — love's being there or not — is constitutive of queer love, deracinated from desire's comparatively rigid organization of presence and absence. If desire circulates in an economy of *Fort/Das,* queer love's economy operates on the tenuous coexistence of *Fort* and *Das,* the affirmation (rather than resignation or celebration) of undecidability. Too close together or maybe too far apart.

While the little pond of "Chemin de Fer" generically bears affinity to the reflective surface of Narcissus's pool or Lacan's mirror, the pond of Bishop's poem problematizes more than recapitulates either account of specularity. The speaker's having seen the pond quickly cedes to the pond's similetic transformation into an "old tear"; that is, moves from an eye to a tear fallen from some other unspecified eye — fragment of pathetic fallacy without specifiable agent. If anything, the pond is specularly unavailable because already, as it were, self-absorbed. Aestheticizing emotion into landscape, the pond sustains itself as pond through the tenaciousness of its "injuries." To reckon the pond, then, as a mirror, is to reckon a mirror that presents not what stands before it, but the sadnesses and resignations that it has itself already weathered. The pond's lucidity describes not the quality of its surface, but the acuity of recollection. Ocularly, the pond's autonomousness forecloses relationality of any sort. Out of the pond's specular desuetude nonetheless arises an auditory landscape whose figurative generativeness exceeds that of the quicksilver simile that turns pond to tear.

As though exhausted by the pond's ocular faculties (the pond's ocular faculties appraised as exhausted), the poem breaks from the visual in an auditory cascade set off by the shot-guns' blast. The shot-gun's shot—ostensibly fired into the air, conflation of the auditory and extravagant force without end, or force configured as auditory—shakes a nearby tree, incites the hermit's hen into onomatopoeia. The shot sends a ripple "over the pond," translating the latter from reflective surface to crossable passage. This recalibration of pond from something seen to something crossed makes possible the poem's final quatrain. "Love," the hermit screams, "should be put into action!"[37] The scream, in turn, occasions ("across the pond") an echo on the verge of the personificatory. Like the opening stanza's "heart" and "ties," the echo can be taken singly as neither figural nor literal; the echo, as both echo and personification of echo, consummates if not the message then the structure of the hermit's utterance, which serves as both exhorting of action and as action itself.[38]

Literally, the echo implies the inefficacy of the hermit's call: the sad fatuousness of love-in-isolation, in relation to nothing but the hermit (himself in relation to no one else)—or the terrible remove of utterance from action. The echo, however, arises as action *and* utterance.[39] It follows that the hermit (like the poem's speaker) is alone and not alone. The poem's speaker—and more extraordinarily, the mechanics of the poem—extends a form of companionship detectable to the reader, if not the hermit himself. The poem's personification of the echo—as "try[ing] and try[ing] to confirm" the hermit's amorous pronouncement—renders nearly gratuitous an actual person across the pond. If only within the logic of the lyric, the echo amounts to a form of aesthetic personhood in its own right. Even as the echo falls short of absolute auditory reciprocity (conceivably analogous to a mirror's specular reciprocity), of literally confirming the hermit's words, its echoic failure nonetheless figuratively makes good on the hermit's utterance in ways a perfect echo never could. An echo shot back across the pond might produce the confirmation that the scream ostensibly solicits, but would also terminate the dialogue between hermit and echo. It is in the suspension, the trying and trying, that the echo becomes the means of indefinitely perpetual emotion. (This form of sustainable emotion counters the nondialectically sustained injuries of the pond-as-tear.) Endless attempts do not preempt a confirmation of love so much as enable the personified echo to keep company with the hermit longer than it otherwise might.

That the echo tries to confirm the hermit's demand without doing so calls to mind Winnicott's account of "good-enough." In the vernacular, the echo is good enough to the extent that it does the best it can, exempt from the expectations of idealization. This form of "good enough," however, has less to do with the psychoanalysis of Winnicott than with the accommodative slacks of pop-psychology.[40] Winnicott's "good-enough," rather, speaks directly to the oscillative equivocations of "Chemin de Fer" between literal and figurative: "too close together or maybe too far apart."

Winnicott's theorization of "good-enough" arises in observation of what he calls a "good-enough mother":

> The mother's adaptation to the infant's needs, when good enough, gives the infant the *illusion* that there is an external reality that corresponds to the infant's own capacity to create. In other words, there is an overlap between what the mother supplies and what the child might conceive. To the observer, the child perceives what the mother actually presents, but this is not the whole truth. The infant perceives the breast only insofar as a breast could be created just there and then.[41]

The hermit's scream, like an infant's cry, asks for an answer that neither it alone nor "external reality" can deliver. The speaker of "Chemin de Fer" — or again, the creative space of the poem, as such — assumes the responsibilities of Winnicottian mother. The good-enough poem — responsible for the echo's own good-enough figurative capacities — both is and is not an extension of the hermit's needs. The hermit, like the poem's speaker, like the Winnicottian infant, is alone and not alone. If, however, Winnicott's good-enough enables a subject assuagingly to imagine external effects as his own doing, Bishop's good-enough oppositely and no less assuagingly allows the hermit of "Chemin de Fer" to imagine his own labors (a scream) as external effects. It allows the hermit to take an echo's figurative properties as literal. In this way, Bishop extends the Winnicottian notion of personate integrity to include not only a phantasmatically empowered subject, but figuratively animated persons on whom the solitary subject depends.

I have introduced the Winnicottian notion of "good-enough" because it illuminates not only the personificatory work of "Chemin de Fer," but also the figurative operations at hand in those Bishop poems where Crane seems most present. Imagine on one side of the water Hart Crane, by nearly every account already drowned, already dead. Imagine on the other side of the water Elizabeth Bishop, sustaining Crane in a transitional space between solitude and relation, in ways nearly unthinkable beyond the "good-enough" of Bishop's poetry. Bishop's investigation of love, loosed from Freudian mandates of idealization, depends on this good-enough space that not only renders undecidable what is real or imaginary, but asserts that such decidability distorts and damages what it preemptively cleaves. This assertion acquires all the more force in the face of a reality that claims Crane as gone. Bishop's poetics, as psychically innovative as Winnicott's own writing, overrides the reality principle in the name of a love whose manipulation of boundaries renders the fact of Crane's loss if not beside the point then point of departure.

Casabianca: The Burning Boy

The echo of "Chemin de Fer" fails, literally, to reiterate the hermit's call, "Love should be put into action": even as it becomes (along Winnicottian lines) the poem's most vivid instantiation of what love, put into action, might be. With the terms of this poem as context, it is time to turn to "Casabianca," one of Bishop's most enigmatically acute lyric appeals to Crane. "Casabianca," written in 1936 and preceding *North and South's* "Chemin de Fer" by two poems, invokes Crane even on a titular level. *Casa* (house) and *Bianca* (white) loosely translate *White Buildings,* the title of Crane's first book of poems. The conversion of "buildings" into "house" marks a shift from what has been built to what might be inhabited. What is inhabitable, a propos "Casabianca," is Bishop's poem. The inhabitant of "Casabianca" is Crane. Not just any Crane, but Crane in his last suicidal moments aboard the *Orizaba.* The ship-deck, as tensile line between living and dying, figurative and irrevocably literal. The ship-deck, then, as urgent occasion for Winnicottian transformation. Stranger than "Chemin de Fer," which offers a good-enough echo as personified exertion of love, "Casabianca" takes love itself as object of personification. Stranger still, "Casabianca," echo of *White Buildings*, takes this personified love as resuscitation of Crane:

> Love's the boy stood on the burning deck
> trying to recite "The boy stood on
> the burning deck." Love's the son
>   stood stammering elocution
>   while the poor ship in flames went down.
>
> Love's the obstinate boy, the ship,
> even the swimming sailors, who
> would like a schoolroom platform, too,
>   or an excuse to stay
>   on deck. And love's the burning boy. (5)

I shall presently elaborate what it might mean for a poem titled "Casabianca" to stage Crane as "the boy . . . on the burning deck," and to renominate this boy as Love. Before this elaboration, however, it is important to specify why such a reading of "Casabianca" has never been ventured, to specify the interpretations of "Casabianca" that have dominated and dictated the poem's reception. The import of "Casabianca" vis-à-vis Crane, mostly simply, has been critically displaced by the fact that Bishop's poem explicitly depends on an antecedent nineteenth-century poem by Felicia Hemans. Hemans's poem, also titled "Casabianca," takes as its subject the son of a ship captain, Giacomo Jocante Casabianca, who refuses to leave ship-deck, even as the ship is going down in the flames of Napoleonic sea-battle. The son will not abandon his post until his father gives him word, but the father will never give word, because he is already dead in one of the ship-cabins below:

> The boy stood on the burning deck
> Whence all but him had fled;
> The flame that lit the battle's wreck
> Shone round him o'er the dead.
> Yet beautiful and bright he stood,
> As born to rule the storm;
> A creature of heroic blood,
> A proud, though childlike form.
>
> The flames rolled on — he would not go
> Without his father's word;
> That father, faint in death below,
> His voice no longer heard.[42]

The Hemans poem ends as one might expect such calamity to end. The ship is strewn across the sea in fiery smithereens, and the boy, inexorably (if not obviously) dies. "But the noblest thing that perished there / Was that young, faithful heart." The Hemans poem, in the sentimental terms for which it is most readily dispatched, describes the pathos of a boy's unconditional allegiance to a father.

In contrast to Bishop's poem, which posits the scene of calamity without calamity's unfolding, Hemans's poem narrativizes calamity as ineluctable sequence: the ship is burning, the father is already dead, and even if he weren't, his and his son's death seem, in the conflagrations of battle, all but inevitable. Allegiance, even literary allegiance, manifests itself as an anxiety not of influence[43] but of abandonment (the abandonment of the child by his father, the abandoning extravagance at which the child finds himself the center). Hemans's poem, read alongside and against Bishop's, poses influence as the least of the boy's worries. Influence serves, if at all, as a misnomer for the boy's misappraisal of silence as obduration:

> "Speak, father!" once again he cried,
> "If I may yet be gone!"
> And but the booming shots replied,
> And fast the flames rolled on.[44]

While many readers of Hemans reckon her dismissably sentimental, her poem both is sentimental (in its familiar relish of the devoted martyr-child) and about a particular failure of sentimentality. If sentimental poetry is meant to operate through circuits of sympathy, Hemans's poem describes a crisis not only of tragic misunderstanding, but (in the father's death) of outright sympathetic breakdown. Hemans's burning boy figures as paradigmatic sympathetic hero, but also, simultaneously, as the awful victim of sympathy's failure, of belief in communicability where there can be none.

I have offered this reading of Hemans's poem as sympathetic breakdown not because Bishop's own poem repeats the pathos of Hemans's burning boy, but because Bishop's poem structurally revises that breakdown's unavoidability. The deceptively straightforward allusive dependence of Bishop on Hemans has foreclosed the possibility of Bishop's poem as an exploration of contact with poets other than Hemans.

Despite the transliterated ghost in "Casabianca" of *White Buildings*, despite the uncanny similarity between the milieu of "Casabianca" and that of Crane's suicide, "Casabianca" has been critically yoked to a history — that of Hemans, that of the Napoleonic war that Hemans recounts — that is taken for granted. Even as I have argued that the disorienting categorical slipperiness of the historical — the equivocal lines between living and dead, empirical and imagined — is constitutive of Bishop's possible understanding of herself in relation to Crane.

Crane's exclusion from the hermeneutic field of "Casabianca" results from the poem's preemptive imbrication with one particular historical context at the expense of others. No less so, Crane's exclusion from "Casabianca" is a consequence of criticism's inadequate treatment of the poem's theorization of love. Love, in Bishop's "Casabianca," doesn't resemble Hemans's account of patrifilial devotion; nor does the love of "Casabianca" seem in any obvious way bound to queer erotics. Bishop's poem does not describe a love between persons, so much as query love's own structural attributes.

Presuming the literary slightness of Hemans's poem, critics can't help but find irony in Bishop's lifting of Hemans's first line. Thomas Travisano, for instance, notes that "here, love is synonymous with pain and seems to exist in a realm of high rhetoric, where it exacts pointless, self-destructive gestures of devotion."[45] Margaret Dickie, pointedly, repeats Travisano's claim of pointlessness, suggesting Bishop's poem as at best a rebuke of love such as the boy's:

> But in "Casabianca," love is so many things that it is finally nothing. The poem suggests that openly declared love is both banal and pointless by contrast to secret passion. Linked to its precursor poem by Felicia Hemans of the boy in the Napoleonic wars who goes loyally down with the ship along with his captain father, who is unconscious and unable to release the boy from his duty, "Casabianca" takes a very cynical view of love's constancy.[46]

Travisano implies that the love of "Casabianca" is banal to the extent that Hemans's poem is banal. Love's banality, for Travisano, becomes all the more intelligible in contrast to "secret passion," even as Travisano's introduction of passion asserts a normative conception of desire (implicitly, the normative reconditeness of queer desire) extrinsic to the poem's own exquisitely impacted frame. That passion, as such, does not crop up in "Casabianca" surely is not equivalent to passion's lyric presence, in secret or under cover. In raising the specter of passion, Travisano forces the love of "Casabianca" into a hallucinated binary that the poem itself intently avoids. It is not, then, that "Casabianca" takes a "very cynical view of love's constancy," but that Travisano himself sabotages the potential interest of love's constancy in his inability to consider love on its own terms — in his preclusive conversion, for instance, of the poem's pulsive figurations and parataxes ("so many things") into "nothing."

Anne Stevenson, sounding a dismissive note similar to Travisano's, condemns Bishop's boy not for being Hemans's boy, so much as for reciting Hemans's poetry. "The boy standing on the burning deck is on fire with love. He tries to escape into poetry by reciting the childish lines of Mrs Heman's 'The Boy Stood on the Burning Deck,' but the love that has torched the ship is too much for him."[47] Both absorbed and repelled by the maudlin surface of a boy's ingenuous commitment to a sinking ship, Stevenson misses the extent to which Bishop's "love" involves not just some potentially masochistic devotion, but also the vicissitudes of communicability itself.

The scene of Bishop's poem is more vexing than Stevenson allows, whose reading reduces the boy's recitation to a sort of nervous whistling in the dark. It's not that the boy erroneously (if not altogether unsuccessfully) escapes to poetry in the face of disaster — it's not, that is, that poetry, "caught in the conflagration of love, never has a chance."[48] It's not this, first of all, for the simple reason that love, in Bishop's poem, is the terrible phenomenon of a boy reciting poetry in the face of fire. Poetry, in "Casabianca," isn't an escape from love, but love's instantiation. Furthermore, Bishop's poem seems less interested in claiming that love's poetic utterance is banal or childish (Travisano's and Stevenson's estimation of the Hemans poem cannot substitute for Bishop's estimation of the Hemans poem), than that love's poetic utterance is a sort of *mise en abyme*:

> Love's the boy stood on the burning deck
> trying to recite "The boy stood on
> the burning deck."

The first lines of "Casabianca" align love not with the destructive force of fire, but with the subject of an earlier poem (Hemans's) returning in a subsequent poet's poem, to speak that earlier poem's conjuring of him.

The enactment of return of "Casabianca" suggests that love is a form of repetition, but more precisely, a particular form of incomplete or imperfect repetition. The boy, after all, does not actually recite the opening of Hemans's poem; he is trying to recite — not unlike the echo of "Chemin de Fer," which does not return the hermit's scream in toto, but tries to do so. To think of the opening lines of "Casabianca" in terms of attempted echo (the recitation tried without necessarily being successfully reproduced), that which the boy tries to recite is less the first line of Hemans's poem (after all, what love quotes is, in fact, the line from Hemans, without error) than the first line of Bishop's poem. Bracketing the Hemans poem of which the readers of "Casabianca" have made a lynchpin, attempted recitation (versus recitation as such, sans "stammer") most directly adheres to the boy's utterance, "The boy stood on the burning deck," as an (echoically) incomplete reciting of "Love's the boy stood on the burning deck." What love (as opposed to the boy) drops from its recitation is love itself. This recitative jettison has great consequences on the level of rhetoric.

Attempted recitation converts "Love's the boy" into "the boy," decreating personification (by which a boy exists in the poem only figuratively) into literalization (by which the boy himself displaces Love as the poem's subject). Love's omission of itself from its own personificatory scene (from its own recitation) misrecognizes figurative event as literal one (a poem about a boy, analogous to Hemans's boy). This misrecognition proleptically cautions against misrecognitions such as Travisano's or Stevenson's (which likewise, in Travisano's words, exemptively read love as "finally nothing"). I say that "Casabianca" cautions against subsequent eschewals of love, rather than anticipates such eschewals, because Bishop's poem enacts love's own recitative curtailment only to return love to the poem if not with a vengeance (the poem is vindictive no more than it is cynical or banal) then with Love's own "obstinan[ce]."

Following love's drop from the first stanza's quotation (its drop from the poem-within-the-poem), love spins into ever greater figurative frenzy — love's the boy, love's the son, love's the boy, love's the ship, and "even the swimming sailors." As much as Bishop's love might initially have seemed a form of repetition, Bishop's love, beyond this, most saliently is a search for personificatory and metaphorical predicates. Why love would (and should) be conceived along these figurative lines becomes clearer, in recalling the insistently figurative buoyance evidenced in the survival of what I've denominated love's drop. A boy wouldn't survive such a drop (from ship-deck to sea); a boy (even a boy in a poem) necessarily would be susceptible to the effects of disaster in ways personification would not. In refusing to extricate the boy from his nonhuman (nonliteral) status as personification, "Casabianca" saves the boy from the literal constraints of fate (which is to say, of history). Bishop's boy, after all, does not, at poem's end, die. The poem concludes with a reiteration of its own opening, differently attempting a recitation of itself that preserves the boy's figurative status. And love's the burning boy. To hear "Casabianca" as *White Buildings,* to imagine the personificatory boy as Hart Crane, is differently to encounter Bishop's Winnicottian good-enough: simultaneously illuminating and blurring the demarcations of literal and nonliteral, on the threshold—trying to recite, trying to echo—of lyric generousness.

Crossing Lines

While I speak of lyric threshold partly in deference to Silverman's earlier theorization of specular threshold, my understanding of thresholds is as much informed by Winnicott's accounts of transitional space. Winnicott's transitional space operates both synchronically (the space, at any given moment, between persons) and diachronically (a psychical progressing of personal transaction, specifically, of the mother's breast from which an infant slowly will be weaned). I have chosen to describe queer love in terms of threshold rather than transitionality for the sake of distancing the vicissitudes of queer love from diachrony's particular temporal trajectories. The sorts of relationships made possible in Bishop's poetry are held, nondiachronically, in a temporal suspension: not unlike the forms of durability I have examined in Crane's and Dickinson's lyric smiles, or Spicer's serial extensions of Billy beyond singularity's own prescribed temporal arc.

The lyric threshold in which literality and figuration blur differs from earlier theorizations of (Bakhtinian or Turneresque) liminality, insofar as lyric threshold designates the indistinguishability of one term from the other, rather than the limbo between them. Lyric threshold likewise differs from constructivist, performative, or more generally poststructuralist accounts of persons, insofar as the threshold does not privilege the factitious (the fabricated, the simulacral) over the genetic, but instead suggests the equivocal intersection and play between literality and figuration, without the latter's energies undermining those of the former. To differently situate this last distinction, conventional optimism attaches to an ideal (whether phantasmatic or futural), whereas queer optimism attaches to an empirical immanence inseparable from and disoriented by the nonempirical operations of lyric imagination. No less so, queer optimism attaches to a lyric imagination inseparable from and disoriented by the empirical.

If queer theory (following deconstruction) has often taken as given the fictiveness of natural categories, queer optimism asks in part for a reparation of the natural. Queer optimism insists that we need not choose between the natural and its discontents. Rather, it insists that we admit to the difficulty of making such a choice, admit to the sacrifices and consequences such a choice entails. In choosing not to cede to the mandate that we fight for fictiveness (figuration) over fact (literalism), we discover a different critical vantage, freed from the compunctions of taking seriously forms of being already foreclosed as ideologically antagonistic to queer undertaking.

The inseparability of lived experience and lyric invention characterizes the turns of Bishop's letter to MacIver, already cited. "I'm afraid I'm really disintegrating, just like Hart Crane, only without his gifts to make it all plausible." What if lyric gift could heal the fear of "really disintegrating?" The pathos of Bishop's letter renders suspect (or at least incomplete) the easy answer: that writing gorgeous poetry could in and of itself shore up a dolorous and panicked ego. Taken less narrowly, the questions raised in Bishop's letter — the provocative constellation of "really disintegrating," "lyric gifts," "plausibility" — might be formulated in terms of the translation "Casabianca" of Crane's *White Buildings* into a house. What if one could live inside a poem? What if one could live there, safely?

Such possibilities inform my reading of Bishop's 1955 "Squatter's Children," a poem whose final stanza meditates on a threshold of its own. The threshold about which Bishop writes resembles, in its lyric capacities, the thresholds I've explored in "Casabianca." As importantly, however, the threshold of "Squatter's Children" tenders a revision of "Voyages I," the first section of one of Crane's most well-known and admired poems. Where in Bishop's poem there exists a threshold, in Crane's poem (more severely) there is a line. The echoic affiliation between "Voyages I" and "Squatter's Children," however, exceeds the translation of a single line. Bishop's poem borrows from Crane's both cast of characters and rhetorical structure. To this end, "Squatter's Children" recounts the children of squatters, those who inhabit a structure that isn't properly (legally) their own, but also signals beyond narrative content a poetic practice of squatting—as though Bishop's return to "Voyages," the final poem of *White Buildings,* literalized those buildings as sites of dwelling. Or are Crane's characters the squatters, in Bishop's poem?

Elizabeth Bishop arranged her 1965 book *Questions of Travel* in two sections, titled "Brazil" and "Elsewhere." David Kalstone, among others, has read the book's bifurcation as one between Bishop's negotiation of the utter unfamiliarity of Brazil (for which she sailed in November 1951, where she lived, on and off, through the early 1970s) and the revenant familiarity of Nova Scotia, where she spent many years of her childhood. The Brazilian poems, Kalstone writes, "themselves resist narrative explanations and links between present and past. The poems record an awakening to a world as if Bishop had no previous history."[49] There is less a connection between the book's two sections, for Kalstone, than an unbreachable fissure. "The questions of how the child survived or 'learned' to be the adult of Brazil are too mysterious to be answered or even asked. The yawning gap between past and present in the book can seem a triumph of repression, yet repression in Bishop's case appears deeply linked to the capacity for discovery and, almost by reflex, for pleasure in the present" (218).

"Squatter's Children," the third poem in the "Brazil" sequence (following "Questions of Travel," the poem after which the book takes its name), troubles the heuristic divisions adduced by Kalstone. The poem's manifest subject is two children at play — a subject more assimilable to the book's second section, "Elsewhere," than to the first—although not necessarily two Brazilian children at play. Kalstone speaks more generally of the "Brazil" sequence's "minute discriminations, the anthropologist's technique." While "Squatter's Children" indubitably discriminates minutely (what Bishop poem doesn't?), its technique seems, anthropologically speaking, dubious. Similarly unfounded seems Victoria Harrison's claim (in a chapter baldly titled "Confronting Brazil"[50]) that "Squatter's Children" is "Bishop's ethnographic exercise" (150).[51] Readings such as Kalstone's and Harrison's hypostasize "Squatter's Children" by locking it into a postcolonial framework to which it is susceptible but hardly unequivocally wedded. "Squatter's Children" only becomes anthropological or ethnographic when the section heading "Brazil" is privileged over the poem's own specific investments.[52]

While those investments can be interpolated to include a literal position on squatting or poverty or homelessness, such interpolations only further consolidate the differences between "Brazil" and "Elsewhere," when in fact, read otherwise, "Squatter's Children" resists the presumed "gap" between past and present (childhood and adulthood, innocence and responsibility, neutrality and desire) by staging a rapprochement between the two. More specifically, the poem's first three stanzas posit a scene of childhood play to which the fourth stanza apostrophically speaks:

> On the unbreathing sides of hills
> they play, a specklike girl and boy,
> alone, but near a specklike house.
> The sun's suspended eye
> blinks casually, and then they wade
> gigantic waves of light and shade.
> A dancing yellow spot, a pup,
> attends them. Clouds are piling up;
>
> a storm piles up behind the house.
> The children play at digging holes.
> The ground is hard; they try to use
> one of their father's tools,
> a mattock with a broken haft
> the two of them can scarcely lift.
> It drops and clangs. Their laughter spreads
> effulgence in the thunderheads,
>
> weak flashes of inquiry
> direct as is the puppy's bark.
> But to their little, soluble,
> unwarrantable ark,
> apparently the rain's reply

consists of echolalia, and Mother's voice,
ugly as sin,
keeps calling to them to come in.

Children, the threshold of the storm
has slid beneath your muddy shoes;
wet and beguiled, you stand among
the mansions you may choose
out of a bigger house than yours,
whose lawfulness endures.
Its soggy documents retain
your rights in rooms of falling rain. (95)

As I earlier suggested, Bishop's poem lifts this cast of characters (children and their dog) and rhetorical structure (observation of childhood ceded to vatic utterance of a speaker who metaphorizes that observation, for whom that observation is inextricable from an order of which the children are not yet aware) from Crane's "Voyages I," whose sixteen lines, comprise exactly half of Bishop's four octaves:

Above the fresh ruffles of the surf
Bright striped urchins flay each other with sand.
They have contrived a conquest for shell shucks,
And their fingers crumble fragments of baked weed
Gaily digging and scattering.
And in answer to their treble interjections
The sun beats lightning on the waves,
The waves fold thunder on the sand;
And could they hear me I would tell them:

O brilliant kids, frisk with your dog,
Fondle your shells and sticks, bleached
By time and the elements; but there is a line
You must not cross nor ever trust beyond it
Spry cordage of your bodies to caresses
Too lichen-faithful from too wide a breast.
The bottom of the sea is cruel.[53]

Contrary to Kalstone's claim that the poems of *Questions of Travel* "record an awakening to a world as if Bishop had no previous history," the extensive echoing between "Squatter's Children" and "Voyages I" construes the former as history made immanent. To momentarily indulge the fantasy of Bishop ethnographically observing the poor children of Brazil, how strange for the ethnographer's transcription of observations to resemble a poem with which Bishop already was familiar. Harrison, in her account of Bishop's "ethnographic exercise," argues that Bishop's imagination animates what, in ethnographic distance, she is unable directly to witness. "Although the speaker's distant perspective finds them almost unrecognizable as children, her imagination's figurations give them movement and character."[54] Following the speaker's more distinct discernment of the mattock, Harrison notes that "as the speaker returns to represent the children, literalism fades and her imagination returns to fill in the tones of their laughter, blending their sounds with the thunder as she had their forms with the sun."[55] Juxtaposed with Crane's "Voyages I," however, Bishop's thunder and lightning, Bishop's animation of specks into children, seem less a fading of literalism into imagination, than a fading of one poet's imagination into another's.

This imaginative fading of Bishop into Crane (and Crane into Bishop) precipitates differences between the poems as instructive as the poems' aforementioned similarities. Practically speaking, similarity marks the points from which those differences become legible as departures. Crane's poem, for instance, introduces its children as "bright striped urchins." The number of children remains unspecified, as does their gender. Being urchins, they are impish, which in this context signifies they are innocents. If they knew the cruelty that the final stanza's speaker knows—if they knew their dangerous proximity to that cruelty—they wouldn't be urchins in the same way; "flay[ing] each other with sand" is less fun for those (such, presumably, as that final speaker) who have suffered flaying on more exacting registers. The speaker's distance from the children is thus reckoned (as Edelman rightly observes) as a perspectival distortion,[56] but also an affective disjunct between violence ingenuously aped and violence vatically admonished.

By comparison, Bishop's poem specifies its children as a "girl and boy," particularizing a relation between the children that "Voyages I" leaves open. That the girl and boy are "specklike" and near a "specklike house" perhaps, following Harrison, designates a literal or epistemological distance. Elsewhere in Bishop, however, the condition of being speck-like more than anything else describes a site of aesthetic equivocating, as in her 1972 poem, "Poem":

> Up closer, a wild iris, white and yellow,
> fresh-squiggled from the tube.
> The air is fresh and cold; cold early spring
> clear as gray glass: a half inch of blue sky
> below the steel-gray storm clouds.
> (They were the artist's speciality.)
> A specklike bird is flying to the left.
> Or is it a flyspeck looking like a bird? (176)[57]

The speaker of "Poem" can't tell if the painting includes a speck-like bird or is smirched by a bird-like piece of fly excrement. To be specklike, here, doesn't incriminate the observer's inability to observe more closely so much as invite the impossibility of adjudicating distinctions between the compositional and the empirical. That the subjects of "Squatter's Children" are specklike raises an analogous set of aesthetic questions.[58] Are these children specklike because so small, or so small because seen from poet's vantage? Or are these children specklike in that they might or might not be intrinsic to Bishop's own composition (let alone derived from any "empirical" ethnographic moment)? Like the flyspeck, might these specklike children have flown from somewhere else? Which is to say, being specklike, in the context of my reading, less describes a problem of distance, than a phenomenon of undecidable liminality. To be "specklike" is maybe to be a small child of Bishop's production or maybe to be children from elsewhere (say, Crane's "Voyages I"), imported onto Bishop's landscape. As such, a speck's relation to composition (maybe or maybe not) recalls a squatter's relation to a house; the undecidability in both instances is constitutive.

Bishop's poem most diverges from Crane's poem on the level of scene. Bishop, whose poetic attachments to the sea are as various and critically parsed as Crane's, locates the children's play "on the unbreathing sides of hills." "Squatter's Children," all the same, is as much a sea poem as "Voyages I," in that the former's storm transforms those hills into "gigantic waves of light and shade." This figurative, chiaroscuro sea recalls the mountains of "Questions of Travel," which "look like the hulls of capsized ships, / slim-hung and barnacled." In both instances, oceanic force is innoculated by metaphor; metaphoricity simulates an experience of the aquatic without the aquatic's consequences. The children of Bishop's poem can wade "gigantic waves" and live to tell, unlike the children of "Voyages I," for whom such waves ostensibly portend devastation. This is to say, likewise, that the sea of Crane's poem is no less metaphorical (if on the other side of metaphoricity). As Edelman writes, "to the extent that the ocean represents in this sequence the Eros of textuality and the textuality of Eros, the water line and the poetic line serve as images of each other.... For Crane as for Whitman, to entrust oneself to the poetic medium and go beyond the lines of past poets... is to commit an Oedipal trespass... [which is] the critical act of poetic initiation" (131).

Crane's final stanza issues an admonition against erotic apocalypse. The admonishing, as it is formulated, spuriously transmutes a temporal problem — namely, the movement from childhood to adulthood as initiation in the perditions of desire — into a spatial one; if the movement into desire were spatial ("a line you must not cross") as opposed to temporal, then the movement and its entailed dangers could be avoided altogether. But the line is spatially tenable only as a metaphor, and so the admonition fails not because the kids can't hear it ("and could they hear me I would tell them"), but because regardless of its being heard, it proscribes a movement that is already inevitable. This inevitability (as critics have noted) surfaces in the stanza's own enjambed lines; to realize more than "there is a line," to realize that "there is a line / You must not cross," the poem's reader already inadvertently crosses the line.

The slipperiness of admonished metaphorical line and the stanzaic lines that couch it is at constant odds with the fidelity and cruelty that follow. That is, the slipperiness by which one suddenly finds oneself on the wrong side of the line is met with slipperiness's opposite. The children must not, beyond that impossibly proscribed line, trust their bodies to caresses "too lichen-faithful." Are the caresses not to be trusted because they are too lichen-faithful to something, someone else? Or because the caresses themselves, even if offered to the children, are faithful the way lichen is faithful to rocks, unremittingly close (less caress than death-embrace) yet (like lichen to rocks) unfeeling? Does the admonisher speak from the experience of having trusted caresses from a heart too lichen-faithful to something else? Or has the speaker given his own lichen-fidelity to a child, amounting (following the logic to its end) to an inadvertent charybdis-like destruction of what was loved?

The sea-bottom is cruel, that is, to the extent that it sustains caresses (the gentlest of touches) as petrified. And the bottom of the sea is cruel to the extent that once there, one can't return. The bottom of the sea is cruel, finally, because it cannot resolve these opposite crises of slip and grip. No one scenario seems, within the poem, more or less available than the others; and yet likewise, no one scenario seems preferable. The children themselves seem destined to such a fate of erotic confusions, as "spry cordage"—simultaneously nimble and roped, roped in their own nimbleness.

"O brilliant kids . . . there is a line / You must not cross" surely echoes in Bishop's "Children, the threshold of the storm / has slid beneath your muddy shoes." Crane's enjambment playfully (sadistically, resignedly) designates that there is a line, but only in crossing said line reveals the line was not to have been crossed. Similarly, Bishop's enjambment designates that there is a threshold (a version of "line" recalling the threshold of Crane's own "Wine Menagerie") but separates the fact of the threshold from the fact of the threshold's moving ("has slid beneath your muddy shoes"). Bishop's threshold, unlike Crane's line, does not signal a proscribed boundary, but a motile force all its own. Bishop's children find themselves on the other side of the threshold, even as they stand in one place, "wet and beguiled." At the same time, however, to be on the other side of Bishop's line (as opposed to Crane's) is not condemning, but enabling of the sort of imaginative labor on which "Squatter's Children" meditates. The threshold of the storm marks the line between the second stanza's hard ground, and this last stanza's kingdom of mud. Bishop's line, that is, doesn't transform the children, but the children's surroundings. Such is one way of describing the relation between "Squatter's Children" and "Voyages I": the former doesn't transform the latter's children so much as relocate them.

If Crane's final stanza proffers admonition against a sort of apocalypse, Bishop's final stanza proffers a corresponding parousia. Beyond the storm's threshold, Bishop's poem promises not just bigger houses than the one the children live in, but a house that is rightfully theirs, "whose lawfulness endures. Its soggy documents retain / your rights in rooms of falling rain." Within the immediate context of Bishop's poem, this dream-house is underwritten by the "soggy documents" of Bishop's own poem;[59] the documents' possessive pronoun could refer to the house's lawfulness, but also to the house itself (a house built of soggy documents, of writing).[60] While the legitimacy of such documents would seem under ordinary circumstances shortlived (water bleeds paper's ink, then dissolves the paper itself), Bishop insists on rights' endurability not in spite of the poem's final deluge, but somehow through it. The poem's final gorgeously counterintuitive image, "rooms of falling rain," conjures less a roofless house (how could that seem an improvement on the speck-like house with which the poem opens?) than a benedictive house made of water. The concluding generosity of "Squatter's Children" acquires all the more force, read as a caretaking of the children of "Voyages I." If their drift to sea is incontrovertible, then Bishop's poem alters the terms of that incontrovertibility. Where there was ocean, there is only metaphorical ocean and Brazilian downpour. And where the sea-bottom could promise only cruelty inseparable from death, the rain of "Squatter's Children" promises "rooms." This revision returns us to Bishop's poem's insistence that the children are not "urchins," but a girl and a boy. Perhaps Bishop and Crane, perhaps Antigone and Polyneices, at play "digging holes," in a poetic time before digging holes meant only burial.

"Pleasure Seas": Allegory and Love

"Casabianca," I have argued, recapitulates Felicia Hemans's eponymous poem in order to describe a relationship not to Hemans or Hemans's poetry, but to the biographical body (as opposed to poetic corpus) of Hart Crane. Bishop's poem reattaches the referents of Hemans's poem to a historical scene different from the Napoleonic battle that is Hemans's subject; namely, to the scene of Crane's ship-deck suicide. Bishop doesn't bring the burning boy of her own poem to the brink of death, so much as extricate the boy from the pathos of dying. This extrication occurs on the level of allegory, in Bishop's transformation of the Hemans-like child into what Steven Knapp has termed an allegorical personification,[61] such that death by fire becomes, in a time beyond that of Bishop's poem, "merely" allegorical death by fire. The extrication occurs more fundamentally on the level of narrative, or more precisely, in the truncation of narrative by which death by fire (even allegorical death, or allegorical fire) is never reached. Narrative is short-circuited in repetitions that consign the allegorical burning boy not only to the safety of poetry, but to the safety of indefinite recitation.[62]

For Bishop's Love, the alternatives are not between death and life, per se, but rather between death and the curtailment of death. In this manner, Bishop's poem recalls the fake frontier of Spicer's *Billy The Kid.* Both Spicer and Bishop treat poetry as a site of invention nonetheless beholden to its own self-allotted limitations. Easy enough to write a poem in which Crane matter-of-factly is alive: as, for instance, Robert Lowell's "Words for Hart Crane," which less delivers words to the poet, than puts words into the restored poet's mouth:

> I,
> *Catullus redivivus,* once the rage
> of the Village and Paris, used to play my role
> of homosexual, wolfing the stray lambs
> who hungered by the Place de la Concorde.[63]

The self-imposed project of "Casabianca," on the other hand, doesn't return Crane to the land of the living (or even ghostly) — doesn't necessarily want to revive Crane as he was. "Casabianca" takes seriously the imaginative faculties of poetry (not to rewrite history or the facticity of death) but rather to articulate a space on the edge of death.

"Squatter's Children," unlike "Casabianca," animates the poetry of Crane as opposed to the person, but to comparable ends. I have tried to show the ways Bishop's rewriting of Crane's "Voyages I" saves the children of that latter poem from their erotic fate (for Crane and Crane critics alike, a fate tantamount to sea-death) by transposing them to a less condemning poetic. This new locale resembles the locale Bishop culls from Hemans, in that safety, in both poems, derives in part from the effects of figuration. Just as Bishop translates Hemans's "real" boy into an allegory, Bishop translates Crane's "real" sea into a metaphor. This practice of redemptive figuration recurs in Bishop's 1939 poem "Pleasure Seas," which variously echoes both "Casabianca" and "Squatter's Children." As we shall see, "Pleasure Seas" continues beyond the experimental stall of "Casabianca." In holding off Crane's going overboard, "Casabianca" treated the sea as a nightmare that impinges on the poem without textually appearing. Despite ship-deck and swimming sailors, despite the unforestallable "[going] down" of the ship itself, the poem does not divulge the word "sea," as though to invoke the water were to condemn the "burning boy" to that water's fate.[64] "Pleasure Seas," by contrast, redefines the sea's own qualities and, in so doing, is able to return to the scene of the "Casabianca" ship-deck without dreading what might otherwise follow. It is in this reconfiguring of the sea that "Pleasure Seas" is linked to "Squatter's Children." The sea of "Pleasure Seas" isn't cruel, as in "Voyages I" (or a tomb, as in Crane's "Melville's Tomb"). Rather the sea, as "Pleasure Seas" puts it, "means *room,*" echoing the room of water with which "Squatter's Children" concludes.

To say that the subject of "Casabianca" is Crane's person and that the subject of "Squatter Children" is Crane's poetry oversimplifies the imbrication of person and poetry that constitutes Crane's particular dilemma. "Hart Crane," Allen Grossman lucidly writes, "was a poet who lived in and through the logic of the poetic principle, wrote poems that told stories about the impossibility of its imperatives, and died the death that always beckons when the exchange of natural for symbolic life is understood as a destiny without alternative."[65] It is this "exchange of natural for symbolic life" that Bishop herself reworks, to both Crane's and her own advantage. That is, whereas Grossman identifies such an exchange as fatal, Bishop resituates such an exchange (if only within her own poetry) as the means by which Crane retroactively negotiates a version of his own ineluctable and perilous poetic demands. Grossman writes of Crane's obscurations as the style "not of the imaginative singer of our poetry but of the imaginary subject (not of 'Wordsworth' but of the solitary reaper, not of 'Keats' but of the nightingale)" (90). Grossman, that is, suggests that Crane's voice delivers not the song of the poet, but the song the poet hears. Both the origin of the poet's song and the subject of the poet's poetry, Crane's poetics complicates the divisions of biographical and literary (the "natural" and the "symbolic") in that the former was lived as a catastrophic confusion with the latter. It is in this sense that one cannot speak of Bishop's return to Crane's suicide as though that enterprise were extricable from a revision of his poetry; and vice versa, that one can't speak of Bishop's return to Crane's poetry (as in "The Squatter's Children") as though revision of Crane's poetic line didn't retroactively color the life with which (for Grossman and myriad Crane critics) that line was so brilliantly, critically, unified. The sea of "Pleasure Seas," in this way, signals both the sea of "Voyages I" and the sea in which Crane drowns; just as the sea of "Voyages I," after the fact of Crane's death, registers less as the intersection of trope and biography than as frank prolepsis.

"Pleasure Seas," from its outset, queries the relation between bodies of water and the bodies that might be endangered by, suspended, or dissolved in them. The poem's investigation begins not with a sea, but with a swimming pool. The pool, for Bishop, differs from the sea in that the former is "walled off," and yet this containment, in relation to a sea's presumed boundless volatility, doesn't guarantee the pool's bathers anything like safety. Bishop's pool can't guarantee safety to the extent that danger isn't a potential property of water so much as intrinsic to the bathers themselves; the pool, as it were, is "perfectly flat" because its occupants require perfect flatness:

> In the walled off swimming-pool the water is perfectly flat.
> The pink Seurat bathers are dipping themselves in and out
> Through a pane of bluish glass.
> The cloud reflections pass
> Huge amoeba-motions directly through
> The beds of bathing caps: white, lavender, and blue.
> If the sky turns gray, the water turns opaque,
> Pistachio green and Mermaid Milk. (195)

The pink Seurat bathers treat the pool as though it were a painting, dipping in and out as though moving from one side of a frame to the other. That the bathers are Seurats might initially imply the safety of the aesthetic: a swimming pool as innocuous as a pastel representation of it; that the bathers can traverse the boundaries of their painterly pool quickly unsteadies such a reading. (The bathers' movement from aesthetic domain to domain beyond the aesthetic [the empirical, that from which a certain mode of the aesthetic is derived] suggests the lability of a poet such as Grossman's Crane, for whom the "pane" dividing poetry from experience seems analogously pervious.[66])

The particular aesthetic conjured, Seurat's pointillism, marks the pool's inhabitants as less stable than the pool they enter. A series of dots, a constellation of contingencies, the pointillist bathers would be scattered by anything less static than their "walled-off swimming-pool." The safety of the pool's boundaries luridly coincides with the strange lack of boundaries by which its bathers are defined. As T. J. Clark writes of Seurat's dot,

> It planted a bomb in the middle of the bourgeois idea of freedom—and order, and individuality, and Art ness, and taste, and "touch," intuition, variety, expressiveness. All the aesthetic categories of the nineteenth century, including most of the modernist ones, disappeared down the black hole of Seurat's technique. A technique that pretended to be a technics—to engineer at last the "elocutary disappearance of the poet, who cedes the initiative to words" [Mallarmé]. And show us a world where "Je est un autre" [Rimbaud].[67]

Contra Jeredith Merrin, one of few Bishop scholars to write about this poem, these opening lines depict something less intuitive than "entrapment and lassitude or dullness."[68] And by extension, the poem's juxtaposition of pool and sea is less intuitive than the distinction between "contained water" and "freer water," as simply a "water/mind analogy." In Merrin's words, the sea, "this other, unconfined water evokes a mind unconstrained—a good thing, surely. This going one's own way suggests the young poet's artistic independence as well as possibly hinting at her sense of social and sexual difference."[69] In contrast to the "walled off swimming-pool," however, Bishop's sea is notable not because it can go anywhere it wants, but because it isn't, unlike the pool, self-defined:

> But out among the keys
> Where the water goes its own way, the shallow pleasure seas
> Drift this way and that mingling currents and tides
> In most of the colors that swarm around the sides
> Of soap-bubbles, poisonous and fabulous. (195)

The poem doesn't pair a single contained pool with any one given sea, but to several various seas "mingling currents and tides"; what matters in the poem's juxtaposition is that the seas are plural. The soap-bubbles, in their own vibrant way, recall the fragility of the "pink Seurat bathers." The tides are as bright as bubbles without being as delicate. And here, within the pleasure seas, we find the scene of dissolution, the stage on which dissolution should take place, without the dissolution. Recall Bishop's later letter to Loren MacIver: "I'm afraid I'm really disintegrating, just like Hart Crane, only without his gifts to make it all plausible." If in "Pleasure Seas," disintegration is already sounded in the swimming pool, then what is there left for the sea to figure? Bishop's seas figure a "mingling of currents" without disintegration. Which is to say, in already aligning danger with the "walled off swimming pool," Bishop aligns the seas with a constantly reintegrative, reconstituting variousness. The counterintuitive stability of such a scheme registers in the sea's correlative to the pool's pointillism:

> From an airplane the water's heavy sheet
> Of glass above a bas-relief:
> Clay-yellow coral and purple dulces
> And long, leaning, submerged green grass. (195)

As in Crane's serial hallucinations of stone, Bishop's bas-relief signals perdurability without oppressiveness. The pleasure seas, with their Whitmanian "leaning grass" are no less sweet for being sculptural. "Dulces," at its most literal, denotes a species of seaweed (as in Longfellow's "the purple dulce is lovely"), but also suggests the happy hypostasizing of the adjectival "dulcet" into nouns: the carved sweetness of a stone's relief:

> And long, leaning, submerged green grass.
> Across it a wide shadow pulses.
> The water is a burning-glass
> Turned to the sun
> That blues and cools as the afternoon wears on,
> And liquidly
> Floats weeds, surrounds fish, supports a violently red bell-buoy,
> Whose neon-color vibrates over it, whose bells vibrate
> Through it. It glitters rhythmically
> To shock after shock of electricity.
> The sea is delight. The sea means *room*.
> It is a dance-floor, a well ventilated ballroom.
> From the swimming-pool or from the deck of a ship
> Pleasures strike off humming, and skip
> Over the tinsel surface: a Grief floats off
> Spreading out thin like oil. And Love
> Sets out determinedly in a straight line,
> One of his burning ideas in mind (195)

"Pleasure Seas" posits this ventilated ballroom quite literally as a last resort—Bishop's seas, unlike Crane's, operate along a horizontal (which is also to say a radically surfacial) axis, ostensibly immune to the pull of sea-bottom.[70] Bishop's seas are marked not by depth (from the outset, rather, they are specified as "shallow"), but by the sheer indefiniteness of their length. Were Crane to jump from such a ship-deck, he might not sink at all (caught in this seascape's antigravity) so much as indefinitely extend across the surface:

> . . . from the deck of a ship
> Pleasures strike off humming and skip
> Over the tinsel surface: a Grief floats off
> Spreading out thin like oil. (195)

A sea with no apparent recourse to its own depth precludes Crane's mythic end—what Riddel, conflating poetry and biography, summarily characterizes as "the pathetic gesture of a man dying into his work." More generally, such a sea redresses the sort of affective topographies that privilege grief over pleasure in the first place. Less stunning than pleasures "skip[ping] over the tinsel surface" is a grief that doesn't sink, but rather "spread[s] out thin like oil." This leveling of pleasure and grief speaks against more familiar narratives that take for granted the latter's being deeper than the former (and concomitantly, take for granted that depth is more persuasive if not altogether more constitutive than surface, no matter how various or vast). Merrin, in reading the "Pleasure Seas," inadvertently demonstrates the very bias Bishop's poem counters. "The pleasure seas," writes Merrin, "are 'shallow,' because Bishop is as usual being scrupulously accurate in her physical description but perhaps also because the pleasure this particular voyager takes in the view is not very deep or covers a deeper sadness."[71] Within Bishop's experimental seascape, however, grief is lighter than water. Grief spreads, but (unsettlingly, for the likes of Merrin) doesn't settle.

It is in her attachment to pleasure's delightful but ultimate frivolousness that Merrin characterizes the poem's final turn to Love:

> The self-consciously artificial broaching of "Love" as a "he" or the allegorical Cupid; the ironic adversion to Petrarchist cliché ("One of his burning ideas in mind") . . . this passage is thickly overlaid with Bishop's urbane defenses against bathos.[72]

Like Merrin, Bonnie Costello finds remarkable Bishop's turn, here, to the allegorical mode: "Bishop does not locate the consciousness of danger within any single perspective of the poem. In order to entertain it she must revert to a perspectiveless, allegorical language of Love and

Grief."[73] Costello further characterizes Bishop's Love as "another inhuman [perspective] which shatters the rest.... At its close, the poem rests outside human concerns, turning instead to nature's easy tolerance of mutability, and to the white color of obliteration.... The unhappy perspective of the omniscient reader, for whom all love's dreams are shattered, is only allegorically and ironically presented."[74] Merrin's turn to irony recalls the irony of Blasing and McCabe, for whom a male-gendered Love within a lesbian's poetry necessarily signals imitation of a canonical (i.e., patriarchal, i.e., "cliché[d]") conception of the amorous without commitment to it. Merrin finds Bishop's profferal of Love inadequate not because it is allegorical so much as because the allegory isn't her own. Costello, by contrast, finds Bishop's profferal of Love inadequate because allegory as such implies a removal (a priori) from the concerns of the human, regardless of allegory's originality or overfamiliarity.

Given the frequency with which Bishop critics fantasize Bishop's unpublished love poems and trawl what Bishop did publish for traces of love, I find it remarkable that in poems such as "Casabianca" and "Pleasure Seas," critics so quickly rule out that Bishop is saying anything interesting (let alone sincere) about love. In assuming that amorous articulations are factitious by Bishop's dint—and more precisely, that such fictions are "defenses" against some more real or dangerous form of love — Merrin and Costello overlook the ways in which the love of "Pleasure Seas" might be allegorical without being inhuman, might be real without being dangerous, might be sincere without unequivocally producing (or at least more egregiously flirting with) some money-shot of lesbian desire:

> ... And Love
> Sets out determinedly in a straight line,
> One of his burning thoughts in mind,
> Keeping his eyes on
> The bright horizon,
> But shatters immediately, suffers refraction,
> And comes back in shoals of distraction.
> Happy the people in the swimming-pool and on the yacht,
> Happy the man in that airplane, likely as not—
> And out there where the coral reef is a shelf
> The water runs at it, leaps, throws itself

Lightly, lightly, whitening in the air:
An acre of cold white spray is there
Dancing happily by itself. (195–96)

In the wake of queer theory, these concluding lines of "Pleasure Seas" are significant in part as uncanny anticipations of what has become a singularly queer-theoretical cliché: namely, post-Bersani, that gay sex literalizes a fantasy of (that is, a propulsive instinct toward) self-shattering, amounting to a temporary self-removal from the psychical oppressions of subjectivity. Though (amazingly) nearly two decades old, Bersani's crucial "Is the Rectum a Grave?" provides the most laconic account of this shibboleth-like shattering, with all its implied political energies. "But if the rectum is the grave in which the masculine ideal (an ideal shared — differently — by men and women) of proud subjectivity is buried, then it should be celebrated for its very potential for death" (222). As removed from this psychoanalytically derived queer theory as Merrin and Costello are, their readings nonetheless dovetail with the conclusions which that theoretical optic, trained on "Pleasure Seas," produce: either Bishop's love veers from "human concerns" via ironic allegory, or Bishop's love (returning to Bersani) "los[es] sight of the self, and in so doing proposes and dangerously represents jouissance as a mode of ascesis."[75]

To imagine the Love of "Pleasure Seas" as a reiteration of the Love of "Casabianca" is not difficult. Both Loves scenically find themselves on a poetic ship-deck; both, in one way or another, are on fire ("one of his burning ideas in mind"). To imagine these Loves as one and the same is to open the possibility of imagining the Love of "Pleasure Seas," the Love who "sets out determinedly" from ship-deck, as Hart Crane. The possible existence in "Pleasure Seas" of Crane's suicide issues into the poem a literal form of self-loss analogous to the tragic literalization of self-loss Bersani locates in the ravage of AIDS. "But if the rectum is the grave in which the masculine ideal . . . of proud subjectivity is buried, then it should be celebrated for its very potential for death. Tragically, AIDS has literalized that potential as the certainty of biological death."[76] Crane's suicide, read through queer theory and back into Bishop, literalizes what the final lines of Bishop's poem luxuriate as the extension of allegory:

> And Love
> Sets out determinedly in a straight line,
> One of his burning ideas in mind,
> Keeping his eyes on
> The bright horizon,
> But shatters immediately, suffers refraction,
> And comes back in shoals of distraction. (195–96)

Bishop's turn to allegory, as it relates to Crane (and more generally, as it relates to nonallegorical death), departs from the realm of the human, which is different from Costello's claim that it "rests outside human concerns." It departs at that moment of death, the limit of the human, as a way of extending (if not preserving) what literal logic can no longer sustain. In this manner, Bishop's allegory recalls what de Man defines as allegory's "fundamental structure": a "tendency of the language toward narrative, the spreading out along the axis of an imaginary line in order to give duration to what is, in fact, simultaneous with the subject."[77] The "straight line" of Bishop's Love, like the "imaginary line" of de Man, gives duration to what is otherwise synchronic (and to the death of one such as Crane, gives duration where, in the order of the human, there is none). Bishop's allegory is not antithetical to the personal. Allegory, here, occupies the terrain between the biographical and the historical;[78] or in Eliot's terms, between an individual and the tradition. Between alone and not alone.

Sea Burial: Of Bells and Buoys

Crane's presence in "Pleasure Seas," however, has already been sounded in the "violently red bell-buoy," a formulation whose specificity hardly follows from the general terms ("weeds," "fish") that precede it. Whether violently red, or violently read, the buoy, both graphically and aurally, suggests the burning boy of "Casabianca," Love. Bishop's heart-red bell-boy, furthermore, may well recall Crane's poem "The Broken Tower":

> And so it was I entered the broken world
> To trace the visionary company of love, its voice
> An instant in the wind (I know not whither hurled)
> But not for long to hold each desperate choice.[79]

The Cranian poet can know love's message only to the extent that he can transcribe the bells' toll, even as their "voice" lasts only an "instant." His only recourse is his own memory of their music:

> . . . counting the strokes
> My veins recall and add, revived and sure
> The angelus of wars my chest evokes:
> What I hold healed, original now, and pure.[80]

The poet's memory must avail precisely because the bells themselves do not. Memory continues the work of echo, because the bells' echoes so emphatically fail. An earlier stanza denominates the bell-ringing as "antiphonal carillons," as though the echo of antiphony were already, aurally, the carrion of dead bodies. And indeed, the carillons become carrion soon enough, "banked voices slain," "terraced echoes prostrate on the plain." The fantasy invoked is of echoes that could take up space, but only that of the dead, a necropolis where living city might otherwise be. The bellsongs all but commit a sort of bell-suicide, leaping from their tower like *Vertigo's* Kim Novak ("campaniles, with reveilles outleaping — "). The poet, within Crane's poem, becomes the site of an echo that retains voice without body, displacing echoes that are themselves more body than voice, and less body than corpse.

If, for Crane, the poet is one who labors to replicate the sound of bells ("to trace the visionary company of love, its voice / an instant in the wind"), Bishop rewrites Crane as bell-buoy, which is to say, as fusion of a boy and the bells he hears. This compression leavens the Cranian poet's dilemma, in that the boy not only already possesses but *is* that which he seeks to recuperate. And unlike the landscape of "The Broken Tower," in which echoes (obsolesced by the poet) accumulate ("Oval encyclicals in canyons heaping / The impasse high with choir") with the heft but not the communicability of persons, the seascape of Bishop's poem is nothing if not echoic medium. The bell-buoy's "neon-color vibrates over" the water, and the bells themselves "vibrate through it."

Bishop's bell, unlike Crane's, is constitutively vibratory, which is as much to say constitutively echoing. Echoes, here, are less carnage-like remainder of song, than song. Crane's poem construes the poet as a scribe of echoes because (1) the carillon's song too quickly fades, and (2) the carillon's echoes as quickly become a chorus of carrion. Bishop's poem, in response, both renders a song's echoes unnecessary as recollection (to the extent that the bell-buoy implies the phantasmatic invention of a poet inseparable from song), and in the freeing of echo from mnemonic burden, envisions echo (newly detachable from referent) with a counterintuitive life of its own.

Epilogue

AFFIRMEZ LA SURVIE

In venturing Elizabeth Bishop's lyric care for Hart Crane in terms of Antigone and Polyneices, I enter a conversation already begun — a conversation first taken up by queer theory in the form of Judith Butler's *Antigone's Claim.* I intend my rehearsal of Butler's work less as précis than as a set of local observations attuned to where Butler's claims seem potentially to jeopardize Antigone's titular own. Even as I articulate what I perceive as limitations within Butler's argument, I agree with Butler's fundamental insight that there is much in Sophocles' *Antigone* from which queer theory can learn. As my previous chapter should indicate, I sympathetically second Butler's wish (following that of George Steiner) for a psychoanalysis hypothetically founded on the lessons of Antigone rather than those of Oedipus. This epilogue differs from *Antigone's Claim* in my understanding of what these lessons — for psychoanalysis, for queer theory — are.

First, though, to succinctly recapitulate the terms of Sophocles' play. Antigone's brother, Polyneices, has been killed by his twin brother, Eteocles. Creon, king of Thebes, forbids Polyneices's burial — the latter is an infidel — and issues an edict whereby anyone who does bury the infidel body will in turn be put to death. Against Creon's orders, out of love for her brother, Antigone buries Polyneices' body. Creon sentences her to death. Antigone dies. Further calamity follows.

Antigone's Claim argues against earlier readings of *Antigone* — specifically, those of Hegel and Lacan — which freeze Antigone and Creon as opposing paradigms: standard-bearers, respectively, of kinship and state power. Far from consolidating the conditions of kinship, Antigone, for Butler, "upsets the vocabulary of kinship that is a precondition of the human" (82). Butler concludes that "if kinship is the precondition of the human, then Antigone is the occasion for a new field of the human, achieved through political catachresis, the one that happens when the less than human speaks, when gender is displaced and kinship founders on its own founding laws" (82). The extent to which kinship founders, however, arguably depends less on what Antigone speaks, than on Butler's subordination of Antigone's own words to a subtext to which Antigone's words, for Butler, ineluctably migrate. The words in question are those Antigone offers in defense of her burying of her brother:

> What law backs me
> when I say this? I will tell you:
> If my husband were dead, I might have had another,
> and child from another man, if I lost the first.
> But when father and mother both were hidden in death
> no brother's life would bloom for me again.
> That is the law under which I gave you precedence,
> my dearest brother, and that is why Creon thinks me
> wrong, even a criminal, and now takes me
> by the hand and leads me away. (196)

This, for all intents and purposes, is Antigone's claim. Like Butler, I find this passage valuable not only for psychoanalytic and queer-theoretical inquiry, but for broader ethical investigations of what an American tradition knows as self-reliance and civil disobedience. I find in Antigone's claim an assertion of queer optimism at perhaps its most austere, sparely unwavering. Antigone's assertiveness dramatizes Hart Crane's formulation of optimism as not only the affirmation of feeling joy, but the affirmation of affirmation. There is no joy, here, for Antigone, but her affirmation is great. Her attachment to Polyneices's absolute singularity likewise dramatizes the negotiation of specificity we have seen in the difficult lucidities of Dickinson — lucidity so committed to its own conditions as to seem, sometimes, to circle back on itself into the unintelligible. Antigone's affirmation likewise dramatizes the nonmelancholic inventiveness by which Spicer "buries" Billy the Kid in the fake frontier of a poem — for Spicer, as for Dickinson, as for Antigone, death does not mark the end of being a person, but occasions a revision of one's repertoire for being a person, for understanding and caring for another person. Antigone's burial of Polyneices, more than a funeral rite, insists that even in death Polyneices is still a person who calls for affection and recognition, even as affection and recognition under these conditions require other terms than those in which they have been hitherto conceived and given. *Queer Optimism* finds in Antigone's claim the buoying valor of one who defends another person's fragility against an edict oppositely demanding that person's — that body's — desecration:[1]

> You shall leave him without burial: you shall watch him
> chewed up by birds and dogs and violated. (168)

You shall, that is, watch Polyneices, this person, slowly cease to be a person. You shall watch his body's irrelevance catch up with his more generally categorical irrelevance, already instituted by king's edict. It is against this edict that Antigone speaks. It is against analogous theoretical exhortings that *Queer Optimism* echoes.[2]

Antigone galvanizes my project's correspondent interest in underarticulated modalities of galvanization. In *Antigone's Claim,* on the other hand, Antigone represents a heroics of foundering. Antigone "emblematize[s]," Butler writes, "a certain heterosexual fatality that remains to be read" (72); she both instantiates and incites displacement and disruption. Even (or rather, especially) Antigone's assertiveness strikes Butler as suspect: how, after all, could a paradigm of equivocation be anything less than equivocal? And here, despite the counterfactual of a psychoanalysis (and in turn, a queer theory) predicated on Antigone rather than Oedipus, we find Antigone once again subject to the unconscious that is Oedipus's legacy. Antigone, Butler writes, "calls her loss her brother Polyneices, insists on his singularity, but that very insistence is suspect" (80). Earlier in her study, opining (against earlier structuralist accounts of the play) the factitious alignment of Antigone/kinship and Creon/state power, Butler asks, "[c]an we assume that Antigone . . . is not, as it were, living the equivocations that unravel the purity and universality of those structuralist rules" (17)? Why, on the contrary, can we not assume Antigone's nonequivocality? Why must we regard her "very insistence" as suspect?

For *Antigone's Claim,* the answer to such questions depends on incest, Oedipus's most direct legacy to Antigone (even as Butler's work wishes to move beyond the Oedipal). Incest, in this reading, not only saturates Antigone's love for Polyneices, but problematizes Antigone's assertion that her crime is committed for Polyneices and Polyneices alone.[3] Butler argues that "[Lacan's] analysis forgets that [Antigone] is also committing a crime, not only defying the edict of the state, but the crime of carrying her love for her brother too far" (53). Normative kinship, following Butler, falters in being equivocally predicated on an incestuous desire never fully consummated:

> If the love toward which [Antigone] moves as she moves toward death is a love for her brother and thus, ambiguously, her father, it is also a love that can only be consummated by its obliteration, which is no consummation at all. (76)

Antigone can claim the singularity of her actions, for Butler, "only by displaying incoherence and inconsistency" (77). It strikes me that it is Butler, not Antigone, who carries Antigone's "love for her brother too far." Or rather: in presuming sororal affection of such intensity as invariably incestuous doesn't carry Antigone's love far enough.

Antigone's Claim makes Antigone undermine that to which she claims unequivocal attachment, even as it holds this undermining in juxtaposition with the nonequivocality of "the edict." Pronounced metonymically by the state, Creon's edict is taken as such in all the ways *Antigone's Claim* asks Antigone's own pronouncement to be taken for granted. Butler writes that Antigone "contest[s] the power of [Creon's] edict, which is delivered as an imperative." And indeed, few readers of *Antigone* — regardless of disposition or training — would disagree with Butler's characterization of the edict as universally applicable, contra the nonuniversality of Antigone's later claim. Returning, however, to Antigone's own account of Creon's law, one finds the germ of the law's own (nonuniversal) equivocating:

> But the unhappy corpse of Polyneices
> he has proclaimed to all the citizens,
> they say, no man may hide
> in a grave nor mourn in a funeral,
> but leave unwept, unburied, a dainty treasure
> for the birds that see him, for their feast's delight.
> That is what, they say, the worthy Creon
> has proclaimed for you and me — for me, I tell you —
> and he comes here to clarify to the unknowing
> his proclamation; he takes it seriously;
> for whoever breaks the edict death is prescribed,
> and death by stoning publicly. (162)

The edict involves both proscription and the consequences of proscription's breach — as a law, it is comprised of two movements. (In the language of J. L. Austin, the former is illocutionary, the latter perlocutionary.) Taken as two movements, however, Creon's law is not actually universal. It is true that upon burying Polyneices, Antigone is sentenced to death. But she is not publicly stoned. Creon alters the consequences of proscription's breach in a manner particular to Antigone. Creon, that is, acts capriciously, with all "the incoherence and inconsistency" (77) Butler reserves for Antigone's defense of singularity. Of Antigone's egregiously nonuniversal punishment, Creon says this:

> I will bring her where the path is loneliest,
> and hide her alive in a rocky cavern there.
> I'll give her just enough of food as shall suffice
> for a bare expiation, that the city may avoid pollution.
> In that place she shall call on Hades, god of death,
> in her prayers. (192)

Where does this leave us? A state power that acts capriciously (and tyranically) wouldn't seem so odd for many of us who have weathered so many decades of arrogant and deplorable executive caprice. "Leaders" such as G. W. Bush or Sadaam Hussein were not queer heros, even as they more or less single-handedly undid and disrupted more families, more systems, more integrities (etc.) than Antigone could ever dream of. Who, in recent history, more grandiosely than Dubya has "achieved" what Butler, speaking of Antigone, denominates "political catachresis?" Who — more even than the most impish and future-abdicating of queers — seems more apt a figuration of the death drive? With recent political regimens in so many ways describable as No Child Left, who needs a queer nonpolitical programmatic (or nonprogrammatic) devoted to the same cause? Why need a queer heroine be aligned with rupture? Butler acknowledges that Antigone is "not quite a queer heroine" (72); but how could she be, in so asphyxiatingly foreclosed a narrative of Oedipal incest? Why would we want her to be, when rupture — in the name of shock, awe, etc. — is one of the few things the world against which "we" often imagine ourselves seems capable? Why then, in turn, can we not note that far more powerful than Antigone's imbrication in and negotiation of an incest taboo is the force of her love governed neither by incest nor taboo? Why can we not imagine affirmation as an act far more radical than negation? Why can we not take Antigone at her word?

Several years following the publication of *Antigone's Claim,* Butler wrote a beautiful and eloquent essay on the occasion of Jacques Derrida's death. Unlike her substitution of Antigone's words with what those words betray, Butler takes Derrida's last words — terribly, consolingly, inconsolably — to heart:

> At his funeral outside of Paris, he left only a few lines to be read by his son Pierre, and among them was a certain imperative, "affirmez la survie." These are the words that survived him, the ones he wanted to be read by his inheritor, the one he knew, even as to affirm that survival means precisely not to know where one's words will go and what kind of inheritance lies in wait for them. Affirm survival, he tells us, and suddenly I am orphaned, since he gives us no instruction, and we are not told how, in the face of suffering, in spite of suffering, this affirmation is to take place.[4]

Derrida's imperative resonates with Crane's own imperative — "All I know through very much suffering and dullness (somehow I seem to twinge more all the time) is that it interests me to still affirm certain things" —[5] and with Antigone's claim. *Affirmez la survie.* How, Butler asks, is this affirmation to take place? I have written *Queer Optimism* as an experiment in such an affirmation — moored not to an unimaginable future ("not knowing . . . what kind of inheritance lies in wait for [one's words]"), but to the beneficent crisis of the present, in which all such experiments must occur. I have written *Queer Optimism* as an analysis of earlier such affirmations, audible could we carefully enough listen. How do they take place? They already are, and already have. In asking the question, they are taking, and no less queerly, no less potentially unfamiliarly, they are giving. Here.

NOTES

Queer Optimism

1. Lauren Berlant and Michael Warner, "Sex in Public," *Critical Inquiry* 24 (Winter 1998): 549.

2. Lauren Berlant, "The Subject of True Feeling: Pain, Privacy, and Politics," *Feminist Consequences: Theory for the New Century,* ed. Elisabeth Bronfen and Misha Kavka (New York: Columbia University Press, 2001), 549.

3. See Michael Warner's *Publics and Counterpublics* (New York: Zone Books, 2005).

4. By the time of this book's publication, Bush's Reign of Error will have nearly (*finally*) run its course. Among the dejecta left in its wake is an archive of political optimism at its most overmuscled and underthought. For instance, back in August of 2004, (the aptly named) Tim Grieve reported that "President George Bush's latest batch of ads doesn't focus on flip-flops. Instead, two new positive ads give a nod to the war and the economy and then trek into values and optimism territory. . . . After all, when you can't run on issues, make an issue out of optimism" ("War Room," August 4, 2004, *salon.com*). Grieve's June 7 "War Room" report as succinctly illustrates this optimism's subsequent faltering: "President Bush continues to talk up the progress the U.S. military is making in Iraq, but his relentless optimism isn't having much of an impact on public opinion ("War Room," June 7, 2005).

5. For a thorough meditation on what Derrida terms the "heterogeneity between faith and knowledge" — which is to say a meditation adequate to this ostensible heterogeneity's complicated provenance and no less complicated philosophical irradiance — see *Religion,* ed. Jacques Derrida and Gianni Vattimo (Stanford, Calif.: Stanford University Press, 1996).

6. I turn to anecdote in the realization of (and subsequently, in the wish to enact) the difficulty of sequestering feelings from metafeelings. Or to conjure Isabel Archer or Maggie Verver, the frustrating and exhilarating perviousness of thinking and living. Anecdotes, in their move to the subjective, sometimes are viewed as escapes from the discursive. I'm not telling this particular story as a retreat from the discursive or critical, but to note the strangeness of having felt like an allegory for my own subsequent academic work.

7. Elaine Scarry, *The Body in Pain: The Making and Unmaking of the World* (New York: Oxford University Press, 1985), 4.

8. Judith Butler, *The Psychic Life of Power* (Stanford, Calif.: Stanford University Press, 1997), 144.

9. Ibid., 149.

10. Ibid. What Butler invokes as "connection" — implying connection between others on political, erotic, and any number of less recognizably charged registers — returns in Lauren Berlant's invoking of "collective attachment." "I propose," Berlant writes, "that we turn optimism itself into a topic probably best phrased as collective attachment. Optimism is a way of describing a certain futurism that implies continuity with the present" ("Critical Inquiry, Affirmative Culture," *Critical Inquiry* 30, no. 2 (Winter 2004): 449). While wary of this optimism's conventional alignment with futurism, I am grateful for Berlant's insistence on returning the term "optimism" to the critical field. While I began this book before the publication of Berlant's own work on optimism, it has been encouraging for me to think of my own project in the vicinity of hers.

11. Judith Butler, *Gender Trouble: Feminism and the Subversion of Identity* (New York: Routledge, 1999), 81.

12. For other references to congealment in Butler's writing, see *Gender Trouble,* xii and 43, as well as *Bodies That Matter* (New York: Routledge, 1993), 244.

13. Butler, *Gender Trouble,* 81.

14. Ibid., 74.

15. Ibid.

16. Ibid., 73.

17. Butler, *The Psychic Life of Power,* 144. "Spawn," with its suggestion of mass hatchings of creatures, arguably resonates within the same implicit science-fictional register as "congealment."

18. Leo Bersani and Ulysse Dutoit, *Forms of Being: Cinema, Aesthetics, Subjectivity* (London: BFI, 2004), 124–25. Bersani's account of a person's hard-wiring for destructiveness, "something as species-specific as the human aptitude for verbal language" (126–27), belies a fantasy of primordiality that recalls and arguably is indebted to Foucault's account of disciplinary subjectivity, even as the former's insistence on interiority surely departs from Foucault's non-psychologizing dermal attentions: "Over the whole surface of contact between the body and the object it handles, power is introduced, fastening them to one another. It constitutes a body-weapon, body-tool, body-machine complex. One is as far as possible from those forms of subjection that demanded of the body only signs or products, forms of expression or the result of labour. The regulation imposed by power is at the same time the law of construction of the operation. Thus disciplinary power appears to have the function not so much of deduction as of synthesis, not so much of exploitation of the product as of coercive link with the apparatus of production" (Michel Foucault, *Discipline and Punish: The Birth of the Prison,* trans. Alan Sheridan [New York: Vintage Books, 1995], 153).

19. "The centrality of redemptive and therapy cultures to the promise of love's formalized satisfactions means that where love provides the dominant rhetoric and form of attachment, so a discussion of pedagogy must be. Popular discourses that merge scientific expertise with a putatively general desire for better techniques of the self — as we see in talk shows, self-help books, and twelve-step semipublics — provide maps for people to clutch in their hands so that they can revisit the unzoned affective domain of which love is the pleasant and thinkable version. In these contexts love — never fully secularized — is the church of optimism for the overwhelmed. The currency that pays the price of entrance is the loss of everything except optimism" (Lauren Berlant, "Love, a Queer Feeling," in *Homosexuality and Psychoanalysis,* ed. Tim Dean and Christopher Lane [Chicago: University of Chicago Press, 2001], 441).

20. See Leo Bersani, *The Freudian Body: Psychoanalysis and Art* (New York: Columbia University Press, 1986), 38–40.

21. D. W. Winnicott, The Use of an Object and Relating through Identification," *Playing and Reality* (New York: Basic Books, 1971), 89–90.

22. Bersani, *The Freudian Body,* 63–64. Whereas Bersani adduces a genetically inexorable correlation (or rather, equivalence) between masochism and sexuality, Lauren Berlant describes optimism — what she denominates "cruel optimism" — in terms of those moments when the inurements of masochism cede to experiences of pain, rather than transliteration of pain into pleasure (or eventually, even, the keloid of pain's acclimation). Optimism, for Berlant, is cruel to the extent that it occasions the erethism of sensitive hope and futural attachment without the ability to achieve either such end. See "Cruel Optimism," *differences* 17, no. 5 (2006): 20–35.

23. Leo Bersani, "Is the Rectum a Grave?" *October* 23 (Winter 1987): 218.

24. Sigmund Freud, *The Ego and the Id,* in *The Standard Edition of the Complete Psychological Works of Sigmund Freud,* ed. and trans. James Strachey, 24 vols. (London: Hogarth Press, 1953–74), 19:29.

25. See Butler, *The Psychic Life of Power,* 139–40.

26. For other queer-theoretical texts nearly unthinkable without the work of Butler or Bersani, see Ann Cvetkovich, *An Archive of Feelings: Trauma, Sexuality, and Lesbian Public Cultures* (Durham: Duke University Press, 2003); Tim Dean, *Beyond Sexuality* (Chicago: University of Chicago Press, 2000); David L. Eng and David Kazanjian, eds. *Loss* (Berkeley: University of California Press, 2003), for which Judith Butler writes an afterword; Didier Eribon, *Insult and the Making of the Gay Self*, trans. Michael Lucey (Durham: Duke University Press, 2004); Brett Farmer, *Spectacular Passions: Cinema, Fantasy, Gay Male Spectatorships* (Durham: Duke University Press, 2000); Diana Fuss, *Identification Papers* (New York: Routledge, 1995); Teresa de Lauretis, *The Practice of Love: Lesbian Sexuality and Perverse Desire* (Bloomington: University of Indiana Press, 1994), whose first chapter takes as epigraph one of Bersani's articulations on Freudian desire; José Muñoz, *Disidentifications: Queers of Color and the Performance of Politics* (Minneapolis: University of Minnesota Press,

1999); Jeffrey T. Nealon, *Alterity Politics: Ethics and Performative Subjectivity* (Durham: Duke University Press, 1998); Esther Sánchez-Pardo, *Cultures of the Death Drive: Melanie Klein and Modernist Melancholia* (Durham: Duke University Press, 2003); The above list intends only to suggest the iceberg's tip; the single essays and articles written under the influence of Bersani or Butler are nearly countless. *Queer Optimism* positions itself not just in relation to the work of two scholars (or three or four), but in relation to the veritable queer cottage industry that these scholars have engendered.

27. See, for instance, Judith Butler's analysis of hate speech in *Excitable Speech: A Politics of the Performative* (New York: Routledge, 1997), or her critique of post 9/11 politics in *Precarious Life: The Powers of Mourning and Violence* (New York: Verso Books, 2004).

28. Gilles Deleuze, *Essays Critical and Clinical,* trans. Daniel W. Smith and Michael A. Greco (Minneapolis: University of Minnesota Press, 1997), 4.

29. Ann Cvetkovich, *Archive of Feelings,* 63.

30. Ibid., 53ff.

31. Ibid., 44f.

32. D. W. Winnicott, "Roots of Aggression," *Psycho-Analytic Explorations* (Cambridge: Harvard University Press, 1989), 458.

33. Curious how both *Loss* and *An Archive of Feelings* seek to depathologize their respective melancholia and trauma, as though these books weren't being published at a time when pathologization itself seems beside the point; as though—if not post-Butler or Bersani, then post-Oprah—melancholia and trauma hadn't themselves long-trafficked in idealized, celebrity-like circuits.

34. I think (to name just a few) of Roland Barthes, Michael Moon, Biddy Martin, Jane Gallop, Lauren Berlant, Henry Abelove, Tim Dean, and, of course, Eve Kosofsky Sedgwick.

35. For a lucid critique of the hermeneutics of suspicion (specifically, vis-à-vis the oeuvre of Slavoj Žižek) along Laplanchian lines, see Tim Dean's "Art as Symptom: Žižek and the Ethics of Psychoanalytic Criticism," *Diacritics* 32, no. 2 (2002): 21–41.

36. Judith Butler, *Giving an Account of Oneself* (New York: Fordham University Press, 2005), 21.

37. Ibid., 21.

38. Think, here, of Thomas Gray's paradigmatic "Ode on a Distant Prospect of Eton College":

> Yet, ah! why should they know their fate,
> Since sorrow never comes too late,
> And happiness too swiftly flies?
> Thought would destroy their paradise.
> No more;—where ignorance is bliss,
> 'Tis folly to be wise.

39. Eve Kosofsky Sedgwick, *Epistemology of the Closet* (Berkeley: University of California Press, 1990), 5.

40. Eve Kosofsky Sedgwick, "Paranoid Reading and Reparative Reading, or, You're So Paranoid, You Probably Think This Essay Is About You," *Touching Feeling: Affect, Pedagogy, Performativity* (Durham, N.C.: Duke University Press, 2003), 137–38.

41. Sedgwick, "Shame, Theatricality, and Queer Performativity: Henry James's *The Art of the Novel*," in *Touching Feeling*, 40.

42. Silvan S. Tomkins, "Shame-Humiliation and Contempt-Disgust," in *Shame and Its Sisters: A Silvan Tomkins Reader*, ed. Eve Kosofsky Sedgwick and Adam Frank (Durham, N.C.: Duke University Press, 1995), 133.

43. "Shame is the affect that mantles the threshold between introversion and extroversion, between absorption and theatricality, between performativity and—performativity" (Sedgwick, *Touching Feeling*, 38).

44. Whereas Sedgwick celebrates shame's blossoming between diachronically ossified self-formations (for instance, between the Henry James of 1875 and the Henry James of 1907), Giorgio Agamben, in "Shame, or On the Subject" notes, following Levinas, that "shame is grounded in our being's incapacity to move away and break from itself" (*Remnants of Auschwitz: The Witness and the Archive*, trans. Daniel Heller-Roazen [New York: Zone Books, 1999], 104–5). "[I]n shame," Agamben writes, "we are consigned to something from which we cannot in any way distance ourselves" (105). From this opposite beginning, and in the quite different context of Auschwitz, Agamben nonetheless reaches a conclusion nearly identical to Sedgwick's own. "It is now possible to clarify," Agamben writes, "the sense in which shame is truly something like the hidden structure of all subjectivity and consciousness" (128). I juxtapose Sedgwick's account of shame with Agamben's to illustrate the persuasiveness of shame, as a trope, beyond my book's immediate queer purlieu. If Sedgwick makes a claim for shame that universalizes its relation to queers, Agamben goes one step further, extending his reading of shame within Primo Levi's *The Reawakening* to pertain to everyone. I introduce Agamben to recall the fact that queer theory's energies are not constitutively different from theories of people as such and, as often, are mutually informing.

45. Tomkins, *Shame and Its Sisters*, 134.

46. Ibid., 138.

47. Sedgwick, "Shame, Theatricality, and Queer Performativity," 65.

48. See Charles Darwin, *The Expression of the Emotions in Man and Animals* (Chicago: University of Chicago Press, 1965), and Mark Hansen, *New Philosophy for New Media* (Cambridge, Mass.: MIT Press, 2004).

49. To look ahead to my book's analysis of Dickinson's account of affects, this mare's nest of nomination and misnomination—as relates specifically to mutations of shame—is the explicit subject of one of Dickinson's undated quatrains:

Faithful was all that I could boast
But Constancy became
To her, by her innominate
A something like a shame (F1716)

50. Sedgwick, "Shame, Theatricality, Queer Performativity," 63.

51. Sedgwick, *Shame and Its Sisters,* 138–39.

52. I find instructive Laplanche's account of an enigmatic signifier's simultaneous transmittability and nonintelligibility: the absorption and circulation of a message's form, irrespective of recognition of the message's content. "The primal scene," Laplanche writes, "conveys messages. It is traumatising only because it proffers, indeed imposes its enigmas, which compromise the spectacle addressed to the child. I certainly have no wish to make an inventory of these messages, for there are, in my sense no objective enigmas: the only enigmas that exist are ones that are proffered, and that reduplicate in one way or another the relationship that the sender of the message has with his own unconscious" ("Seduction, Persecution, Revelation," *Essays on Otherness,* ed. John Fletcher [London: Routledge, 1999], 170–71). In suggesting the circulation of something like melancholy from one theoretical text to another, I imagine Butler (or Bersani) not as "the sender[s] of the message," but rather as themselves recipients of an enigma prior to their own work. That Bersani and Butler have importantly helped to revitalize critical interest in Laplanche's work is beyond this introduction's immediate purview, although I make note of this, if only to reiterate that my critiques of Bersani and Butler are neither absolute nor preempting of indebtedness or admiration.

53. Lee Edelman, *No Future: Queer Theory and the Death Drive* (Durham: Duke University Press, 2004), 6.

54. The interminable gadflying of *No Future* strikes me as its own peculiar form of generosity, insofar as it is near impossible for readers not to feel *something* toward Edelman's work. How not to feel grateful for a book that solicits intense feeling from nearly anyone who reads it? I nonetheless balk at the possibility of a revamped queer ethics predicated on "the corrosive force of irony" (*No Future* 23), predicated on the slap-happy eschewal of The Child, as though there were only one ideological Child. As though there weren't within cultural discourse (not just the specter, but) the tenable, exquisitely precocious, touched and touching figure of a Queer Child. "The cult of the Child," Edelman writes, "permits no shrines to the queerness of boys and girls, since queerness ... is understood as bringing children and childhood to an end" (19). Such claims seem so patently misguided and foreclosing that it's difficult to know how to respond, beyond the obvious fact that *there's nothing queerer than childhood*: cf. Henry James's Maisie, or JonBenet Ramsey, or the Ludovic of "Ma Vie en Rose," or my own childhood home videos, which motivate in me a certain pathos not because childhood ends where queerness begins, but because my own queerness, as I bat my seahorse eyelashes or wander through leaf-piles, is so effusively, if

confusedly, in full-gear. Were one to claim that Edelman's hypostasizations of the Child seem to do more harm than good, Edelman, impeccably, might say, *of course,* more harm than good. In fact (of course), Edelman already says as much: "[T]he queerness of which I speak would deliberately sever us from ourselves, from the assurance, that is, of *knowing* ourselves and hence of *knowing* our 'good.' Such queerness proposes, in place of the good, something I want to call 'better,' though it promises, in more than one sense of the phrase, absolutely nothing" (5). *Queer Optimism* is for those wanting ("in more than one sense of the phrase") something "better" than "nothing." Edelman's immodest proposals inevitably have rankled many scholars. In their introduction to *Curiouser: On the Queerness of Children,* Steven Bruhm and Natasha Hurley similarly question Edelman's preemptive inscription of the Child into a predetermined ideological matrix: "What is the effect," Bruhm and Hurley write, "of projecting the child into a heteronormative future? One effect is that we accept the teleology of the child... as heterosexually determined" (*Curiouser: On the Queerness of Children,* ed. Steven Bruhm and Natasha Hurley [Minneapolis: University of Minnesota Press, 2004], xiv). *Curiouser's* essays importantly challenge simplifying or evacuating narratives of childhood sexuality, rescuing children from hypostasized forms of innocence. My own project, on the other hand, seeks to rescue (not children, but) *optimism from innocence.*

On a different register, Susan Fraiman addresses the foreclosure, in *No Future,* of a queer pregnant body. "My interest here," Fraiman writes at the close of her book *Cool Men and the Second Sex,* "is not in the merits of campaigns for gay 'normalization' and marriage rights but rather in Edelman's suppression of procreative queerness even as he brings up lesbian and gay parenting. By tying this firmly and exclusively to *adoption,* Edelman keeps the category of queerness apart from the feminized, reproductive body, which is imagined as scarcely any closer or more familiar than China or Guatemala" (*Cool Men and the Second Sex* [New York: Columbia University Press, 2003], 133). Fraiman's interceding is timely (and not just because the pregnancy of Katie Holmes has brought home to all checkout-aisle tabloid-readers how utterly queer pregnancy itself can be)—albeit the queer *unheimlich* of pregnancy has been available for scrutiny, at very least, since Rosemary's Baby, Sigourney Weaver's Ripley, etc. Neither my interest nor Fraiman's, however, is in a pregnancy that could assert its queerness only along these limited, science-fiction (or Scientological) lines. Rather, I admire Fraiman's assertion of a queer theory that could accommodate (and not merely chide) the complicated lexicons of maternal affect. Here, again, I think of Winnicott, whose own meticulous and insightful theorizations of maternity salubriously supplement those enabled by Fraiman's work, or (psychoanalytically) the work of Melanie Klein.

55. My methodological attachment to the local is informed by Sedgwick's revitalizing engagements with Silvan Tompkins's notion of weak theory (versus the strong theory of which Edelman's polemic is a keen example). See "Paranoid

Reading and Reparative Reading, or You're So Paranoid, You Probably Think This Essay Is About You," in *Touching Feeling.*

56. The argument (if not the polemical affect) of Edelman's recent study implicitly recalls various moments in Bersani's corpus, but more explicitly conjures a proposition made by Peggy Phelan, in her 1995 essay, "Dying Man with a Movie Camera, *Silverlake Life.*" Phelan writes: "Let's suppose that lesbians and gay men in the academies and institutions of the contemporary United States have a particularly potent relation to grief. Exiled from the Law of the Social, many gay men and lesbians may have introjected the passionate hatred of mainstream homophobia and taken up an embattled, aggressive, and complex relation to the death drive. The aggressivity of this relation, the theory goes, makes it possible for us to survive our (first) deaths. While we wait for the next, we perform queer acts" (Peggy Phelan, "Dying Man with a Movie Camera, *Silverlake Life:* The View from Here," *GLQ* 2, no. 4 [1995]: 380.) Such "queer acts," folded back into Edelman's *No Future,* would entail acting as though there were no future, executing actions directly (if not solely) motivated by the death drive. Phelan's essay, meditating on the utterly harrowing documentary, "Silverlake Life," is itself harrowing in the austere deference with which Phelan approaches her topic. "Harrowing," etymologically denoting an implement that could either extirpate bodies or hollow the ground in preparation for other burials, seems to capture what such an "embattled" relation to the death drive might feel like. The harrow of both Phelan's essay and "Silverlake Life" stands in stark opposition to the effulgence of Edelman's often pyrotechnically brilliant, gymnastic observations. The affective disjunct between Phelan's and Edelman's texts seems illustrative of an evolving ease with which the death drive has come to be articulated and invoked. Where is the harrow in Edelman's writing? With what has the harrow been replaced?

57. Edelman's aligning of Lacanian truth and Edelmanian queerness may mislead one to think that *Wunsch* itself is Lacan's word for "truth." This is not the case, as Lacan makes clear in both the seminar from which Edelman quotes and in *Ecrits,* in which Lacan, traversing languages, aligns *Wunsch* with "its English translation *wish*" and "the French *desir.*" This is to say that Edelman tries to compel an equivalence between truth (denoted in Lacan's text as *vérité,* rather than the Freudian *Wunsch*) and queerness, when in fact queerness, following Lacan, has more to do with wishing — a *true wish* (which, contra Edelman's purposes, resonates in an optative rather than antioptative register) rather than *true truth.* The fancy footwork by which Edelman's text elides wishing in favor of stringent verity seems symptomatic of what I shall go on to describe as *No Future's* coercive absolutism, whose Lacanian origins seem if not intentionally falsifying, then (forgive the pun) wishy-washy. Many thanks to Tim Dean for bringing to my attention the translational confusions of my own initial analysis of these passages. For an insightful critique of *No Future* along lines more psychoanalytically sustained than my own, see Dean's "An Impossible Embrace:

Queerness, Futurity, and the Death Drive," in *A Time for the Humanities: Futurity and the Limits of Autonomy,* ed. James J. Bono, Tim Dean, Ewa Plonowska Ziarek (New York: Fordham University Press, 2008).

58. Eve Kosofsky Sedgwick, "Paranoid Reading, Reparative Reading," *Touching Feeling,* 125.

59. There isn't space in this introduction to do justice to Edelman's complicated and saponifying rhetoric of embodiment and figuration. I shall return, elsewhere in these pages, to Edelman's insistence on queer *figurations* of the death drive — as though readers of Edelman might otherwise think they could slink into a phone-booth only to reappear, cape and tights, as *TODESTRIEBE.*

60. This claustrophobia might account, in part, for the ellipses that conclude *No Future's* second epigraph, by Virginia Woolf. "Yes, I was thinking: we live without a future. That's what's queer." One could variously speculate how Woolf's "queer" differs from Edelman's, when Woolf continues, beyond Edelman's ellipses: "That's whats [*sic*] queer, with our noses pressed to a closed door" (Virginia Woolf, *The Diary of Virginia Woolf,* vol. 5 [London: Chatto & Windus / The Hogarth Press, 1984], 355).

61. Butler, *Giving an Account of Oneself,* 41.

62. G. W. Leibniz, "Discourse on Metaphysics," in *Philosophical Essays,* ed. and trans. Roger Ariew and Daniel Garber (Indianapolis: Hackett Publishing Company, 1989), 38. Subsequent references to this essay, unless otherwise noted, are to this edition and cited parenthetically within the text.

63. Gilles Deleuze, *The Fold: Leibniz and the Baroque,* trans. Tom Conley (Minneapolis: University of Minnesota Press, 1993), 68.

64. Ibid.

65. "I hold, therefore, that, according to these principles, in order to act in accordance with the love of God, it is not sufficient to force ourselves to be patient; rather, we must truly be satisfied with everything that has come to us according to his will" (G. W. Leibniz, *Discourse on Metaphysics,* trans. Roger Ariew and Daniel Garber [Indianapolis: Hackett Publishing Company, 1991], 37–38). The noncultivatability of optimism, in this context, is an effect of a person's chronic inability to know as much as God does. Leibniz's conception of God, in this respect, is analogous to Freud's conception of an unconscious. Both God and the unconscious delineate what a person at any given moment cannot know. Several years following Leibniz's writing, in response to Hobbes's condemnations of humanity, Shaftesbury similarly describes an epistemological predicament that Leibnizian optimism abandons altogether, and that psychoanalysis later takes as point of departure. "In an infinity of things, mutually relative, a mind which sees not infinitely can see nothing fully, and must therefore frequently see that as imperfect which in itself is really perfect" (quoted from Shaftesbury's *The Moralists: A Philosophical Rhapsody,* in Radoslav Andrea Tsanoff's *The Nature of Evil* [New York: Macmillan, 1931], 113).

66. Leibniz, *Theodicy: Essays on the Goodness of God and the Freedom of Man and the Origin of Evil,* ed. Austin Farrer (Chicago: Open Court, 1998), 154.

67. Jonathan Lear, *Happiness, Death, and the Remainder of Life* (Cambridge, Mass.: Harvard University Press, 2000), 50.

68. Ibid.

69. Ibid., 129.

70. Ibid., 27.

71. Ibid., 98.

72. "Lyric" more or less nonproblematically describes the poetics of Hart Crane, Emily Dickinson, and Elizabeth Bishop, but perhaps seems a misdesignation for that of Jack Spicer, who rejected conceptions of lyric poetry for what he termed serial poetry. As my chapter on Spicer will argue, however, Spicer's relation to seriality is no less ambivalent or confused than is his relation to lyric form. What it means, exactly, to read lyrically remains an open (if not potentially inexhaustible) question, albeit my intuitive regard for the genre is indebted to Sharon Cameron's *Lyric Time: Dickinson and the Limits of Genre* (Baltimore: Johns Hopkins University Press, 1979). I take the lyric's license, in part, as the readerly luxury of inhabiting local instances of a given body of poetic work, without metaleptic compunction to dilate these local formulations into representatives of any larger poetic event. Wai Chee Dimock's translation of readerly dilemma into the landscapes of fractal geometry provides a useful vocabulary for thinking about the necessity of multiple optics, as well as the theoretical difficulty of sustaining these optics simultaneously. See Dimock, *Through Other Continents: American Literature Across Deep Time* (Princeton: Princeton University Press, 2006), 73–106.

73. "For several decades, a group of unreproachably intelligent and resourceful readers from several countries performed an annihilating elucidation of Mallarmé's writing. . . . The Mallarméan text is treated as if it were sick, as if it were *deficient in narrativity*. The assumption has been that Mallarmé's work could be appreciated only if it were first straightened out. . . . Criticism is perhaps always motivated by the more or less secret project of substituting itself for the texts which it studies; it does away with its objects by embracing them" (*The Death of Stéphane Mallarmé* [New York: Cambridge University Press, 1982], vii–viii).

74. See Christopher Herbert's "The Conundrum of Coherence," *New Literary History* 35, no. 2 (2004). Herbert's critique of New Criticism's privileging of coherence inadvertently dovetails with Judith Butler's critique of ontological coherence. Herbert writes that "[t]hanks to the intervention of a post-modern angle of vision upon the ideal or fetish of coherence, however, it has become possible to divest this idea of its cloak of timeless necessity and to see it, rather, as a creed with a particular history that it behooves us to seek to understand if we wish to avoid being its dupes by default" (185). While Herbert allows

for the possibility of incoherence's own possible fetishization, such an observation seems at best belated. Coherence, within literary criticism (not to mention queer theory) has become a much-kicked dead horse, even as incoherence, in being posited as corrective "angle of vision," refuses the extensiveness of its own possible blind spots and astigmatisms. For other critiques of New Criticism lexically analogous to critiques of optimism, see Terry Eagleton's *Literary Theory: An Introduction* (Oxford: Basil Blackwell, 1983), and John Paul Russo's "The Tranquilized Poem: The Crisis of New Criticism in the 1950s," *Literature and Language* 30, no. 2 (Summer 1988). Russo claims that in the event of New Criticism, "the poem was not tranquil, only tranquilized; artificially drugged and immobilized were the political, social, historical implications of the text" (198). For readings of lyric poetry beyond New Criticism, see the aptly titled *Lyric Poetry beyond New Criticism,* ed. Chavira Hosek and Patricia Parker (Ithaca, N.Y.: Cornell University Press, 1985).

75. Contrary to John Middleton Murray's 1921 malediction that Eliot's *The Sacred Wood* (the volume in which "Tradition and the Individual Talent" first appeared) would unlikely "impress any large section of the public" (*New Republic* 26 [April 13, 1921]: 194–95), James Longenbach has recently, unsurprisingly called *The Sacred Wood* "perhaps the most influential volume of literary criticism published in the century." Louis Menand has called Eliot the link "between the first academic critics — Richards, Empson, Leavis, the New Critics — and the whole sequence of nonacademic critics stretching back to Kant, and from Kant back to Plato" (*New England Quarterly* 69, no. 4 [December 1996]: 554–79); René Wellek has called him "by far the most important critic of the 20th century in the English-speaking world" (*Sewanee Review* 64, no. 3 [Summer 1956]: 398–443); and Harold Bloom, who has often spurned Eliot for his rejection of the Romantic poets (even as Bloom's work on influence would be impossible without Eliot's articulations of tradition), has called him a "cultural oracle of the academies" (*Raritan* 6, no. 1 [Fall 1988]: 1–25). It is worth noting, for the sake of contextualizing an intellectual climate that eventually could enable the intersection of Eliot's interests and queer theory's, that the *Raritan* issue that featured Bloom's essay on Eliot (as part of a celebratory section called "Eliot at 100") also included an essay by Leo Bersani. In the issue just previous, *Raritan* had published the second installment of Sedgwick's essay, "Epistemology of the Closet."

Eliot's reputation as a critic depends largely on the essay in question. And the influence of "Tradition and the Individual Talent," it nearly goes without saying, goes unmatched, both in its saturation of the critical field (titularly sounded early on in Cleanth Brooks's *Modern Poetry and the Tradition* (Chapel Hill: University of North Carolina Press, 1939), and F. R. Leavis's *The Great Tradition* (London: Chatto & Windus, 1948).

76. For an extensive account of impersonality's premodernist history, as well as its varying instantiations within the modernist poetics of Eliot and Pound, see Maud Ellmann's excellent *The Poetics of Impersonality: T. S. Eliot and Ezra*

Pound (Brighton, Sussex: Harvester Press, 1987). My reading of Eliot's "Tradition and the Individual Talent" can't help but produce a winnowing, simplified version of Eliot, what James Longenbach has termed " 'a straw-man' Eliot" ("Hart Crane and T. S. Eliot: Poets in the Sacred Grove," *Denver Quarterly* 23, no. 1 (1988): 102). For the sake of my introduction's argument, I stand by this simplification, as it is this received version of Eliot that most uncannily shares the queer-theoretical argot I have outlined. Just as my book is occupied less with Freud than with Freud's reception, it is occupied less with Eliot than with Eliot's reception, particularly the reception of Eliotic impersonality, as most acutely drawn in "Tradition and the Individual Talent." For more generous treatments of Eliot's shifting understanding of tradition as imbricated with poetic individuality, see Longenbach's essays "Hart Crane and T. S. Eliot: Poets in the Sacred Grove" and "Guarding the Hornèd Gates: History and Interpretation in the Early Poetry of T. S. Eliot" (*ELH* 52, no. 2 (Summer 1985): 503–27), the latter of which broaches Eliot's sense of history, within "Tradition and the Individual Talent," as it emerges from Eliot's earlier study of F. H. Bradley. See also John Paul Riquelme's *Harmony of Dissonances: T. S. Eliot, Romanticism and Imagination* (Baltimore: Johns Hopkins University, 1991), 25–44, and Sanford Schwartz's *The Matrix of Modernism: Pound, Eliot, and Early Twentieth-Century Thought* (Princeton, N.J.: Princeton University Press, 1985), esp. 170–83.

77. T. S. Eliot, "Tradition and the Individual Talent," *The Sacred Wood: Essays on Poetry and Criticism* (London: Methuen & Co. 1948), 52–53.

78. Furthermore, the following passage — what Eliot, in the spirit of science, calls "analogy," but what as veritably works as metaphor — effects within Eliot's criticism a metaphorical rupture (the confusion of which, looking ahead to Crane, we might call catachrestic) potentially at odds with the essay's manifest argument. This strange analogy points to a resistance within Eliot's metaphor to the argument of which it is put in the service. The metaphor, as it successively swerves and alters through the course of Eliot's argument for impersonality, will foster within Eliot's essay a confusion in whose space something like the personal can be restored. I shall differently consider the reparative capacities of metaphoricity in subsequent chapters.

79. Eliot, "Tradition and the Individual Talent," 54.

80. I'm not the first to note the confusions of what F. W. Bateson calls "the notorious episode of the 'finely filiated platinum' " ("T. S. Eliot: 'Impersonality' 50 Years Later," 631). "The essay has been criticized recently," Bateson continues, "more than once because of this episode, which is, I agree, annoying and embarrassing" (631). Bateson's account of "the notorious episode" (a pitch of rhetoric that suggests sexual as much as metaphorical scandal) comes from a 1969 essay from the *Southern Review*, in which Bateson fascinatingly recalls the publication history of Eliot's essay. "The essay," Bateson writes, "as is not always remembered, was originally published in two installments . . . and it was necessary for him, as for any other writer of a 'serial,' to end the first installment with

a statement that would whet the reader's appetite for its sequel a month later. Dipping desperately into his memory Eliot bethought him of the stinks class [!] at school" (631).The passage, that is, that ends the first installment of Eliot's essay, is precisely the one in question, wherein he invites the reader to consider the action of platinum in a gaseous chamber. A month later, the essay resumes, "The analogy was that of the catalyst." Bateson, in the final analysis, is as little moved by this passage as I am moved. "Nowadays," Bateson opines, "when the essay can be read as an uninterrupted whole, the platinum episode is best skipped. As I have said, it can be justified as a sophisticated 'To be continued in our Next' device under the conditions of its original publication, but it adds nothing of interest to the theoretical argument. If it is ignored or excised, on the other hand, the essay will be immediately recognized as probably the most original single critical essay that Eliot ever wrote" (632). Coincidentally, the *Southern Review* was edited in those years by Donald Stanford, whose correspondence with Elizabeth Bishop — many decades earlier — I shall consider in the book's final chapter.

81. Eliot, "Tradition and the Individual Talent," 54.

82. Eliot's recourse to the scientific is itself curious (if not suspicious), in light of his essay "The Perfect Critic" (positioned in *The Sacred Wood* just two essays before "Tradition and the Individual Talent"), in which he reproves "a distinguished critic" for "that familiar vague suggestion of the scientific vocabulary which is characteristic of modern writing" (2). For further reading on Eliot's varying relation to scientism, see Benjamin Lockerd, *Aethereal Rumours: T. S. Eliot's Physics and Poetics* (Lewisburg, Pa.: Bucknell University Press, 1998), 23–32.

83. Eliot, "Tradition and the Individual Talent," 54.

84. My book moves thematically rather than chronologically. While the move backward from Eliot and Crane to Dickinson may seem flatly anachronistic, my conception of Dickinson's optimism is in fact a progression from Crane's (even if, strictly speaking, preceding it), and not vice versa. Insofar as my book takes as its subject both these poets (as articulators of queer optimism) *and* their critical reception (as instances of pessimistic optics inadequate to their queer-optimistic enterprise), the chronological order of poets is less determining than their relative contemporaneity within a shared critical field.

85. See Mark Seltzer's *Serial Killers: Death and Life in America's Wound Culture* (New York: Routledge, 1998). From the fantasy of a serial killer who seems "abnormally normal" (10), who looks like anyone else in the neighborhood, to the aesthetic implications of a serial killer's composite sketch, Seltzer's argument depends on a seriality inextricable from depersonalization. "The shift in terms [from 'stranger-killing' to serial killing] registers a progressive migration or inflection in the understanding of 'impersonal' violence — a shift in the understanding of the conditions of personation and impersonality. The brutality of serial violence is consistently linked to its impersonality, as if its brutality consists above all in the feeling of sheer typicality" (42).

86. Elizabeth Bishop, *One Art: Letters,* ed. Robert Giroux (New York: Farrar, Straus & Giroux, 1994), 188 (July 3, 1949).

87. Eliot, "Tradition and the Individual Talent," 54–55.

88. Dante, *The Inferno,* trans. Robert Pinksy (New York: Noonday Press, 1998), 125.

89. Ibid., 123.

90. Feeling eternal importantly differs, theoretically speaking, from being so. My attachments here, as throughout, accept the impossibility of the latter without ceding the potential hopefulness of the former.

91. I am defining sodomy along the expansive lines articulated by Jonathan Goldberg: "sodomy is, as a sexual act, anything that threatens alliance — any sexual act, that is, that does not promote the aim of married procreative sex" (*Sodometries: Renaissance Texts, Modern Sexualities* [Stanford: Stanford University Press, 1992], 19). Sodomy, thus conceived, threatens *some* forms of alliance even as it indubitably enables and cultivates others. I denominate the four poets in question "sodomites" with every alliant affection.

1. Hart Crane's Smile

1. I think here of investigation's etymological denoting of a kind of bob and weave, a rhythm composed of both immersion and the rising for air (*in – "into" + vestigare – "to trace out"*).

2. Eric J. Sundquist, "Bringing Home the Word: Magic, Lies and Silence in Hart Crane," *ELH* 44, no. 2 (Summer 1977): 381.

3. Ibid.

4. Christopher Nealon, *Foundlings: Lesbian and Gay Historical Emotion before Stonewall* (Durham, N.C.: Duke University Press, 2001), 41.

5. *The Letters of Hart Crane,* ed. Brom Weber (New York: Hermitage House, 1952), May 16, 1922, 87. Hereafter cited as *Letters.*

6. Crane, *Letters,* 113 (January 5, 1923).

7. Crane's differentiation between "positive" and "ecstatic" seems all the more salubrious in a critical climate that uncritically presumes Crane as an avatar of the ecstatic. Nealon describes Crane's poetics as an "ecstatic lyricism." Thomas Yingling likewise regards Crane as ecstatic — as do Lee Edelman, Tim Dean, and Robert K. Martin. The ubiquity in queer Crane readings of such pronouncements both spurs my own interest in imagining a nonecstatic Crane and intimates that the skeptical age invoked by Crane might presciently describe not only the time of Crane's writing, but the time of our own.

8. Hart Crane, *Complete Poems of Hart Crane,* ed. Marc Simon (New York: Liveright Publishing Corporation, 1986), 18. Subsequent references to Crane's poetry are to this edition, and cited parenthetically by page number within the text.

9. Catachresis, sometimes more loosely defined as a mixed metaphor, describes (from Quintilian, Puttenham, and on) "the practice of adapting the nearest available term to describe something for which no actual term exists." Metaphor, for Quintilian, involves *translatio*; catachresis, *abusio*. As a form of abuse, catachresis seems serendipitously congenial to the violences and improprieties by which queer subjects of all sorts get interpellated. For instance, Edelman's mobilizing of catachresis not just as a queer trope, but as a trope for a particular queer sensibility seems evident in his writing that "catachresis . . . as a verbal abuse . . . has the air of something dangerous and disreputable" (12). For more on catachresis, see Quintilian, *Institutio oratoria,* or more recently Patricia Parker, "Metaphor and Catachresis," in *Ends of Rhetoric: History, Theory, Practice,* ed. John Bender and David Wellbery (Stanford, Calif.: Stanford University Press, 1990), and Lee Edelman, *Transmemberment of Song: Hart Crane's Anatomies of Rhetoric and Desire* (Stanford, Calif.: Stanford University Press, 1987).

10. "Expressions of long duration — certainly ten seconds or more, and usually 5 seconds — are likely to be false. Most felt expressions don't last that long. Unless someone is having a peak experience, at the height of ecstasy, in a roaring rage, or at the bottom of depression, genuine emotional expressions don't remain on the face for more than a few seconds. Even in those extreme states expressions rarely last so long; instead, there are many shorter expressions. The long expressions are usually emblems or mock expressions" (Paul Ekman, *Telling Lies* [New York: W. W. Norton, 1992], 147). Ekman's work, motivated by thinkers such as Erving Goffman and Silvan Tomkins, extends the nineteenth-century observations of Guillaume-Benjamin Duchenne du Bologne's *Mechanisme de la physionomie humaine.* Darwin, also following Duchenne, likewise notes that indelible smiles might be a sign of idiocy. "There is another large class of idiots who are persistently joyous and benign, and who are constantly laughing and smiling. Their countenances often exhibit a stereotyped smile" (Charles Darwin, *The Expression of the Emotions in Man and Animals* [Chicago: University of Chicago Press, 1965], 197.)

11. Think of Wordsworth's conception of poetry as emotion recollected in tranquility, or of Proust's madeleines.

12. For a brilliant, if differently keyed, account of the nonfrivolous, epistemological and political stakes of style within queer theory, see Lee Edelman's "Antagonism, Negativity, and the Subject of Queer Theory" (*PMLA* 121, no. 3 [May 2006]: 821), a rejoinder to Judith Halberstam's dismissively grousing insistence that queer theory "abandon the neat, clever, chiasmic, punning emphasis on style and stylistic order that characterizes both the gay male archive and the theoretical writings about it" ("The Politics of Negativity in Recent Queer Theory," *PMLA* 121, no. 3 [May 2006): 823).

13. Joseph Riddel, "Hart Crane's Poetics of Failure," *ELH* 33, no. 4 (December 1966): 487. Hereafter cited parenthetically in the text.

14. Riddel, quoting from Nietzsche, *The Birth of Tragedy* (Garden City, N.Y.: Anchor Books, 1956), 126.

15. Nietzsche, *The Birth of Tragedy,* 126.

16. This oscillation within Crane's poetry between fluid and nonfluid (resonant enough in Crane's book titles, *White Buildings, The Bridge, Key West*) is reflected in Crane criticism, whose trope of choice in describing fluidities in Crane's poetry is booze. R. P. Blackmur paradigmatically characterizes the language of "Lachrymae Christi" as "in the flux of intoxicated sense" (R. P. Blackmur, "New Thresholds, New Anatomies: Notes on a Text by Hart Crane," in *Hart Crane: A Collection of Critical Essays,* ed. Alan Trachtenberg [Englewood Cliffs, N.J.: Prentice-Hall, 1982], 61), and its principle of association (which Crane would later himself denominate the logic of metaphor) as "resembl[ing] the notion of wine . . . the notion of extralogical, intoxicated metamorphosis of the senses [which both] controls and innervates Crane's whole sensibility" (Blackmur, 60). To discuss Crane's poems as though liquor were both origin and constitutive energy conjures an especial problematic of intentional fallacy, in simultaneously claiming that poetic meaning lies beyond the purview of the poem proper, but that meaning as such would speak in the slurs of a "rum-scallion."

In his important essay "Danced Undone: Performances of Exhaustion and Resignation in Crane's Lyrics," John Vincent notes that for Riddel, exhaustion (as particularization of Crane's brand of failure) "*happens to* rather than is *performed in* Crane's poems" (Vincent, *Queer Lyrics: Difficulty and Closure in American Poetry* [New York: Palgrave, 2002], 130). Intoxication, following a Blackmurian trajectory, happens to *and* is performed in Crane's poems. Or rather, performance within Crane's poems implicitly (or as in the case of Blackmur, explicitly) is imagined as under the influence. Thus, Vincent's lucid analysis of exhaustion within Crane as phenomenological experience of interpersonal boundary nonetheless depends on the rush (the lush?) that speeds against boundary, and which sometimes breaks through. Exhaustion, then, becomes an affective figuring of what is left after "self-shattering" (Vincent, 143) or "breach" (145) or outward radiation of waves" (145). Exhaustion is related to intoxication (alcoholic, erotic, syntactical, or some composite of the three) as its endgame, and intoxication itself presumes a certain sort of flux, within Crane's poetry, as definitionally operative.

The conjoining in Crane (or at least in Crane's critics) of poetry and alcohol suggests one of Crane's consanguinities (to use one of Crane's words) with Whitman. Leaving booze and flux (of Crane, of Whitman) aside, I'm interested in thinking about moments in Crane in which the argot of flux seems acutely inapplicable. This is much less to say that flux isn't ubiquitous as a style throughout Crane's writing (it is), than that the poetry reacts against itself in decisive moments, and that the flotsam of these nonfluid formulations has a particular quality, and in particular relation to the lyric tide on which it washes up. While

Vincent's interest in exhaustion might seem like a comparable site of poetic inertia, his is a sort of "I'm too tired to move," which smacks of (drips with, smells like) the movement that has precipitated it; the formulations that interest me are extrinsic from the narrative of dissipation altogether. It is not, to recall a temporality described by Renu Bora, that one asks what made these formulations immobile: they could, it seems, exist in no other way.

Fluidity, in Crane's poetry, is commensurate with what is most unintelligible within it. Or rather, fluidity marks the threshold beyond which Crane's most challenging formulations become jettisonable in their inscrutability. Past this point, the challenges of poetry whose meaning is always on the move (which is to say, elsewhere) seem nearly indistinguishable from those of poetry that won't budge. This resistance seems in its inaccessibility to force novel ways of engagement; if meaning, per se, can't be gleaned from these "new thresholds" of imperviousness, then how, meaning aside, do the formulations recall earlier formulations, what are the sounds of these words, and what is the ambiance of these sounds? This is to say that what has become textually nonfluid in its impenetrability itself instances a sort of liquidity (at least insofar as the cues solicited by these tough coinings would seem to recalibrate the hermeneutic project of understanding Crane as a sort of (Kristevan) semiotic. Being before language (Kristeva) and being after (Crane, with his rococo of Elizabethan jazz-age bricolage) amount to uncannily similar scenarios. For a discussion adjacent to this poetic recidivism, see Christian Thorne's "The Revolutionary Energy of the Outmoded," *October* 104 (Spring 2003). "Underlying retro culture is a vision of a world in which commodity production has come to a halt, in which objects have been handed down, not for our consumption, but for our care. The apocalypse is retro culture's deepest fantasy, its enabling wish" (114).

17. Thomas Yingling, *Hart Crane and the Homosexual Text* (Chicago: University of Chicago Press, 1990), 155.

18. T. S. Eliot, *Collected Poems, 1909–1962* (New York: Harcourt, Brace, 1991), 26. Subsequent references to Eliot's poetry are to this volume and parenthetically cited by page number within the text.

19. Gilles Deleuze describes similar affective phenomena in Proust. "The wordly sign does not refer to something, it 'stands for' it, claims to be equivalent to its meaning. It anticipates action as it does thought, annuls thought as it does action, and declares itself adequate" (Gilles Deleuze, *Proust and Signs,* trans. Richard Howard [Minneapolis: University of Minnesota Press, 2000], 6).

20. I mean to distinguish the repetitiveness of Eliot's smiles from the repetitiveness of Crane's. The latter repetitiveness is essentially accretive, whereas the former—consonant with a psychoanalytic logic of repetition—is compulsively (if ambivalently) undermining. Consider Cathy Caruth's observation (in a different context) that "[t]he accident is thus not a reality that can simply be known once and for all, but an encounter with the real that must take place each time

anew in the accident of where the words happen to fall" (*Unclaimed Experience: Trauma, Narrative, and History* [Baltimore: Johns Hopkins University, 1996], 107).

21. For a perspicuous account of Crane's logic of metaphor, see John Irwin, "Hart Crane's 'Logic of Metaphor,'" in *Critical Essays on Hart Crane*, ed. David R. Clark (Boston: G. K. Hall, 1982).

22. Hart Crane, "General Aims and Theories," in *The Complete Poems and Selected Letters and Prose of Hart Crane*, ed. Brom Weber (New York: Liveright Publishing Corporation, 1966), 222.

23. The logic of metaphor, as understood by both Crane and critics such as Irwin, enacts a rhetoric of desire. Desire, that is, glossed as a fundamental relation to absence. One desires what one lacks, what one isn't, and along these lines, Crane's metaphorical vehicles persistently reach toward a tenor they can only begin to imagine. The logic of metaphor, thus formulated, requires of its readers a hermeneutic position that is also an eroticized position: desire, here, scaled to the level of rhetoric, of occluded, even botched, syntax. Not only are Crane's poems about love (as he describes, for instance, "Voyages" as a love poem for welkin-eyed sailor Emil Opffer), but they construct for the reader a structure whose inhabiting renders reading and desiring coincident practices. Along these lines, Crane's poetry, at its most fluid (which is to say, at its most characteristically difficult and analytic), affirms conceptions of desire-as-elsewhere but also creates within itself a terrain in which 'the ideal reader' could construe satisfaction as a practice of cultivating, even enjoying, readerly deferral.

24. Cited in full.

25. For instance, Warner Berthoff (*Hart Crane: A Re-Introduction* [Minneapolis: University of Minnesota Press], 20) seconds Sherman Paul's description of the poem's voice as that of a "driven sexual adventurer" (*Hart's Bridge* [Urbana: University of Illinois Press, 1972]); Robert K. Martin writes that "the speaker of 'Possessions' confronts the deadly repetition of 'cruising,' the obsessive searching of the city streets for a sexual partner" (*The Homosexual Tradition in American Poetry* [Austin: University of Texas Press, 1979], 127).

26. See Tim Dean, "Hart Crane's Poetics of Privacy," *American Literary History* 8, no. 1 (Spring 1996): "Crane's expectation that 'the audience for [his] work will always be quite small'...has been taken to support this interpretation insofar as the poet's audience is restricted to those with the capacity (derived from gay experience) to understand the connotations of Crane's 'homosexual code.' Indeed, 'The Tunnel' section of *The Bridge* invokes such a code in the form of the 'tearoom' sign of a lighted match, by which gay men secretly make themselves known to each other even today" (90).

27. Blackmur, "New Thresholds, New Anatomies," 57–58.

28. *O My Land, My Friends: The Selected Letters of Hart Crane*, ed. Langdon Hammer and Brom Weber (New York: Four Walls Eight Windows, 1997), 279.

29. This whiteness anticipates the "white wind" that ends the poem, as well as the "white paraphrase" that ends the poem just preceding "Possessions," as well as the adverbial "whitely" of "Lachrymae Christi," the poem that follows. These whitenesses in turn inform the book's title, *White Buildings,* the collective whiteness of which pays homage to the monstrous whitenesses of Melville and Poe. Doing justice to the relation between Crane's whiteness and theirs would require more space than this note. For an account of the paronomasic affinities between whiteness and witness in Melville, see Eyal Peretz, *Literature, Disaster, and the Enigma of Power: A Reading of Moby Dick* (Stanford: Stanford University Press, 2003).

30. "But there arose in our pathway a shrouded human figure, very far larger in its proportions than any dweller among men. And the hue of the skin of the figure was of the perfect whiteness of the snow" (Edgar Allan Poe, *The Narrative of Arthur Gordon Pym* [New York: Penguin Books, 1999], 217).

31. Dean, "Hart Crane's Poetics of Privacy," 92.

32. Leo Bersani, *Homos* (New York: Columbia University Press, 1995), 77. Hereafter cited parenthetically in the text.

33. D. W. Winnicott, *Playing and Reality* (New York: Routledge, 1989), 1. Subsequent references cited parenthetically in the text.

34. Edward Brunner, *Splendid Failure: Hart Crane and the Making of* The Bridge (Urbana: University of Illinois Press, 1985), 206–7.

35. Allen Grossman, "Hart Crane and Poetry: A Consideration of Crane's Intense Poetics with Reference to 'The Return,' " in *The Long Schoolroom: Lessons in the Bitter Logic of the Poetic Principle* (Ann Arbor: University of Michigan Press, 2000), 97.

36. Ralph Waldo Emerson, "Nature," in *Essays and Lectures* (New York: Library of America, 1983), 10.

37. Bersani, "Is the Rectum a Grave?" 218.

38. Marius Bewley, "Hart Crane's Last Poem," in *Hart Crane: A Collection of Critical Essays,* ed. Alan Trachtenberg (Englewood Cliffs, N.J.: Prentice-Hall, 1982), 150.

39. Riddel, "The Poetics of Failure," 473.

40. Dean, *Hart Crane's Death Drive,* 62.

41. Edelman, *Transmemberment of Song,* 268.

42. Allen Grossman, for instance, honors the sonorities of this suicidal pathos. "The four-line poem called 'The Return' . . . was in effect a final communication, a suicide note. On one of the four manuscript pages relating to 'The Return' Hart Crane's mother, Grace Hart Crane, searching like so many others for the 'cause' of her son's death, notes (the annotation, now erased, is still sufficiently legible) that she found a version of this poem in his suitcase — on top — and asks whether is bears any 'significance to his death.' " (87). While Grossman designates "The Return" as a suicide note, his essay nonetheless thrice denominates "The Broken Tower" as Crane's "death-poem."

2. *Emily Dickinson's Queer Pain*

Note to epigraph: Significantly (and perhaps bemusingly), this passage concludes the concluding essay of a collection titled *Compassion: The Culture and Politics of an Emotion* (New York: Routledge, 2004). The provocation of ending a volume titled *Compassion* with so searingly bleak an entreaty — spinning outward from a description of Arendt's own ethics to an exhortation to readers; hence the final pronomial shift from "her" to "one" — is the sort of incitement that fueled my first counterimagining of alternate "co-builders" and alternate ways of building the world. My turn to Nelson likewise is meant to reiterate that while my book's principal focus is queer theory, the affective energies of queer theory are not definitively different from those of other disciplines, so much as more saliently (one could say flamboyantly) present. In situating my book (to the degree that I do) within queer theory, I inevitably limit my radius of inquiry — a necessary predicament of all critical enterprises. I no less wish, however, that *Queer Optimism* remain conversant with disciplines and fields beyond itself.

1. Sandra Runzo, "Dickinson's Transgressive Body," *Emily Dickinson Journal* 8, no. 1 (Spring 1999): 60.

2. Virginia Jackson's recent study, *Dickinson's Misery: A Theory of Lyric Reading,* persuasively argues against critical presumptions of how a Dickinsonian lyric is understood and cautions against what premature designations of the "lyrical" invariably jettison (materially, interpretatively, theoretically) from our engagement of Dickinson's writing practices. "Why," Jackson asks, "so idealize and so renounce the lyric? I have been suggesting that the lyric has come to seem so ideal and so ludicrous because it has been progressively identified with a form of personal abstraction that cannot quite be disowned, and yet cannot quite be embraced by modern critical culture. That is why Dickinson is such a perfect and pathetic figure for it, though that is the last thing she may have wanted to be" (*Dickinson's Misery* [Princeton, N.J.: Princeton University Press, 2005], 236). Jackson's book is an important one, especially for its agile and sophisticated account of the critical motivations and consequences of both materialist and formalist reading. The title of her book, however, strikes me as sensationalist: one might say that, within the academy, *Misery Sells.* Even as misery is far less operative a term in Jackson's analyses than *pathos* (a category that includes but is nonequivalent to misery), how much more alluring if not lurid it is to be promised a new account of *Dickinson's misery,* rather than *her pathos*? Jackson isn't the first scholar to move quickly between two such terms. I think, for instance, of Rei Terada's brilliant *Feeling in Theory: Emotion after the Death of the Subject* (Cambridge, Mass.: Harvard University Press, 2001), whose account of feeling more specifically is of *negative feelings,* specifically fear.

3. Sandra Runzo, "Dickinson, Performance, and the Homoerotic Lyric," *American Literature* 68, no. 2 (Spring 1996): 348.

4. Ibid., 350.

5. There invariably are queer readings of Dickinson that exceed the parameters I have sketched. Sometimes such work, however, frustratingly slips too quickly from the strangeness of Dickinson's texts to some correlatively lived strangeness modeled on Dickinson's lyrics. Given the scrupulous elusiveness characteristic of Dickinson's lyric traversals of the figurative and literal, such heuristic applications of Dickinson's experiments cannot help but distort both Dickinson and the queer experiences on whose behalf she is made to speak. H. Jordan Landry's essay, "Animal/Insectual/Lesbian Sex: Dickinson's Queer Version of the Birds and the Bees" (*Emily Dickinson Journal* 9, no. 2 [Fall 2000]: 42–54) speciously invokes Dickinson's own "hopes to instate a more fluid self, sexuality, and subjectivity not wholly fixed by the social" (50). Landry argues that through a "zoological" tropology of birds and bees, Dickinson's poetry and letters effectively proliferate otherwise inarticulable scenes of lesbian desire. Given the imaginative capaciousness of her writing, Dickinson's lyric conceptions of selfhood or sexuality veer from "the social" without the aid of insects; and Dickinson's insects, for that matter, are themselves so fastidiously odd as to gain little from their sublation into fundamentally generic lesbian narratives. More generally, Landry's article's attachment to fluidities of self so much reiterates Butlerian (and even Bersanian) modes of personate fluidity that fluidity looks less boundary-troubling or subversively labile than overexposed, if not predictable. In respect to such predilections for fluidity, see Brad Epps's insightful, "The Fetish of Fluidity," in *Homosexuality and Psychoanalysis,* ed. Tim Dean and Christopher Lane (Chicago: University of Chicago Press, 2001).

6. Suzanne Juhasz, "Amplitude of Queer Desire in Dickinson's Erotic Language," *Emily Dickinson Journal* 14, no. 2 (Fall 2005): 24.

7. Ibid., 26.

8. Ibid., 27.

9. This and all subsequent citations of Dickinson's poetry, unless otherwise noted, refer to *The Poems of Emily Dickinson: Reading Edition,* ed. R. W. Franklin (Cambridge: The Belknap Press of Harvard University Press, 1999), and are cited in the text by the letter F, followed by Franklin's particular numbering of the poems (to be distinguished from Thomas Johnson's 1955 edition of Dickinson's poems).

10. Juhasz, "Amplitude of Queer Desire," 31.

11. Ibid., 32.

12. Georges Poulet, "Appendix: Time and American Writers," *Studies in Human Time,* trans. Elliott Coleman (Westport, Conn.: Greenwood Press, 1956), 347.

13. Albert Gelpi, *The Mind of the Poet* (Cambridge, Mass.: Harvard University Press, 1965), 72.

14. Jane Donahue Eberwein, *Dickinson: Strategies of Limitation* (Amherst: University of Massachusetts Press, 1985), 31.

15. Ibid., 45.

16. Robert Weisbuch, *Emily Dickinson's Poetry* (Chicago: University of Chicago Press, 1975), 97.

17. Eberwein, *Dickinson,* 45–46. Such accounts of pain — explicitly privileging pain's epistemological and ethical rewards over those of pleasure — are unique to studies neither of Dickinson, nor of literature more generally. Scanning library shelves and journal indices, the currency of pain-scholarship is astonishing, and all the more requiring an external vantage from which to ask *why so much of this, and at what cost.*

18. Marianne Noble, "The Revenge of Cato's Daughter: Emily Dickinson's Uses of Sentimental Masochism," in *The Masochistic Pleasures of Sentimental Literature* (Princeton, N.J.: Princeton University Press, 2000), 147. Subsequent references to this essay are cited parenthetically in the text.

19. Emily Dickinson, *Selected Letters,* ed. Thomas H. Johnson (Cambridge, Mass.: The Belknap Press of Harvard University Press, 1986), letter no. 93.

20. Such a claim is countered by Dickinson herself: it is a safe bet that for every claim (or more likely, set of contradicting claims) one Dickinson poem makes, another poem will venture its opposite. For example, pain, in the following poem, doesn't destroy illusion, but *provides* it:

> There is a pain — so utter —
> It swallows substance up —
> Then covers the Abyss with Trance —
> So Memory can step
> Around — across-opon it —
> As One within a Swoon —
> Goes safely — where an open eye —
> Would drop Him — Bone by Bone —
> (F515)

21. See Robert McClure Smith's "Dickinson and the Masochistic Aesthetic," *Emily Dickinson Journal* 7, no. 2 (Fall 1998): 1–21.

22. Judith Butler, *Gender Trouble: Feminism and the Subversion of Identity* (New York: Routledge, 1999), esp. 134–42.

23. Sharon Cameron, *Choosing Not Choosing: Dickinson's Fascicles* (Chicago: University of Chicago Press, 1992), 27.

24. My assertion of Dickinson-poem-as-lyric-text does not necessarily contradict the argument of Virginia Jackson, already cited. For the purposes of these pages, my understanding of "lyric" is less generically rigid (and therefore, less hermeneutically foreclosing) than that pursued by Jackson. Furthermore — in a suspension of intentional fallacy's *who-dun-it* — I am less attached to how Dickinson ideally imagined her poem (as written, as received, if received at all), than how Dickinson's poem might be imagined.

25. Gilles Deleuze, *Masochism: Coldness and Cruelty and Venus in Furs* (New York: Zone Books, 1991), 74.

26. Ibid., 71.

27. Ibid.

28. Ibid., 18.

29. That the poem's second stanza makes reference to a sun might for some readers eventuate this reading of "setting" as the *only* reading. The terms of the second stanza, however, do not necessarily dictate those of the first. As evidenced in "Her Smile was shaped like other smiles," it hardly goes without saying, in reading Dickinson, that a later stanza necessarily would further (let alone conclude or corroborate) the claims of an earlier one.

30. Elizabeth Phillips, one of few critics to attend to this poem, suggests (outrageously, if only because so assuredly) that the bird in question has been shot. I quote Phillips's account of this poem in full, as it posits a claim opposite mine, namely, that the poem is uninteresting; and by extension, that the phenomenon it attempts to describe is likewise. "There is a small group of verses that seem hardly worth mentioning except for the record of Dickinson's interest in writing about other people. As usual, they have no names.... Other verse, in the same category, may describe a woman the poet has observed.... The strained simile of the bird that has been gun-shot and the spasms of sound breaking like a strand of beads suggest that the poet is trying too hard. Perhaps the verse is well forgotten, but it belongs to the record of an effort to describe another human being whose pain the poet perceives" (*Emily Dickinson, Personae and Performance* [University Park: Pennsylvania State University Press, 1988], 183).

31. This spectacle of a convulsive hold shares a vocabulary with the spectacle, in Whitman's poetry, of seizures. For an account of the seizure as it relates to Whitman's conceptions of identity, see my "Whitman on the Verge," *Arizona Quarterly* 61, no. 3.

32. This line begins the final stanza of the poem already quoted, "Then quiver down, with tufts of tune—."

33. Sigmund Freud, *The Ego and the Id,* in *The Standard Edition of the Complete Psychological Works of Sigmund Freud,* ed. and trans. James Strachey, 24 vols. (London: Hogarth Press, 1953–74), 19:29.

34. See Judith Butler, *The Psychic Life of Power* (Stanford, Calif.: Stanford University Press, 1997), 132–34.

35. For an excellent analysis of this poem, see Virgina Jackson's *Dickinson's Misery,* 185–90.

36. The second stanza's refusal of the mechanical is signaled even in the suffix of "merriment," "ment," which attests to an adjective's alchemization (or "setting") into a noun, without account of the transformation (from adjectival to nominal) beyond the retroactive grammatical retagging. Along similar lines, think of the reiterated nominal suffixes of "A nearness to Tremendousness," where "ness" likewise designates a grammatical change already transpired. This suffixative insistence ("nearness," "Tremendousness," "Boundlessness," "contentment") in turn reinforces the poem's interest not in how a feeling is produced, but in how a feeling might (or might not) be located.

37. G. W. Leibniz, *New Essays on Human Understanding,* trans. and ed. Peter Remnant and Jonathan Bennett (New York: Cambridge University Press, 1981), 370.

38. G. W. Leibniz, "Discourse on Metaphysics," in *Philosophical Essays,* trans. Roger Ariew and Daniel Garber (Indianapolis: Hackett Publishing Company, 1989), 62.

39. Jane Donahue Eberwein, " 'Graphicer for Grace': Emily Dickinson's Calvinist Language," *Studies in Puritan American Spirituality* 1 (1990): 183.

40. Ibid., 195 n. 17.

41. Sharon Cameron, *Lyric Time: Dickinson and the Limits of Genre* (Baltimore: Johns Hopkins University Press, 1979), 57. Subsequent references to this text are cited parenthetically in the text.

42. Jane Eberwein reads this poem along lines similar to Cameron's, positing that "[t]he speaker can neither voice a prayer when unsure whether any person or power will hear it nor completely articulate even to herself her own final sentence, in which the subordinate 'if' clause dangles helplessly to express her stammering and skeptical wishfulness" (*Dickinson: Strategies of Limitation,* 26). Eberwein, like Cameron, finds this poem's final stanza remarkable less for what it says or successfully ventures, than for its failure: "Lack of language here reflects lack of anything to say — lack of any clear conception even of desire. . . . The total breakdown — possibly of the speaker, surely of the poem — comes in the final stanza with its unresolved pileup of phrases that fail to constitute a sentence or articulate an idea. . . . If this speaker's 'Business is Circumference,' she has gone bankrupt." Ibid., 129)

I will argue against this characteristic account of the poem's "breakdown," as I have earlier argued against correlative accounts of Cranian failure. On a rhythmic level, for instance, this final stanza is exquisitely, insistently patterned: despite lack of immediate conceptual clarity, the stanza's triple rhyme of "Despair," "care," and "affair" (a poetic feat few could execute so subtly), locked into the double rhyme of "be" and "Misery," suggests less "breakdown" than virtuosic compression. Compression (of rhymes or meaning) is not identical to breakdown or implosion. To salvage this final stanza from presumptions of its own failure is the first step in taking it *seriously* as poetic utterance, no less intentional (albeit perhaps differently intentional) than the stanzas that precede it.

43. See Jacques Derrida's foreword to Nicolas Abraham and Maria Torok, *The Wolf Man's Magic Word,* trans. Nicholas Rand (Minneapolis: University of Minnesota Press, 2005).

44. Allen Tate, "New England Culture and Emily Dickinson," *The Recognition of Emily Dickinson: Selected Criticism since 1890,* ed. Caesar R. Blake and Carlton F. Wells (Ann Arbor: University of Michigan Press, 1968), 166.

45. Ibid., 156.

46. Tate's speculations find recent amplification in the work of James McIntosh, who writes that "[Dickinson's] transcriptions of Christian ideas and her

reworkings of Christian texts are not dogmatic but experimental, heuristic, and in their own way pastoral.... Her Protestant heritage provides her with figures for poetry and with textual strategies to 'keep Believing nimble' " (*Nimble Believing: Dickinson and the Unknown* [Ann Arbor: University of Michigan Press], 2000).

47. The ostensible machinics of Dickinsonian grace themselves recall Jonathan Edwards's account of grace, in which tropaic and lexical fastidiousness verge on a physics suggesting nothing so much as Newtonian law: "It likewise seems reasonable to me to suppose that the habit of grace in adults is always begun with an act of grace that shall imply faith in it, because a habit can be of no manner of use till there is occasion to exert it; and all habits being only a law that God has fixed, that such actions upon such occasions should be exerted, the first new thing that there can be in the creature must be some actual alteration" (Jonathan Edwards, "Miscellanies").

48. R. P. Blackmur, "Emily Dickinson: Notes on Prejudice and Fact," in *Language as Gesture* (New York: Harcourt, Brace, 1952), 33. All subsequent references to this essay are cited parenthetically in the text.

49. Paul de Man, *The Rhetoric of Romanticism* (New York: Columbia University Press, 1984), 265.

50. Ibid.

51. Ibid., 264. The terms in which de Man recounts Kleist's *Marionettentheater* uncannily no less accurately describe the profoundly intense mechanicality of "I got so I could take his name." Of Kleist's work, de Man writes that "this scene abounds in stage business to the point of achieving the pantomimic liveliness associated with texts such as Diderot's *Nevue de Rameau.* We are told when and how the interlocutors nod and smile, sniff tobacco, express enthusiasm or, on the contrary, manifest their doubts or hesitations; K & C, with the alternating symmetry of a dance figure in a ballet, cast down their gaze to the floor or lift it to eye-level.... This stress on staging, on the mimesis of the diegetic narratives — the text *shows* people engaged in the act of *telling* — emphasizes the self-consciousness of the representational mode within the hermeneutic context of a persuasion" (269). For Dickinson's own account of ballet, not inapposite to my own considerations of Dickinsonian grace, see her poem "I cannot Dance opon my Toes," (F381) in which the speaker feels gleefully possessed with what Dickinson overdeterminedly calls "Ballet Knowledge." Such a poem suggests Dickinson as both Kleistian puppet and puppeteer, held apart by the lines of Dickinson's own writing. "The aesthetic power is located neither in the puppet nor the puppeteer but in the text that spins itself between them" (de Man, 285). "I cannot Dance opon my Toes" likewise is the source of this chapter's subtitle, "One Claw opon the Air."

52. Ibid., 267.

53. Ibid., 269.

3. *Jack Spicer's* Billy The Kid

1. Judith Butler, *The Psychic Life of Power* (Stanford: Stanford University Press, 1997), 134.

2. Later pages will clarify what I mean by auratic, as the term pertains directly to Billy the Kid. To raise the possibility of an aura that is mechanically reproduced inevitably invites judgment as misreading or conflation of Benjaminian terms. After all, Walter Benjamin's "The Work of Art in the Age of Mechanical Reproduction" — written in the thirties but first published in 1955, as Spicer was ruminating the ends of seriality a propos the end of the lyric — ascribes the auratic to the work of art in its singularity, opposite its posterior reproducible iterations. As Richard Wolin writes, "[a]s an object of religious veneration and worship, the work of art acquires a sense of uniqueness, an authenticity, a *hallowed* character.... The aura testifies to the *authority* of art in its cultic form, its condition of inimitable uniqueness, a singularity in time and space which is the hallmark of its authenticity" (*Walter Benjamin: An Aesthetic of Redemption* [Berkeley: University of California Press, 1994], 187–88). While Benjamin argues that late-nineteenth- and early-twentieth-century reproductive technologies — specifically film — lead to a politically generative "decline of the aura," it is precisely film and film's proliferative capacities that most bring Billy's auratic status to the fore: if not in terms of authenticity, then in terms of a uniqueness, a hallowedness, unto itself. Beatrice Hanssen writes that "mechanical reproduction brought about both a temporal and spatial displacement" (*Walter Benjamin's Other Histories: Of Stones, Animals, Human Beings, and Angels* [Berkeley: University of California Press, 2000], 73). Billy the Kid's authenticity — although authenticity, in the case of both Billy and Spicer's poem to him is, as we shall see, from outset an erroneous characterization — springs rather than suffers from the confusions of temporal and spatial displacement. Much would be gained from a more sustained collation of Benjamin and Spicer. For the sake of economy, I'll only note that the reproduction most at stake for Benjamin involves the negotiation of singularity at its most assiduously literal. By contrast, Spicer's version of reproduction — under the strictures (and nonstrictures) of Billy's seriality — floods the market with forms of verisimilitude proximate enough to antecedent as to seem the same *and* nonidentical enough — however minimally — as to seem novel. This, if reductively, is to recall the temporal and material differences between seriality and Freudian repetition; the latter of which shares with Benjamin's essay a cathectic relation to originality that in the context of Billy the Kid is far more problematically diffuse. To look ahead to a later section of this chapter, the separability of auratic original from its proxies becomes for Spicer as difficult to maintain as the separability of singular lyric from the serial poetry for which Spicer equivocally stumps as the lyric's undoing.

3. Or at very least takes for granted the translation of one conception of melancholy (psychical) into another (textual); no matter how arduously (following Freud and Lacan) one takes the psychical as linguistically structured, a psyche (psychoanalytically speaking) must necessarily ultimately differ from a poem.

4. See, for the latter, Leo Bersani, "Is the Rectum a Grave?" *October* 23: 206–9.

5. Butler, *The Psychic Life of Power,* 138.

6. Leo Bersani, "Psychoanalysis and the Aesthetic Subject," *Critical Inquiry* 32 (Winter 2006): 167.

7. For instance, anal intercourse (as addressed in Bersani's "Is the Rectum a Grave?") is thrilling (or ought seem so) not because it occasions an obliterative askesis of one ego against another, but because it radically (because so nearly literally) reproduces the man who is fucked as his own potential external world. Such a reading admittedly is tenuous, its limitations most immediately arising in the presumed identificatory relation between one man (or one man's penis) and another. I nonetheless find salutary the experiment of thinking about the earlier essay's erotic dynamics within the aesthetic terms of Bersani's later "Psychoanalysis and the Aesthetic Subject," written nearly two decades after the fact. The aestheticization of sex does not (as might otherwise be presumed) clean sex up, so much as reinvigorate the aesthetic as a way of differently considering sex in terms structurally more inventive than those axiomatically attached to differentials of power.

8. Ibid., 161.

9. Ibid., 169.

10. One could say that Jack Spicer's serial poem, in its indirect advances toward Billy, circles an exquisite corpse, *cadavre exquis.* Spicer's poem circles less in the manner of vultures than of Emerson, who writes in his essay, "Circles," that "every action admits of being outdone," that "the heart refuses to be imprisoned . . . already tends outward with a vast force, and to immense and innumerable expansions" (404–5). If the serial possibilities of Emerson's exhortations are not already apparent, the latent seriality of Emerson's contemplations resounds unequivocally in a formulation from the same essay's next paragraph: "[e]very ultimate fact is only the first of a new series" (405).

11. Walter Noble Burns, *The Saga of Billy the Kid* (Garden City, N.Y.: Garden City Publishing Co., 1925), 70.

12. Lewis Ellingham and Kevin Killian, *Poet Be Like God: Jack Spicer and the San Francisco Renaissance* (Hanover, N.H.: University Press of New England, 1998), 135.

13. Mark Seltzer, *Serial Killers: Death and Life in America's Wound Culture* (New York: Routledge, 1998), 10.

14. Ibid., 46.

15. John L. Spicer, "The Poems of Emily Dickinson," *Boston Public Library Quarterly* (July 1956): 141.

16. Spicer, "The Poems of Emily Dickinson," 135.

17. Walt Whitman, "Song of Myself," *Leaves of Grass*, ed. Sculley Bradley (New York: W. W. Norton, 1973), 68.

18. Frank O'Hara, "Second Avenue," *Frank O'Hara: Selected Poems*, ed. Donald Allen (New York: Penguin Books, 1994), 64.

19. Ellingham and Killian, *Poet Be Like God*, 65.

20. "The audience was familiar with this type of lecture series, as [Robert] Duncan and [Robert] Creeley had each offered them in the past, again at the Tallmans' home. As the reading was about to begin, Jack ran out of brandy and pleaded with Warren to run out and buy him some. There was a liquor store a block away, so in the nick of time, Warren was there and back, sneaking in the back door with another pint" (*Poet Be Like God*, 334).

21. *The House That Jack Built: The Collected Lectures of Jack Spicer*, ed. Peter Gizzi (Middletown, Conn.: Wesleyan University Press, 1998), 55. All subsequent references cited parenthetically in the text.

22. T. S. Eliot, "Tradition and the Individual Talent," 53.

23. In trying not to interfere with the poem, "you have to interfere with yourself. You have to, as much as possible, empty yourself for this. And that's not noninterference. I mean, it's almost an athletic thing. It takes a huge amount of practice to be able to avoid blocking a person when you're not supposed to block the person on the play.... It takes a huge amount because you have this natural impulse. You know.... And the business of being able *not* to do something, especially things which are so important to you, are you, takes a tremendous amount of patience" (*The House That Jack Built*, 14).

24. As in Cocteau's 1949 *Orphée*, from which Spicer's radio-analogy is culled. In Cocteau's film, the radio serves as homoerotic liaison between Orpheus (Jean Marais) and Cegeste, another young poet whose cryptic poems are transmitted to Orpheus through the radio of a car. For Spicer's most extended engagement with Cocteau's retelling of the Orpheus myth, see *Heads of the Town up to the Aether* (1960).

25. "According to Spicer's motley procession of metaphors, the poet is a host being invaded by the parasite of the dictating source of the poem; this source is "Martian"; the poem is the product of the dance between the poet and his Martian source" (*The House That Jack Built: The Collected Lectures of Jack Spicer*, 2).

26. For instance, how can the arrangement of building blocks (even as the metaphorization of poetic form-making) illuminate a poetry so intent on arrangements not of blocks, but cocks? I think, as just one example, of the opening poem of *Heads of the Town up to the Aether*, itself a brusque revamping of Shakespeare's sonnet #144, "Two loves I have, of comfort and despair":

> Two loves I had. One rang a bell
> Connected on both sides with hell

The other'd written me a letter
In which he said I've written better

They pushed their cocks in many places
And I'm not certain of their faces

Or which I'd kissed or which I didn't
Or which of both of them I hadn't. (118)

It's not merely that the figures of Spicer's poetry seem incompatible with the figures through which he discusses them, but that the sexiness of the former seems unattended by the latter vocabulary, which would claim cocks as affectively or erotically neutral, as though all building blocks were, in the hands (or, as it were, mouth) of Spicer, effectively indistinguishable.

27. I want to note here the passage's anti-Semitism, but more generally to acknowledge the magnitude and variousness of Spicer's poetic articulations of anti-Semitism (or racism, or misogyny, or certain forms of homophobia). Spicer's anti-Semitism comprises a subject of inquiry in its own right, most recently addressed in the work of Maria Damon, who recently has written an essay on Spicer's anti-Semitism for a critical collection that includes a shorter version of this chapter. For present purposes, I want to point to the "New York Jew Salesmen of Amethyst pajamas" as an exclusion from the poem's frontier not only of Jewishness, but also a certain form of New York urbanity, as well as a sort of gayness (signaled in the amethyst pajamas) different from Spicer's own. An antecedent to this excluded figure is to be found in Arthur Penn's film "Left-Handed Gun," in a Billy-loving dandy who delivers to a prisoned Billy not a set of amethyst pajamas, but an impossibly pristine stack of linens no less foppish in their anticowboy crispness. I shall have more to say of Penn's dandy-figure in this chapter's final section.

28. Susan Stewart, *Poetry and the Fate of the Senses* (Chicago: University of Chicago Press, 2002), 156.

29. An archive of such poems would include Milton's "Lycidas," Shelley's "Adonais," Keats's "Endymion," Whitman's sequence, "Live Oak with Moss," Cavafy's "Kaisarion," to name just a few. Such poems depend on the beautiful boy's death, departure, or more general distance from the moment of writing. Whitman's is an important exception to this rule, one that Spicer takes to heart, even as Spicer's Billy *is* (by some accounts) already dead, *is* departed, yet nonetheless somehow as immanent as Whitman's "friend" ("And his arm lay lightly over my breast—And that night I was / happy").

30. Neil Hertz, "Lurid Figures," *Reading de Man Reading,* ed. Lindsay Waters and Wlad Godzich (Minneapolis: University of Minnesota Press, 1989), 87.

31. Leo Bersani, "Sociability and Cruising," *Umbr(a): A Journal of the Unconscious* (2002): 21.

32. Ibid., 11.

33. Bersani, "Is the Rectum a Grave?" 208.

34. Bersani, "Sociability and Cruising," 13.

35. And here, one might think of Spicer's own struggles with his boyfriend at the time, Russ Fitzgerald, whose wandering eye and hankerings toward promiscuity threatened the relationship Spicer so dearly sought to sustain. For an account of Spicer's relationship with Fitzgerald, see Ellingham's and Killian's *Poet Be Like God,* 118–39.

36. "Dear Lorca, Loneliness is necessary for pure poetry. When someone intrudes into the poet's life (and any sudden personal contact, whether in the bed or in the heart, is an intrusion) he loses his balance for a moment" (Spicer, *After Lorca,* in *The Collected Books,* 48)

37. The idiomatic compressiveness of Spicer's "it was hell" dilates in relation to "Imaginary Elegies," an earlier Spicer poem that similarly collates hell in relation to a proliferating contingent of denizens, suspended by Spicer between conceivability and nonconceivability with a gentleness that complicates the affective coarseness by which Spicer, within criticism, too often is characterized:

> Hell somehow exists in the distance
> Between what happened and what never happened.
>
> [. . .]
>
> But look now, in this room, see the moon-children
> Wolf, bear, and otter, dragon, dove.
> Look now, in this room, see the moon-children
> Flying, crawling, swimming, burning
> Vacant with beauty.
> Hear them whisper.

38. Gilles Deleuze, *Cinema 2: The Time Image* (Minneapolis: University of Minnesota Press, 2003), 129.

39. Ibid.

40. Ibid., 147.

41. A sprinkling of gold leaf looking like hell flowers
A flat piece of wrapping paper, already wrinkled, but wrinkled
again by hand, smoothed into shape by an electric iron
A painting
Which told me about the death of Billy the Kid.
Collage a binding together
Of the real
Which flat colors
Tell us what heroes
really come by (79)

Marjorie Perloff's essay "The Invention of Collage" helpfully provides both artistic and literary contexts in which one might think through Spicer's own poetic representation of collage-making. "And here," Perloff writes, "it may be helpful to remember that *collage,* literally a pasting, is also a slang expression for two people living (pasted) together—that is to say, an illicit sexual union—and that the past participle *collé* means 'faked' or 'pretended' " ("The Invention of Collage," *New York Literary Forum* 10–11 [1983]: 5–47).

42. Deleuze, *The Time Image,* 128.

43. Ibid., 27.

44. What "just one touch" flirts with, and what it abdicates, is something along the lines of Whitman's erethism:

> I merely stir, press, feel with my fingers, and am happy,
> To touch my person to some one else's is about as much as I can stand.

In Whitman, "just one touch" would become shorthand for a supreme epidermal sensitivity, whereas in Spicer, "just one touch" removes Billy's body altogether. Spicer's lines, that is, trade the g-spot sensitivity of Whitman for a weird, painterly carefulness.

45. Once again, delicacy equivocates in its enjambment between dermal and nondermal residences, from how Billy might feel or be felt, touch or be touched, to the possibilities of his being seen.

46. Spicer's aestheticization of Billy the Kid, in this context, is a significant precursor to Richard Prince's uncanny series of cowboy photographs, culled from iconic Marlboro Man advertisements.

47. Just as *Billy The Kid* problematizes categories of poetic impersonality (whereas poetry should travel through the poet like a radio transmission, *Billy The Kid* begins with a radio that is starkly insufficient), it likewise troubles what usually is considered Spicer's unequivocal attachment to magic as correlative to if not version of poetry. Hence, in the spring of 1957, Spicer organizes a poetry workshop called "Poetry as Magic" (see *Poet Be Like God,* 79–98). Magic, as Blaser comments in the appendix to Spicer's collected poems, "was [for Spicer] a matter of disturbance, entrance, and passion, rather than abracadabra" (*Collected Books,* 353). Still *Billy's* veto of magic, as it relates to its vexed relation to impersonality, in fact impinges on the "matter" of "entrance." Hence the first section's strange false starts.

48. Clayton Eshleman, "The Lorca Working," *Boundary* 27, no. 1 (1977): 31–50.

49. John Keats, "Endymion," *Complete Poetical Works* (Oxford: Oxford University Press, 1988), 89–90.

50. Burns, *The Saga of Billy the Kid,* 76.

51. Ibid., 277.

52. John W. Poe, *The Death of Billy the Kid* (Boston: Houghton Mifflin, 1933), 28.

53. Ibid., 29–30.

54. Ibid., 31.

55. Burns, *The Saga of Billy the Kid,* 281.

56. Poe, *The Death of Billy the Kid,* xxxvii.

57. Ibid., 34–35.

58. Spicer, *The House That Jack Built,* 55.

59. Burns, *The Saga of Billy the Kid,* 284.

60. Other writers before Spicer have argued Billy out of his fate. In 1955, for instance, Harvard professor C. L. Sonnichsen published *Alias Billy the Kid,* a *National Enquirer*–like account of the "true" events of that fateful night. Sonnichsen introduces the figure of Brushy Bill Roberts, who confessed in 1950 that he, in fact, was Billy the Kid, and that the man shot in Maxwell's bedroom was another Billy altogether, Billy's partner Billy Barlow, "younger than Billy the Kid, but about the same size" (48n). Further complicating the fact of Billy's death, for Sonnichsen, is the suspicious disappearances of both Billy's death certificate and the certificate forged to replace that original. Among the legal documents Sonnichsen appends to his study is a 1951 letter from a New Mexico district attorney to William Morrison, an inquiring investigator and Sonnichsen's co-author:

> Dear Sir:
>
> I wish to acknowledge receipt of your letter of August 9, 1951 requesting a certified copy of the coroner's verdict on the death of Wm. H. Bonney, alias Billy the Kid.
>
> I am sorry I cannot comply with your request because of the fact that such a record is not now, and never has been, among the records of this office. I am sorry, also, that I am at a loss to direct you to the office where you could obtain a copy of such a record. (109–10)

(C. L. Sonnichsen and William V. Morrison, *Alias Billy the Kid* [Albuquerque: University of New Mexico Press, 1955]).

61. The facial limbo of these lines instances a correlative to Deleuze and Guattari's theorization of faciality in *A Thousand Plateaus*: "All faces envelop an unknown, unexplored landscape; all landscapes are populated by a loved or dreamed-of face, develop a face to come or already past" (Deleuze and Guattari, *A Thousand Plateaus: Capitalism and Schizophrenia,* trans. Brian Massumi (Minneapolis: University of Minnesota Press, 2000), 172–73).

62. Jack Spicer, *Billy The Kid* (Stinson Beach, Calif.: Enkidu Surrogate Press, 1959), 6.

63. Burns, *The Saga of Billy the Kid,* 231.

64. One could add to this collection Warhol's 1967 film *Lonesome Cowboys,* whose "floundering form" Mark Finch describes as "a series of loosely connected confrontations" (Finch, "Rio Limpo: 'Lonesome Cowboys' and Gay Cinema," in *Andy Warhol: Film Factory,* ed. Michael O'Pray [London: British Film Institute, 1990], 114).

65. Richard Meyer, "Warhol's Clones," *Yale Journal of Criticism* 7, no. 1 (Spring 1994): 100.

66. Ibid., 102.

67. Which is to say (in contrast to the amorous declaration of "For Billy") *that I love you in spite of the fact not that you might already be dead, but that you cannot die.*

4. Elizabeth Bishop's Crane and the Good-Enough Poem

1. Diana Fuss, *Identification Papers* (New York: Routledge, 1995), 91.

2. For a sense of Bishop criticism engaged with Bishop's homosexuality (manifest both a propos Bishop's relationship with Soares and more generally), see Crystal Bacon, " '. . . That World Inverted': Encoded Lesbian Identity in Elizabeth Bishop's 'Love Lies Sleeping' and 'Insomnia,' " in *Divisions of the Heart: Elizabeth Bishop and the Art of Memory and Place,* ed. Sandra Barry, Gwendolyn Davies, and Peter Sanger (Wolfville, Nova Scotia: Gaspereau, 2001), 199–207; David Jarraway, " 'O Canada!': The Spectral Lesbian Poetics of Elizabeth Bishop," *PMLA: Publications of the Modern Language Association of America* 113, no. 2 (March 1998): 243–57; Corinne Blackmer, "Ethnoporn, Lesbian Childhood, and Native Maternal Culture: Reading *National Geographic* with Elizabeth Bishop," *GLQ: A Journal of Lesbian and Gay Studies* 4, no. 1 (1998): 17–58; Margaret Dickie, "The Love Poetry of Elizabeth Bishop: Silent and Silenced," in *Semantics of Silences in Linguistics and Literature,* ed. Gudrun Grabher, Gudrun, and Jessner, Ulrike (Heidelberg: Winter, 1996), 271–89; Carmen Oliveira, "Luminous Lota," in *"In Worcester, Massachusetts": Essays on Elizabeth Bishop: From the 1997 Elizabeth Bishop Conference at WPI,* ed. Laura Menides, Laura Jehn, and Angela Dorenkamp (New York: Peter Lang, 1999), 83–91; Gary Fountain, " 'Closets, Closets, and More Closets!' Elizabeth Bishop's Lesbianism," in *Queer Representations: Reading Lives, Reading Cultures,* ed. Martin Duberman (New York: New York University Press, 1997), 247–57.

3. Mutlu Blasing is one of few critics to remark upon Bishop's poetic relation to Crane, as opposed to the more numerous critics, content to generalize Bishop's and Crane's respectively vast importance to an American poetic canon, as though inclusion in a list constituted if not relationship then at least membership to the same exclusive club. Blasing, however, lodges her analysis within a poststructuralist framework that renders moot the differences (between historical and personal) to which I (and more importantly, Bishop's poetry) am most attached. Blasing sometimes refers to the "historical" in opposition to the personal, but more often collects the energies of history under what she calls the patriarchal. Blasing argues that "we need to place [Bishop] all the more firmly within a patriarchal tradition so as to see how her revisions of it signify politically as well as poetically" (Blasing, *Politics and Form in Postmodern Poetry: O'Hara, Bishop, Ashbery, Merrill* [Cambridge: Cambridge University Press, 1995], 65). Blasing reads Bishop's location within such a tradition as necessary, but also necessarily ironic ("styles that observe historical conventions

are able increasingly to question the rhetoric of their forms" [71]), as though Bishop's performance of form didn't corroborate form's ineluctable hold but rather deformed it from the inside—a poetics implicitly commensurate with a Butler-derived model of performativity.

In a reading of Bishop's "The Moose," Blasing identifies Crane in Bishop's formulation "craning backward." But Crane's relation to Bishop is underwritten (which is to say unwritten) by Blasing's invoking of Crane as merely one of several instantiations of the patriarchal: " 'The Moose' audibly recalls a number of American poets, some not heard before in her verse, and in the rest of my discussion I want to explore the poem's native ground. Walt Whitman, Robert Frost, and Hart Crane provide models her poem may be read against, whether they are all consciously invoked or not. For Bishop's recuperation of these models is less a matter of 'anxiety of influence' than one of entering a traditional narrative framework of journeys.... Not only is narrative a patriarchal structure—as Edward Said, for example, has argued—but entering the linear, causal time of narrative also means, in this case, entering the history (necessarily patriarchal) of how personal, temporal experience has been traditionally figured" (96–97). Blasing's triptych of patriarchal poets seems, from the outset, dubious. Whitman's relation to an American poetic tradition, while grandiose, seems as feasibly nonpatriarchal, in the myriad ways Whitman critics such as Michael Moon illuminate. Crane, even more extravagantly, seems antithetical to a patriarchal tradition—what could be less patriarchal than the frequent hypostasizing of Crane (all the more so in Bishop's time than ours) as a suicidal, alcoholic homosexual most poetically renowned for having written a massive failure? More frustrating than the looseness of Blasing's terminology is Blasing's implied equivalency between Bishop's uptakes of Whitman, the Good Gray Poet, Frost (whom Bishop, in a letter to Lowell, dubbed the Bad Gray Poet [Bishop, *One Art,* 365]), and Crane; as though invoking the "patriarchal" nullified what might otherwise count more vividly, particularly, as a relationship between two poets. For instance, Blasing intimates that the caricatured maleness inherent in conceptions of patriarchy is equally manifest in the likes of Whitman, Crane, and Frost, or, more precisely, that the differences within these quite diverse malenesses are subordinate to what holds them under the single patriarchal aegis. Maleness and talent aside, Crane and Whitman are most easily consignable to the status of patriarchal because they are dead, whereas Frost, as a less debatable representative of something such as patriarchy, may as well be dead. As Bishop distraughtedly asks Pearl Kazin, following the death of Dylan Thomas, "Why do some poets manage to get by and live to be malicious old bores like Frost... and some just don't!" (*One Art,* 276). Within Blasing's account (and likewise, in Bishop's own disparagings of Frost), patriarchy has the effect of making even living poets seem historical.

Patriarchy, for Blasing, derives its equalizing force from its coincidence with a Lacanian symbolic order: "[Bishop's] conventional stanzas and meters, together with her grammatical syntax, place her within the symbolic order" (71); "She only discovers that, *within* the symbolic economy she has entered, nature becomes female. What has brought her to this figuration is her contract with a particular tradition, written by men, of poems about journeys like the one she has made" (95). At her most good-intentioned, Blasing imagines the incontrovertibility of the symbolic as foundational to a poetry whose meaning is always collective. "Yet such meaning as poetry discloses on its historical and figural road can be only a shared meaning—that is, historical and rhetorical. She writes her experience as it is written by the resources—historical, formal, and figurative—of the common language of poetry" (103).

Along these lines, patriarchy doesn't discriminate between the living and the dead (between Crane and Whitman, who are dead but seldom seem patriarchal as such, and Frost who can seem utterly patriarchal at his most vivacious) to the exact degree that "the common language of poetry" subordinates individual personality to commonality. Writing within the symbolic, Bishop's being alive is as coincidental as Crane's not being so: the symbolic order (like the conventional or traditional — or in the tradition's oppressive, male mode, the patriarchal) doesn't care about the aliveness or deadness of an individual person, because it doesn't care about personal singularity. Such a revelation (in the wake of Barthes or Foucault, in and of itself unsurprising) doesn't resolve Bishop's problematic relationship with Crane, so much as dispense with it as an object of inquiry.

4. For criticism on Bishop and Moore, see Kathryn Kent, *Making Girls into Women: American Women's Writing and the Rise of Lesbian Identity* (Durham, N.C.: Duke University Press, 2003); Pickard Zachariah, "Natural History and Epiphany: Elizabeth Bishop's Darwin Letter," *Twentieth Century Literature: A Scholarly and Critical Journal* 50, no. 3 (Fall 2004): 268–82; Kirstin Hotelling Zona, *Marianne Moore, Elizabeth Bishop, and May Swenson: The Feminist Poetics of Self-Restraint* (Ann Arbor: University of Michigan Press, 2002); Fiona Green, "Locating the Lyric: Marianne Moore, Elizabeth Bishop and the Second World War," in *Locations of Literary Modernism: Region and Nation in British and American Modernist Poetry,* ed. Alex Davis and Lee M. Jenkins (Cambridge: Cambridge University Press, 2000), 199–214; Margaret Wooster Freeman, " 'Efforts of Affection': Mentorship and Friendship in Moore and Bishop," in *American Literary Mentors,* ed. Irene C. Goldman-Price and Melissa McFarland Pennell (Gainesville: University Press of Florida, 1999), 147–60; Ann Keniston, "Efforts of Influence: Moore and Bishop," *Contemporary Literature* 36, no. 2 (Summer 1995): 384–91; Jeredith Merrin, "Marianne Moore and Elizabeth Bishop," in *The Columbia History of American Poetry,* ed. Jay Parini and Brett Millier (New York: Columbia University Press, 1993), 343–69; Betsy Erkilla, "Elizabeth Bishop and Marianne Moore: The Dynamics of Female Influence," in *Marianne Moore: Woman and Poet,* ed. Patricia Willis (Orono, Me.: National Poetry Foundation, 1990), 335–50; Bonnie Costello, "Marianne Moore and Elizabeth Bishop: Friendship and Influence," *Twentieth Century Literature: A Scholarly and Critical Journal* 30, no. 2–3 (Fall 1984): 130–49.

For criticism on Bishop and Lowell, see Lloyd Schwartz, "Dedications: Lowell's 'Skunk Hour' and Bishop's 'The Armadillo,' " *Salmagundi* 141–42 (Winter 2004): 120–24; Lorrie Goldensohn, "Robert Lowell's 'Dropping South: Brazil,' " *Salmagundi* 141–42 (Winter 2004): 145–50; Josef Raab, "The Poetics of Life: Robert Lowell and Elizabeth Bishop," in *Poetics in the Poem: Critical Essays on American Self-Reflexive Poetry,* ed. Dorothy Baker (New York: Peter Lang, 1997), 195–219; Charles Tomlinson, "Poetry and Friendship," *Parnassus: Poetry in Review,* 16, no. 2 (1991): 102–7; C. K. Doreski, "Robert Lowell and Elizabeth Bishop: A Matter of Life Studies," *Prose Studies* 10, no. 1 (May 1987): 85–101; Martha Carlson-Bradley, "Lowell's 'My Last Afternoon with Uncle Devereux Winslow': The Model for Bishop's 'First Death in Nova Scotia,' " *Concerning Poetry* 19 (1986): 117–31; David Kalstone, "Prodigal Years: Elizabeth Bishop and Robert Lowell (1947–49)," *Grand Street* 4, no. 4 (Summer 1985): 170–93.

5. See Robert Cording, "Elizabeth Bishop and George Herbert: 'Self-Distaste' and Self-Understanding, in *"In Worcester, Massachusetts": Essays on Elizabeth Bishop: From the 1997 Elizabeth Bishop Conference at WPI,* ed. Laura Jehn Menides and Angela Dorenkamp (New York: Peter Lang, 1999), 235–45; Jeffrey Powers-Beck, " 'Time to Plant Tears'; Elizabeth Bishop's Seminary of Tears" *South Atlantic Review* 60, no. 4 (November 1995): 69–87; Joseph H. Summers, "George Herbert and Elizabeth Bishop," *George Herbert Journal* 18, no. 1–2 (Fall–Spring 1995): 48–58; Brett Millier, "Modesty and Morality: George Herbert, Gerard Manley Hopkins, and Elizabeth Bishop," *Kenyon Review* 11, no. 2 (Spring 1989): 47–56.

6. The temporal predicament of Bishop and Crane broaches one hypothetical response to Carolyn Dinshaw's question, "How does it feel to be an anachronism?" See *GLQ's* double issue on Queer Temporalities (13, nos. 2–3), especially the roundtable discussion between the likes of Edelman, Dinshaw, Halberstam, and others. For my own anecdotal speculations on queer intergenerationality, see "Agape," *The Massachusetts Review* 49, nos. 1–2 (Spring–Summer 2008): 106–17.

7. See, especially, Kathryn Kent's chapter on Bishop and Moore in *Making Girls into Women.*

8. "A symbolic position is never commensurate with any individual who happens to occupy it; it assumes its status as symbolic precisely as a function of that incommensurability" (Judith Butler, *Antigone's Claim: Kinship between Life and Death* [New York: Columbia University Press, 2000], 14).

9. Harold Bloom, *The Anxiety of Influence: A Theory of Poetry* (New York: Oxford University Press, 1973), 11.

10. Ibid.

11. Susan McCabe, *Elizabeth Bishop: Her Poetics of Loss* (University Park: Pennsylvania State University Press, 1994), 109.

12. Ibid., 114.

13. Margaret Dickie ignores the male pronoun altogether, symptomatically twice replacing it with the definite article: "The qualifications here, negatives that enfold negatives, make it difficult to read this poem as a plea for the 'gay eyes,' for release from the 'tension' of 'nothing.' As in the second poem where the ecstatic moment is muted, the negative contructions here hide the power of the 'gay eyes' and the force of the adjective" ("Half is Enough: Elizabeth Bishop's Love Poetry," in Margaret Dickie, *Stein, Bishop, and Rich: Lyrics of Love, War and Place* [Chapel Hill: University of North Carolina Press, 1997], 95). The force, however, of 'the adjective' "gay" surely changes within the poem, depending on the gender to which "gay" is ascribed. If "gay" is taken to signal a sexual predilection (and not simply a synonym for "happy"), Dickie's omission amounts to a falsifying simplification of one of the poem's possible *mise en scènes*, that of a homosexual woman potentially writing a love poem for a homosexual man.

14. That this poem might speak to Crane is less important as a definitive possibility than as a conjecture, situated within a need for more theoretically articulate accounts of the desires such a possibility might entail. If these were, however, to be Crane's "gay green eyes," I would look, as antecedent, to the opening lines of Crane's poem "Cutty Sark":

> I met a man in South Street, tall—
> a nervous shark tooth swung on his chain.
> His eyes pressed through green glass
> —green glasses, or bar lights made them
> so—
>   shine—
>   GREEN—
>   eyes—
> stepped out—forgot to look at you
> or left you several blocks away—
>   (Crane, *Complete Poems,* 71)

15. I shall speak directly to the incestuous wake of *Antigone* criticism in my book's epilogue.

16. Kaja Silverman, *The Threshold of the Visible World* (New York: Routledge, 1996), 1.

17. Ibid.

18. Ibid., 37.

19. Ibid.

20. Bishop's first letter to Stanford (written in 1933, while Bishop was a student at Vassar) begins, "I had been forewarned by Mr. Winters that you were going to write to me."

21. See Thomas Francis Parkinson's *Hart Crane and Yvor Winters: Their Literary Correspondence* (Berkeley: University of California Press, 1978). Further entangling Winters and Crane with Bishop and Stanford, Parkinson notes that

the first two chapters of his book first were printed in *Southern Review,* and singles out that journal's editor for especial thanks—*Southern Review*'s editor, at that time, being none other than Donald Stanford.

22. Elizabeth Bishop, *One Art: Letters,* ed. Robert Giroux (New York: Farrar, Straus & Giroux, 1994), 18 (March 5, 1934).

23. And might the third member of this literary threesome, Robert Bridges, nominally reiterate, within some epistolary unconscious, Bishop's study of *The Bridge*?

24. Bishop, *One Art,* 27–28 (September 7, 1934).

25. In distinction from Winters's encomial review of Crane's 1926 *White Buildings,* a review rejected — on account of its enthusiasms — by the differently minded editor of the literary magazine *The Dial.* Again, to suggest the intricate near-nearness of Bishop and Crane, *The Dial's* then-editor was Marianne Moore, who would commence a life-long friendship with Bishop just a few years thereafter.

26. Brian M. Reed, *Hart Crane: After His Lights* (Tuscaloosa: University of Alabama Press, 2006), 5.

27. Except, perhaps, for those enthralled by the unhappy mythology of doomed young poets, or those persuaded by Lee Edelman's own enthralled call for a necessary and ethical figuring of the death drive.

28. Silverman, *The Threshold of the Visible World,* 40.

29. Elizabeth Bishop, *One Art: Letters,* ed. Robert Giroux (New York: Farrar, Straus & Giroux, 1994), 18 (March 5, 1934).

30. Silverman, *The Threshold of the Visible World,* 20.

31. Bishop, *One Art,* 28 (September 7, 1934).

32. Hart Crane, *The Letters of Hart Crane,* ed. Brom Weber (New York: Hermitage House, 1952), 305–6 (April 20, 1924).

33. Bishop, *One Art,* 188 (July 3, 1949).

34. See Sedgwick, *Epistemology of the Closet,* 202.

35. Silverman, *The Threshold of the Visible World,* 2.

36. Elizabeth Bishop, *The Complete Poems, 1927–1979* (New York: Farrar, Straus & Giroux, 1983), 8. All subsequent references to Bishop's poetry are to this edition and parenthetically cited by page number within the text.

37. This scream's message is lexically identical to Silverman's own exhortation, already cited, that we ought imagine "new uses to which [the psychic activity at the heart of love] might be put."

38. The poem's final attachment to echo indicates not only the other side of the pond, but the verso of a Narcissus myth. At the limits of the pond's narcissistic industry arises Echo, in love with Narcissus but in significant revision of the Greek myth, independent of him; where might there have been narcissus blooms we find only "scrub-pine and oak."

39. The echoic utterance on one level resembles an Austinian perlocutionary utterance, whose performative fruition arrives after the fact of utterance itself. The echo, however, significantly differs from Austinian utterance in that the

latter depends on the presence of subject and object, whereas the echoic former displaces Austinian hierarchy with a subject that refractively doubles.

40. In this context, I think specifically of *Saturday Night Live*'s Stuart Smalley, parodic paragon and purveyor of pop-psychological acceptance. When Smalley proclaims that "he's good enough, he's smart enough, and dog-gonnit people like me," he presumably does not have Winnicott in mind. Or at very least, has not read his Winnicott *well enough*.

41. D. W. Winnicott, *Playing and Reality* (New York: Brunner-Routledge, 1989), 12.

42. Felicia Hemans, *Selected Poems, Letters, Reception Materials,* ed. Susan J. Wolfson (Princeton, N.J.: Princeton University Press, 2000), 428–30.

43. Bloom, *The Anxiety of Influence.*

44. Hemans's poem elegiacally ends with a heart which (for myself, perhaps for Bishop) inevitably evokes the Hart of Crane:

> But the noblest thing that perished there
> Was that young, faithful heart.

Hemans's lines likewise evoke the burning heart of Crane's own poem, "Possessions," "The pure possession, the inclusive cloud / Whose heart is fire shall come." Crane's futural tense, on one level striking the chord of oracles, might less vatically posit an invitation to future readers; which is to say that Crane's "shall" points beyond the "inclusive[ness]" of the poem itself. The poem's hermeticism, if imagined in terms of a Whitmanian poetics that asks for a futural reader to make sense of it, seems less exclusionary, less frustrating, than strangely generous. If difficult to find meaning in the poem, then perhaps the poem asks for meaning to be found elsewhere — the poem, on this reading, is less about self-possession than an offering of itself as someone else's possession.

45. Thomas J. Travisano, *Elizabeth Bishop: Her Artistic Development* (Charlottesville: University Press of Virginia, 1989), 33.

46. Dickie, *Stein, Bishop, and Rich,* 93.

47. Anne Stevenson, *Five Looks at Elizabeth Bishop* (London: Bellew, 1998), 45.

48. Ibid.

49. David Kalstone, *Becoming a Poet: Elizabeth Bishop with Marianne Moore and Robert Lowell* (New York: Farrar, Straus, & Giroux, 1989), 214.

50. In Victoria Harrison, *Elizabeth Bishop's Poetics of Intimacy* (Cambridge: Cambridge University Press, 1993).

51. Anne Stevenson, writing outside the argot of postcolonial theory, discusses "Squatter's Children" in terms of Bishop's compassion for "the poor": "'Jeronimo's House,' 'Faustina" and Part IV of 'Songs for a Colored Singer' beautifully convey the poet's pity for and empathy with the poor black population of Florida. The popular ballad 'The Burglar of Babylon,' with the more subtle lyric 'Squatter's Children,' carry that sympathetic empathy to Brazil. But

in all these poems, strong discipline in the writing stiffens the sentiments displayed, as though the poet were afraid of giving offence through condescension" ("The Geographical Mirror," *Five Looks at Elizabeth Bishop*, 107). I don't mean to disavow Bishop's compassion, but rather to extricate "Squatter's Children" from discourses (of "ethnography" or "social conscience") that peremptorily dictate the objects of a poem's compassion, hypostasizing the terrain of a social conscience, and, indeed, of the political itself. My reading of "Squatter's Children," in imagining it beyond its immediate Brazilian context, does not intend to depoliticize the poem so much as to politicize it differently. The way critics describe (or more often, overlook) the relation between Bishop and Crane signals a new field for queer theoretical work, requiring new tools. Neither this work nor its tools are unpolitical (in either immediate import or subsequent use).

52. David Bromwich, in his elegant and often perspicacious essay, "Elizabeth Bishop's Dream-Houses" (*Raritan* 4, no. 1 [1984]: 77–94) is one of few critics to note the ways in which poems such as "Squatter's Children" present a set of hermeneutic problems generically distinct from other Bishop texts: "[F]ew readers are likely to know even a single region as intimately as [Bishop] knew two hemispheres; and to make her geography poems interesting we have to read them as poems about something else.... I think these are the only poems Bishop ever wrote that dwindle as one comes to see them more clearly. One has to move away from these in order to learn what must have been clear to her from the first: that geography carries an interest as a figure of the soul's encounter with fate (or as she puts it, with 'what we imagine knowledge to be')" (125).
As much as I differ with Bromwich's concluding grandiosity—his rearticulation of a geography as so specific an allegorical figure is as foreclosing (if in opposite ways) as more recent readings that zealously broach Bishop's *literal* geographies as *only* such—I find largely salutary Bromwich's later polemical claim that Bishop "exploits the genre [of travel sketch]... to break with it" (127).

53. Crane, *Complete Poems of Hart Crane*, 34.

54. Harrison, *Elizabeth Bishop's Poetics of Intimacy*, 150.

55. Ibid., 151.

56. "For the poet here speaks not from the shore, but from the sea; and he is situated not so much *in* the water as *under* it.... From his subaquatic station Crane offers the warning that cannot, as he knows, bridge the distance between himself and the 'urchins' on the beach.... The extraordinary angle of this particular line of vision is suggested in the opening phrase of the poem when Crane's perspective locates the 'brilliant' children 'above the fresh ruffles of the surf" (Edelman, *Hart Crane's Transmemberment of Song*, 131).

57. A similar wavering between the compositional and empirical occurs at the start of "Crusoe in England":

> A new volcano has erupted,
> the papers say, and last week I was reading
> where some ship saw an island being born:

at first a breath of steam, ten miles away;
and then a black fleck — basalt, probably —
rose in the mate's binoculars
and caught on the horizon like a fly.
(Bishop, *The Complete Poems,* 162)

Here, the composition occurs within the lens of a binocular. The "fleck," probably of basalt, but at the same time maybe not, might be a fly caught on the "horizon" of the lens' frame. While the final line's simile ("like a fly") attempts to normalize the optical moment, the similetic can only be partly assuaging; just as looking like a speck amounts, ultimately, to being a speck, looking like a fly, in these lines' context, can't definitively rule out the possibility of simply being one. That Crusoe reads about the volcano in the papers doesn't necessarily lend to its credibility, i.e., doesn't make the fleck anything more than "basalt, probably." This generative capacity of potentially erroneous newspapers recalls the generative error from which Bishop wrote her much earlier "Man-moth." For an alternative treatment of the speck of "Poem" and the fleck of "Crusoe," see Sarah Riggs's "Binocular Optics: Elizabeth Bishop" in *Word Sighting: Poetry and Visual Media in Stevens, Bishop and O'Hara* (New York: Routledge, 2002), 59–60. Riggs discusses these aesthetic abruptions as the intersection of "optical and linguistic indeterminacy." I, on the other hand, see these moments not as evidence of indeterminacy, but undecideability; which is to say, not of the impossibility of distinctions as such, so much as the inability, in a given instance, to decide between equally plausible (if ultimately incommensurate) interpretations.

58. Thomas Travisano, in a reading of the poem's final stanza, notes that "Bishop's indelicate figures blossom on the canvas against a ground of suggestive syntactic ambiguity" (*Elizabeth Bishop: Her Artistic Development,* 122). Travisano, lyrically, would align the "indelicate figures" with the "fresh squiggled iris" of "Poem," whereas I think "ambiguity" begins with the specklike figures themselves, as opposed to the "ground" on which they eventually stand. Stevenson similarly describes the poem's scene as "painterly" (107), albeit, like Travisano, she offers little account as to how.

59. More often, critics take the promised mansions as gifts from nature, not Bishop. Stevenson writes that "one must take 'mansions' here to mean nature's" (108), and Lorrie Goldensohn, hallucinating a sentimental familial structure where there is none, writes "these children willfully orphaned from the immediate familial world of the mother's ugly voice, are reparented in the bigger house of nature — much as the orphaned Bishop herself must have wished reparenting" (*Elizabeth Bishop: The Biography of a Poetry* [New York: Columbia University Press, 1992], 42). Such readings depend on (among other things) the exclusion of Bishop as outsider to the scene she observes, as opposed to inclusion as author in a scene she produces.

60. More tenuously, the "soggy documents" recall an earlier Crane poem, "My Grandmother's Love Letters":

> There are no stars tonight
> But those of memory.
> Yet how much room for memory there is
> In the loose girdle of soft rain.
>
> There is even room enough
> For the letters of my mother's mother,
> Elizabeth,
> That have been pressed so long
> Into a corner of the roof
> That they are brown and soft,
> And liable to melt as snow.
> (Crane, *Complete Poems,* 6)

This poem, like "Squatter's Children," ruminates on another set of soggy documents, Crane's grandmother's love-letters, and offers itself as both those love letters' correlative and keep-safe. While the poem strains to "carry back the music to its source / And back to you again / As though to her," the object of apostrophe, Elizabeth, might (if only with the fantasy of this footnote) carry the music forward, as though Bishop might hear the poem's impossible nominal call, impossibly, as hers.

61. Steven Knapp, *Personification and the Sublime: Milton to Coleridge* (Cambridge, Mass.: Harvard University Press, 1985), 2.

62. A simpler version of such redemptive recursiveness occurs in a film such as "The Stepford Wives," in which repetition, like a skipped record, betrays the extent to which a person is already beyond the realm of ordinary consequence. While the Stepford wives repeat their lines ("I'll just die if I don't get that recipe") as an indication of the degree to which they no longer count *as persons,* Love, in "Casabianca," on the other hand, latches onto auto-echolalia as a counterintuitive preservation of personhood.

63. Robert Lowell, *The Collected Poems of Robert Lowell,* ed. Frank Bidart and David Gewanter (New York: Farrar, Straus & Giroux, 2003), 159.

64. In a sense, "Casabianca" reverses the *New York Times* 1932 headline about Hart Crane, "Poet is Missing at Sea," suspending the poet above a sea that is itself missing.

65. Allen Grossman, "Hart Crane and Poetry: A Consideration of Crane's Intense Poetics with Reference to 'The Return,' " *The Long Schoolroom: Lessons in the Bitter Logic of the Poetic Principle* (Ann Arbor: University of Michigan Press, 2000), 85.

66. "Such as" Crane, albeit not at all exclusively so — this is to say that Bishop's relation with Crane, for all its alluring specificities, oftentimes instantiates a more generic problematic; for instance, this problematic of aesthetic perviousness, which would consume much of Bishop's later correspondence with Robert Lowell.

67. T. J. Clark, *Farewell to an Idea: Episodes from a History of Modernism* (New Haven: Yale University Press, 2001), 107–8. "Dipping themselves in and out," the bathers's movement might also conjure the diphtheria (inflammation of the heart) that kills Seurat at age thirty-one, a year earlier than the death of Crane.

68. Jeredith Merrin, "Elizabeth Bishop: Gaiety, Gayness, Change," in *Elizabeth Bishop: The Geography of Gender,* ed. Marilyn May Lombardi (Charlottesville: University Press of Virginia), 155.

69. Ibid., 156.

70. Lee Edelman rightly calls attention to the sea's verticality in Crane's "At Melville's Tomb," a poem governed by the centrifugal gravity of a whirlpool ("the calyx of death's bounty"). "By figuring Melville's shadow as 'high in the azure steeps,'" Edelman writes, "Crane himself implies, near the end of his poem, that 'steep' and 'deep' can be figuratively exchanged.... The antitheses thus become figurally conjoined, bound up in one another much like imagination and despair, or Eros and Thanatos" (*Transmemberment of Song,* 126–27).

71. Merrin, "Elizabeth Bishop: Gaiety, Gayness, and Change," 156. Bonnie Costello similarly writes that in turning from the initial swimming pool, "the poet turns from the mirror to the sea, still a reflective surface, now deep and unmasterable." If "Pleasure Seas" submits a scene of mastery, that mastery turns on a crisis independent of depth. Bishop's "shallow pleasure seas," after all, are shallow. Costello's attachment to a certain Melvillean (which is as well to say Cranian) formulation of topography, like Merrin's, too quickly attaches to a phantasm of danger: "Increasingly," Costello writes, "the poem's comic mood becomes ominous." The sort of "comic" that Costello invokes is inseparable from "ominous[ness]" in that the former de facto gives way to something else. The pleasures of Bishop's poem, however, not only aren't subordinate to grief (the way shallows, ordinarily, would be subordinate to depth), but rather (in the form of Love), have the last say (Costello, *Questions of Mastery,* 33).

72. Merrin, "Gaiety, Gayness, Change," 158.

73. Costello, *Questions of Mastery,* 35.

74. Ibid., 36.

75. Leo Bersani, "Is the Rectum a Grave?" 222.

76. Ibid.

77. Paul de Man, "The Rhetoric of Temporality," in *Blindness and Insight: Essays in the Rhetoric of Contemporary Criticism* (Minneapolis: University of Minnesota Press, 1997), 225.

78. To claim allegory's peculiar historical investments is to distinguish my reading from the likes of Cindy Weinstein, whose account of allegory's labors nonetheless importantly resuscitates the textures and stakes from which such rhetoric alchemizations arguably are inseparable. "However great the differences may be between a new critical conception of allegory, like Angus Fletcher's, and a deconstructive paradigm of allegory, like Paul de Man's, surely they are

united by a turning away, indeed an erasure, of history." Even as I posit a correspondence between Bishop's and de Man's respective understandings of allegory, it is not in the service of history's erasure, but in the service of history's salvage, that I find the two writers most sympathetic. If allegory traditionally is positioned as an erasure of history, Bishop's allegory is historically crucial in its capacity to overlook *and inhabit* what otherwise is conceivable only as historical calcification (Cindy Weinstein, *The Literature of Labor and the Labors of Literature* [New York: Cambridge University Press, 1995], 9).

79. Crane, *The Complete Poems,* 160.

80. Ibid.

Epilogue

1. At the limit that is Polyneices, personhood is both most accessible and most vulnerable along bodily lines. Personhood need not always attach so intensely to the body (for instance, a tour through the late novels of Henry James suggests bodies as personate integrities composed of emotion and intellect). Honoring Antigone's own honoring of singularity, I therefore don't intend this particular elision of persons and bodies beyond the text at hand.

2. It is partly for the sheer fact of Antigone's intelligibility (if not in speech then in deed) that Edelman's *No Future* decries Butler's account of *Antigone.* Over and against such intelligibility (which for Edelman always already speaks for a hegemonic future that would require some new nonintelligible population as sacrifice for the becoming-intelligible of another), Edelman favors the death-driven squawk of Hitchcock's *The Birds.* Edelman's own account of the imperatives of the unintelligible nonetheless inevitably rely on the sorts of eloquence *No Future* incessantly excoriates. Edelman writes thus: "But one thing in this must be perfectly clear: my point is not to equate the birds with homosexuality nor to suggest that they be understood as 'meaning' same-sex desire. Neither is Hitchcock's film, as I read it, an allegory of gay coming-out. Insofar as the birds bear the burden of *sintho*mosexuality, which aims to dissociate heteronormativity from its own implication in the drive, it would, in fact, be more accurate to say that the meaning of homosexuality is determined by what the film represents in *them*: the violent undoing of meanings, the loss of identity and coherence, the unnatural access to jouissance, which find their perfect expression in the slogan devised by Hitchcock himself for the movie's promotion, '*The Birds* is coming'" (132). Edelman revels in "the meaning of homosexuality" in metonymic relation to "the violent undoing of meaning," even as he prefaces his fugue on meaning's undoing with the cross-purposed insistence that "one thing in this must be perfectly clear," and closes (again, it would seem, at cross-purposes with itself) with an assertion of "perfect expression." How can Edelman's argument (with the avian burdens it likewise bears) accommodate,

let alone sustain, its own momentary insistence on perfect clarity, its own delight—against the delight of incoherence—in "perfect expression"? Alongside the birds' flight "in the face of meaning" (140), how and when can the death drive make room for a queer theorist's own inclinations toward meaning; for a queer theorist who doesn't embrace sinthomosexuality's unraveling of legibility so much as inform other queers that this unraveling is their singular duty; for a queer theorist who calls the shots and pulls if not our own queer marionette strings then the wings whose death-driven "relentless rhythm" (14) we are called on to follow?

These questions seem no more answerable than there seems just one task for which queers are singled out. Many more questions (rhetorical and otherwise) might be asked of Edelman's study, and many more "ethical task[s]" than the one Edelman proffers might be held out to queers and to queer theory: *Queer Optimism* hopes already to have made this clear. There are birds and then there are birds.

3. John Seery, in a recent essay, argues (to my mind, preposterously) that Butler doesn't attend enough to *Antigone*'s incestuous humidities. "Surprisingly," Seery writes, "for someone who claims that she is reprising (or discovering) an incestuous reading of Antigone against those who ignore it or insist otherwise, Butler doesn't really explore the nature of the incest, and in fact, pays little heed to it" ("Acclaim for *Antigone's Claim* Reclaimed [or Steiner, contra Butler]," *Theory and Event* 9, no. 1, paragraph 70).

4. Judith Butler, "On Never Having Learned How to Live," *differences* 16 (2005): 34.

5. Crane, *The Letters of Hart Crane,* 113 (January 5, 1923).

INDEX

Michael D. Snediker is assistant professor of English at Queen's University in Kingston, Ontario, Canada.